Nantucket
Only Yesterday

Nantucket Only Yesterday

An Island View
of the
Twentieth Century

Robert F. Mooney

Wesco Publishing
Nantucket, Massachusetts
2000

Nantucket Only Yesterday
Copyright © 2000 by Robert F. Mooney

ISBN: 0-9627851-2-1

First Edition
2000

Manufactured in the
United States of America
Design by Robert A. Frazier

Wesco Publishing
P.O. Box 1540
Nantucket, MA 02554

To the people of Nantucket,
who made this island
a place to preserve.

PHOTO CREDITS

These photographers have graciously offered their work for publication:
Stan Grossfeld—pages 210 and 216;
Cary Hazlegrove—pages 144 and 212;
Jack Weinhold—pages 175, 244, and 250;
Rob Benchley—pages 142, 248, and 252;
Michael Galvin—pages 179 and 246;
Terry Pommett—back cover/jacket flap.

Other photographs in this volume are used courtesy of the collections of:
NHA—pages 1, 15, 18, 30, 37, 55, 80, 117, 118, 140, 146, 181, 182;
. Nantucket Conservation Foundation—page 146 (top);
Alma K. Coffin and Marilyn Coffin Brown —front cover,
frontis, 17, 57, 80, 117;
Nantucket Magazine—pages 6, 17, 38, 58, 115;
Robert F. Mooney—pages 76, 78, 101, 112, 113, 252;
Joan Keenan — page 182;
Henry Fee—page 214;
Grace Grossman—page 248.

ACKNOWLEDGMENTS

The author gratefully acknowledges the assistance and
cooperation of the people and organizations
who helped in the creation of this book:

Elizabeth Oldham, for editorial assistance.
Robert Frazier, for design and production.
Lee Rand Burne, for historical research.

The Nantucket Atheneum, the island's historic public library, for
research facilities and its microfilm record of island newspapers.

The Nantucket Historical Association (NHA) for its invaluable
photograph collection in the Edouard A. Stackpole Library.

Nantucket Magazine, the island's premier quarterly, for permission
to use material and photographs previously published in its pages.

Alma K. Coffin and Marilyn Coffin Brown, for permission
to use photographs from the collection of William W. Coffin.

All the Nantucket people who willingly
contributed information and interviews.

Especially my wife, Elizabeth Bowker Mooney,
who endured and supported me in this effort.

This is a personal view of the past hundred years on Nantucket.
In a work of this scope, it is inevitable that errors and omissions
will occur. These are the responsibility of the author,
to be corrected by future critics and historians.

CONTENTS

Turn of the Century	7	1900
	15	*Captain John Killen*
The Carfree Years	19	1904–1918
	30	*The Great Auto Fight*
The Good Old Days	39	1919–1929
	55	*Pasture to Airport*
Hard Times	59	1930–1940
	76	*Two Chiefs*
	78	*Rev. Joseph M. Griffin*
Wartime & Peacetime	81	1941–1950
	101	*WW II: A Memoir*
	113	*Charles F. Sayle Sr.*
	115	*José Formoso Reyes*
Starting to Move	119	1950–1960
	140	*The New Nantucket*
	142	*Edouard A. Stackpole*
	144	*Albert F. Egan Jr.*
The New Nantucket	147	1961–1971
	175	*Walter Beinecke Jr.*
	179	*Joseph Lopes*
Growing Pains	183	1972–1980
	210	*Mildred Jewett*
	212	*James M. Lentowski*
	214	*Henry Fee*
More People, More Problems	217	1981–1989
	244	*William B. Macomber*
	246	*Vito Capizzo*
	248	*Bernard & Grace Grossman*
	250	*Rev. Edward B. Anderson*
Here Comes Everybody	253	1990–2000

Nantucket
Only Yesterday

As the century opened, large summer hotels like the Sea Cliff Inn served the tourism industry.

Foreword

Nantucket Island has often been called a microcosm of America, but it is more than that. It is a way of life. All islands are special, but Nantucket's location and traditions have combined to shape her character as one of America's most memorable places. Almost thirty miles at sea off the coast of Massachusetts, Nantucket was once the center of an international whaling industry, sending her ships around the world in pursuit of the largest prey on earth. The surrounding waters, once a barrier to the outside world, have now become the island's greatest attraction. Modern transportation now brings the island an international clientele, seeking to spend their leisure in pursuit of that most elusive prey, pleasure.

At the beginning of the twentieth century, the year-round population of Nantucket was close to 3,000, and declining. By the end of the century, that number had tripled, and a single concert of the Boston Pops brought a crowd of 12,000 to celebrate the peak of the summer season.

Across many years, the inhabitants of the island continued to take on the character of the island itself. Those proud and independent islanders stubbornly tried to uphold the traditions of their self-contained community, like their whaling forebears, observing the world surrounding them. For many years, Nantucket could safely ignore the outside world, secure behind its geographical boundaries. However, the insistent demands of the modern world would not be denied; progress begat change, and with change came the New Nantucket.

One cannot turn back the clock or the calendar. I do not believe the island should live in the past. I only hope to describe the island as it was, how and and why it changed, so that the Nantucket of the future will never forget the Nantucket of the past.

—Robert F. Mooney
October 2000

An Island View
of the
Twentieth Century

Top: Main Street in 1900. Bottom: The Middle Gully road in Siasconset in 1900.

As the turn of the century dawned, the United States looked forward with faith in the future. After easily winning the little three-month war with Spain, the country was confident, and only Britain was involved in a major conflict—the Boer War in South Africa. The world was full of optimism, and the Nantucket newspaper, the Inquirer and Mirror, *expressed the hope that the new century would bring peace and goodwill to the world.*

There would be a national election that year, and the reelection of President William McKinley was assured. His vice-president, whom many considered too young for the presidency, was New York Governor Theodore Roosevelt, the hero of the Spanish-American War. Within a year, President McKinley was fatally shot, and Theodore Roosevelt, at 42, became the country's youngest president.

Turn
of the
Century

On Nantucket Island, there was less confidence and more concern for the future. Many islanders longed for the past, when the island had made its reputation and fortunes from the sea, sustaining itself and taking pride in its maritime heritage. Now all the great ships were gone, the future was uncertain, and the island seemed to drift along, dreaming of the past.

Nantucket in 1900 had a population of 3,006, a figure that was falling every year. From the peak of the whaling era in the 1830s, when the island sustained almost 10,000 people, the population had declined as men left the island for the California Gold Rush, the Civil War, and employment opportunities on the mainland, leaving a town of widows and old men. The statistics for 1899 told the distressing story: births, 34; marriages, 17; deaths, 81.

Nantucket was known for its mild climate, its quiet streets, and the absence of modern conveniences—an atmosphere often described as "quaint." There were no automobiles, no motion pictures, and only a few electric and telephone lines. The appearance of the old town had not changed much since the reconstruction of the downtown area following the Great Fire of 1846, which devastated the town in one fiery night. Thereafter, the streets were widened and planted with shade trees, so that by 1900 the large elms spread a canopy of green over Main Street. The downtown was rebuilt using red brick and brownstone, imparting an impression of permanence and prosperity to the business district. Little business was being done, however, and islanders worried about the future of their island home. All commerce was centered in the Lower Square of Main Street, in small shops and markets, where people met daily to chat and stroll along the brick sidewalks. Horses pulled wagons at a leisurely pace, the drivers often stopping to talk to neighbors. It was a pleasant and sociable way of life, and people liked it that way.

Then, on an afternoon in May 1900, Nantucket rolled into the twentieth century when the first motor vehicle ever seen on the island wheeled off the steamboat and chugged its way up Steamboat Wharf, followed by a crowd of curious onlookers. The vehicle was a Stanley Steamer, piloted by native Nantucketer Arthur R. Folger accompanied by his son, the popular young doctor, George A. Folger. The islanders gazed with curiosity and wonder, and the newspaper reported that it was "a decidedly smooth-running vehicle."

Life moved slowly on Nantucket, in rhythm with the seasons. Although the island had seen the beginning of the tourism business with the building of the summer hotels, most islanders were ambivalent toward its effect on their lives as they tried to preserve the identity of the old town and its traditional way of life. Nantucket was very much an island, dependent upon the steamship, which arrived every day from New Bedford, weather permitting. The waterfront was an active place, with fishing vessels, cargo schooners, and catboats clustered about the wharves and moorings. In 1896, a terrific storm had created a cut at the Haulover, at Coskata, making an island of Great Point and Coatue, and for more than a decade Nantucket fishermen could sail up-harbor straight into the Atlantic. Nantucket was also a port of call for the Gloucester fishing fleet, and the whole town welcomed the arrival of those graceful schooners when they came in for supplies. The most prominent business on the waterfront was that of the jovial Captain John Killen, an Irish immigrant who had come up from the fishing fleet and ownership of its shore facilities to become the major supplier of essential commodities. He imported ice from the Kennebec River in Maine and coal from the rail yards of New Bedford, supplied the fishing fleet and the homes of the town.

Communication with the mainland depended on the privately owned steamship line, which carried all mail, freight, and passengers to Nantucket and Martha's Vineyard. The line operated one boat a day in the winter and two in the summer, weather permitting, making the trip from New Bedford to Nantucket in four or five hours. The New Bedford stores ran weekly advertisements in the Nantucket newspaper for goods to be ordered by mail. The city furniture store of C. F. Wing opened a branch in Nantucket and advertised a free mattress with every bedroom suite ordered in January. Complaints arose about the length and uncertainty of the New Bedford service, and islanders proposed Hyannis as the shortest and most efficient port of call for Nantucket.

In 1900, twenty-seven miles of electric power lines served to illuminate the streets in town, but did not extend to the outskirts. There was local telephone service but no long-distance line until 1916. In the Folger Block, at the corner of Main and Orange Streets, a telegraph office was available to send emergency messages to the mainland, via a cable to Martha's Vineyard. In 1900, the powerful printing press of the *Inquirer and Mirror* was installed in the rear of the

Folger Block, making it the news hub of the island for the next sixty-six years. The paper sold for four cents a copy.

Also in 1900, the stately Nantucket Atheneum on Lower India Street, which had been a private library and museum since its inception, voted to become a free and public library in July. Prior to that date, one of the most famous and literate towns in Massachusetts was one of only seven without a public library. But Nantucket did have a railroad; the line ran during the summer season from Steamboat Wharf to Surfside Beach and then on to Sconset. The popular little railroad provided a pleasant ride and a festive time for the summer clientele, and soon led to the development of Sconset as the jewel in the crown of Nantucket's tourism industry. The village had been popularized for its healthy climate and restful atmosphere back in the 1880s, and its colorful cast of Broadway actors and actresses had spread the word of Sconset's attractions to the big city, where theaters closed and everyone suffered in the days before air conditioning. Sconset held a special appeal for the theater people, and they also contributed greatly to its success as a resort and way of life.

The most notable event in Sconset's happy history and the big story of 1900 was the midsummer opening of the Siasconset Casino, truly a night to remember. The casino was built by private contributions from Sconset summer residents who became the proprietors of the building, but the public was welcome to its social events. Opening night was spectacular, with the building gaslit and lending a festive glow to the sleepy village. Horses and carriages arriving from Nantucket filled the streets, while twenty-three special "pleasure wagons" and passengers on a special train from Nantucket arrived to create a throng around the building. When the casino doors opened, 840 people surged into the building, a crowd described as "the largest and most select audience ever before gathered under a public hall roof on the island."

The crowd was not disappointed as the Sconset theater colony put on an evening of music and comedy, the Spanish dancers whirled about in full costume, and the band played on—truly Nantucket's celebration of the new century. That first evening at the casino launched the village of Sconset as what some would call Nantucket's answer to Newport.

Another event that took place that summer had far-reaching consequences. In the middle of August, another Stanley Steamer, owned by the famous yachtsman Howard Willets, arrived on the island, The driver attempted to navigate through heavy traffic on Federal Street, and although the townspeople might have tolerated the new vehicles, the Nantucket horses were terrified of them. Willets came too close to Joseph Hussey's horse, which became frightened and bolted. Hussey was thrown from his carriage, suffering body bruises and thereby becoming Nantucket's first victim of an automobile accident.

That was just the beginning of the long battle between Nantucket and the automobile, a war that was waged in the streets, the courts, and the legislature, resulting in a total ban on the vehicles for several years, making Nantucket the only place in the country to successfully outlaw the automobile. That law was repealed in 1918, principally due to the pressure from outlying summer residents who wanted to drive their pleasure vehicles everywhere.

Nantucket was a town of walkers and talkers. People walked everywhere and enjoyed the company of their neighbors. Although the population was declining, the farmers and fishermen tended to have large families whose boys and girls went to work at an early age. The island yearned for a revival of its maritime trade, which was always beset by problems of weather, distance, and declining capital investment. The local fishermen had a hard life and made little money. The farmers were always in debt to the bank. Yet friends and relatives helped one another. There were no luxuries, no vacations, but many good times. Like most New Englanders, Nantucketers lived a hardy and independent life, and did not complain.

One of the pleasant experiences of local life was the daily shopping trip to the grocery store, usually the task of the woman of the house. The grocer or butcher wore a white shirt and straw hat, and advised young wives on the best values. The butcher would chop and wrap the meat or chicken, creating a bloody scene that fascinated the children. The grocer would hustle around the store, hooking items from the tall shelves, bag up everything, write down the prices on the paper bag and add the list in his head—and always got it right!

A big event for children was the arrival of the ice man, with his horse-drawn cart carrying big chunks of ice. Housewives posted a colored card in the front window, which was rotated to display the needed size of ice to be delivered. The iceman would chop and chisel the chunk until it was the proper size and lug it into the kitchen on his back, which was covered by a rubber mat. The same ice wagon, with a minimum of cleaning, was converted to a coal wagon in winter.

Winters seemed more severe in the early years of the century. Heavy snows at Christmas and the new year were common, and the prospect of a "hard winter" was always predicted. Nantucketers took advantage of nature, with sledding and sliding in the streets and ice skating and boating on the ponds. The best times were free and provided by nature. Family entertainment revolved around church and fraternal events; church suppers and Sunday events, with the children joining in with their parents. There was little night life on the island. Nantucketers in the Victorian era were a self-sufficient, hardy people who lived in a demanding climate, but they accepted their life and made the most of it.

The islanders found many recreational pleasures and pursuits provided by nature and their own talents during all seasons. Two new unpaved bicycle paths were laid out to Sconset and Surfside, and bicycling was a very popular sport. In the summer, beach parties and picnics were common, with harbor sails and sight-seeing cruises always in fashion. In the fall, the biggest event was the annual Nantucket County Fair, a panorama of agricultural Nantucket, with something to be enjoyed by everyone. The fairgrounds were situated at the mid-island site later in the century to be occupied by the offices of the electric company. The three-day fair included horse racing, cattle shows, and domestic arts and exhibitions, with many prizes awarded.

The peaceful pleasures of the inhabitants could not compensate for the depressed state of the island's economy. The hoped-for revival of the maritime trade never developed, and the waterfront seemed to decline each year. The summer tourist season was too short and did little for the majority of islanders. Nantucket real estate was widely available for rent or for sale. Farms and cottages were advertised at bargain prices, but no buyers could be found. Every proposed real estate development had failed. Among the properties offered for sale were the Surfside Hotel, several cottages on Brant Point, an eleven-room house and barn on Union Street, and fifty acres of waterfront on the South Shore; all were looking for buyers.

Business was very slow on the island, but a business directory published in 1909 paints a picture of island life during the decade. Heads of households were listed to include many farmers, fishermen and tradesmen, teachers and clerks. Six real estate agents, seven doctors, and four dentists were practicing, but sadly only one lawyer who could afford to advertise. The town was blessed with four blacksmiths and sixteen livery men, a formidable force in the horse-drawn society, which would later play a prominent role in the fight against the automobile.

Business began early on Main Street, where the post office opened at 5:30 A.M. and didn't close until 9:00 P.M. in the summer, 7:00 P.M. in the winter—hours dictated by the departure and arrival of the steamboat. There were twenty-six boarding houses in town, providing homes for working men and single women, and nineteen mostly seasonal hotels, which seemed to open and disappear annually.

Social life revolved around the dozen or so fraternal and social

13

societies usually segregated by gender and providing weekly or monthly meetings and activities for men and women—virtually the only evening entertainment in Nantucket.

Business in Nantucket in the early 1900s was conducted by individuals whose names would endure on the island. A partial list would include James Andrews, boatman; Albert G. Brock, insurance; Congdon's Pharmacy; Glidden's Fish Market; Israel Lewis, undertaker; and Willard B. Marden, plumber. The two island banks, the Nantucket Institution for Savings and the Pacific National Bank, doing business in 1900, would survive the century with slightly altered names and different owners.

Probably the most lasting of Nantucket institutions would be the *Inquirer and Mirror,* which moved from one end of Orange Street to the other, and at the end of the century raised its 1900 price of four cents a copy to a dollar.

Captain Killen, center, drives the last spike to complete the Nantucket Railroad.

Captain John Killen
CAPTAIN OF THE WATERFRONT

JOHN KILLEN WAS BORN IN IRELAND IN 1848 AND CARRIED to Nantucket by his parents when only five years old. He was fascinated by the seaman's life, and ran away from home at fifteen to ship out of New Bedford as a cabin boy. Later, he made one whaling voyage out of Nantucket with his boyhood friends—a "plum pudding" voyage of only a few months.

He spent most of his sea-going years in the coastal trade during the era when big wooden schooners were the workhorses of the maritime fleet, and he soon rose to become mate and master of several schooners. In 1882, he had built and named for his wife the Mary A. Killen, a 1,000-ton schooner. He skippered this ship in the southern trade, often with his wife and son on board. On one winter night when they were on shore, Captain Killen was caught in a blinding snowstorm and wrecked off Scituate, losing his ship and its cargo of sugar.

The captain returned home to Nantucket, where he later purchased the coal, wood, and ice business that he operated for the rest of his life as J. Killen and Son. In 1902, he built the first artificial ice plant on the island. He soon became the most important man on the busy Nantucket waterfront, owning several waterfront vessels, most of Old North Wharf, and Straight Wharf, which was generally known as Killen's Wharf.

Captain Killen lived in the Greek Revival mansion on the corner of Federal and Broad Streets, which had been built by Frederick C. Sanford in 1847. Here he raised a family of three sons and two daughters. He was greatly respected as a businessman and good citizen, becoming elected to the Board of Selectmen for eight years. When it came time to drive the golden spike for the Nantucket Railroad, the burly Captain Jack was the man with the hammer. The captain's name stood for industry and integrity; he proudly advertised his coal and ice company with the slogan "We have kept you warm in winter and cool in summer, and are still on deck!"

After his death on Christmas Eve in 1927, at the age of 80, the captain left a widow and five children, but no will. Family disagreement subjected his valuable properties to lengthy and expensive court proceedings, during which the mighty Killen empire deteriorated, symbolized by the big coal shed bearing the Killen name, slowly sinking into the waters of Nantucket Harbor. The property became the modern boat basin and Straight Wharf, where thousands of tourists now land on the spot from which Captain Jack once ruled the waterfront.

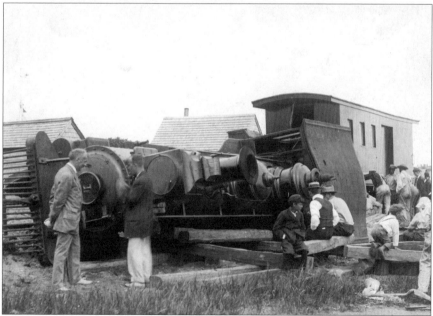

Top: A peaceful view of Post Office Square in Sconset at the turn of the century.
Bottom: Less than peaceful, the 1909 wreck of the Nantucket Railroad engine *Dionis*.

Top: First airplane wreck on Nantucket, April 27, 1918. Bottom: Passengers from the steamer *Sankaty* walk across the ice at Brant Point; the baby in foreground is Albert "Bud" Egan.

The second decade of the new century witnessed the rise of the motor vehicle, the sinking of the Titanic, and the catastrophe of World War I. The United States celebrated the opening of the Panama Canal and victory in Europe, which promised world peace and progress. Nantucket awakened to the era of the automobile, the airplane, and the telephone—bringing the island closer to the mainland, for better or for worse.

The Carfree Years

The water and the weather accounted for much of what was newsworthy in the early part of the century. In the summer of 1901, the U. S. Navy and the Marine Corps landed on Nantucket for an unusual engagement: the North Atlantic Squadron, commanded by Admiral Higginson, arrived in the Chord of the Bay with the battleships *Alabama, Kearsarge,* and *Massachusetts* and staged a week of maneuvers on Coatue. Because of the opening of the Haulover at the Head of the Harbor, Great Point and Coatue were a separate island, and the Marines established a tent encampment known as Camp City. The Marines staged an amphibious landing, complete with five-inch guns and live ammunition, while the Navy unlimbered its heavy guns to sink the condemned *Lightship No. 19* in a practice battle off Gay Head, Martha's Vineyard. Although no one on the island participated in the action (later described as practice for the Pacific landings of World War II!) the Navy sent its band ashore to play for a concert on the Lower Square on August 17, whereafter the summer residents invited the Navy and Marine officers to a farewell reception on August 23 at the Sea Cliff Inn. This proved to be a patriotic occasion for the island and a prelude to the welcome arrival of the U. S. Navy during World War I, sixteen years later.

The miracle of wireless telegraphy came to Nantucket during 1901, when the first wireless telegraph office was established in Sconset on August 3. This project was promoted by the *New York Herald* in order to scoop news of incoming Atlantic shipping one day before the vessels reached New York. The first message came from the steamship *Lucania* on August 16. The station was later taken over by the Marconi Wireless Company in 1904, and became famous for its early reception of steamship traffic, which was relayed to the mainland by telegraph line. One of the first two wireless operators on Nantucket was David Sarnoff, who would later be the founder of RCA, the Radio Corporation of America.

Nantucket had its own customs office in the Pacific Club Building, which also housed the weather bureau; and although it did no international business, it was a reminder of the island's maritime heritage. The government closed it down in 1913, but until that date vessels could be registered and proudly claim Nantucket as their home port. The weather bureau was moved to Cash's Court, off Orange Street, in 1904, where it remained until it moved to the airport. The weather was always a favorite subject of islanders' conversation.

Outside of town, a pattern of dirt roads led to the settlements and farms that were situated in outlying areas of the island. Many small farms were scattered across the island from Wauwinet to Madaket, farms that provided the main food supply for the islanders and a marginal living for the farmers. At one time, James Gibbs listed a total of ninety-four known farms on the island. Many of the farmers and their families led solitary lives, going to town only when necessary for business or for important public occasions.

One major agricultural venture was the cultivation of the natural cranberry bog near Gibbs Pond in 1905. Hundreds of workmen and horse-drawn vehicles were imported to perform the extensive digging and ditching of the bog, which when it was finished was the largest in the world. The creation of a Nantucket farmer named Fred Maglathlin, the bog later became one of the island's most successful agricultural pursuits, as it is to this day.

The town began to pave streets as early as 1904, when Federal Street was concreted and cobblestones later were covered on Orange, India, Fair, and Centre Streets. The streets were not paved to accommodate automobile traffic but to satisfy neighborhood complaints about the noisy and unsafe surfaces of the cobbles. The town took advantage of the situation and installed sewer and water pipes before the paving was laid down, a far-sighted project for the times. Still resisting the automobile, the town embarked upon a continuing project to cover the cobblestones, which was a controversial issue: the proponents argued for smoother and quieter streets; the opponents wanted to preserve the traditional ways of Nantucket. Veteran attorney Allen Coffin objected to the paving: "Noise is louder over the leveled vitrified brick (on upper Main Street) than over the cobbles . . . . Covering a good cobblestone road with concrete is wasting money for no good purpose," he said.

Some of the streets in town have now had the cobblestones restored or have been newly cobbled, mainly because of the low-maintenance factor. (When the cobblestones reappeared, *The New York Times* columnist Russell Baker, a longtime summer resident, wrote humorously about Nantucket in an article titled "The Taint of Quaint," in which he had some rather outlandish suggestions for further use of cobblestones.)

Severe weather conditions prevailed in the early years of the century, which accentuated the island's sense of isolation. Along with the declining economy and the loss of population, the island was struck by the worst of winter weather, with heavy snows, howling gales, and freeze-ups of the harbor. Each December seemed to bring heavier snows, and the snow of January 1905 was recorded as the greatest on record: 21.4 inches in twenty-four hours, with a northeast gale creating thirty-foot drifts. Then the harbor froze solid from February 2 to February 25, imprisoning the steamship *Nantucket* for three weeks. In 1908, Nantucket's weather bureau recorded the most severe storm in its history, with a wind velocity of 130 miles an hour on January 23, accompanied by ten inches of snow and heavy seas in the harbor. On November 9, changing currents closed the channel at the Haulover, north of Wauwinet, thus reuniting Great Point and Coatue to the rest of Nantucket. The next day a horse and team drove down to Wauwinet from the Coskata Life-Saving Station for the first time in twelve years. From the time when the cut was made, everything, including horses, had to be carried out to the station by boat and barge.

Changes came slowly in Nantucket. Some traditional island institutions remained active, while others originated early in the century. The Catholic church on Federal Street, the Church of St. Mary, Our Lady of the Isle, which had been constructed in 1897, finally became an official parish in 1903, when the Reverend Thomas J. McGee, a native of Oak Bluffs and graduate of Holy Cross College, became the first pastor of the Nantucket church and said his first Mass on June 7. The Catholic population of the island had grown to several hundred with the arrival of Irish, French Canadian, and Portuguese workers in the agricultural and construction businesses.

The Nantucket Atheneum, which had been a private institution since its founding, became a public library in 1900. The Maria Mitchell Association, founded in 1902, honored the memory of Nantucket's greatest woman, who began her career as the first librar-

ian of the Atheneum and went on to become a professor of astrono-
my at Vassar College. The cornerstone for St. Paul's Episcopal
Church was laid in 1902, and the church was consecrated in June.
The Methodist Church had so declined in membership by 1901 the
building was offered for sale, but the only interested buyer was the
Town of Nantucket, which thought it might be appropriate for con-
version to a town hall; but town meeting rejected the idea, so the
church was repaired and continued in operation, though it would see
hard times. At the end of the century it gained a new lease of life
when First Lady Hillary Clinton, visiting Nantucket with the
President, was instrumental in having the church declared a
"National Treasure," which greatly assisted in the fund-raising effort.
The Coffin School, founded in 1827 for descendants of Tristram
Coffin, the "first settler," reopened as a manual training and home
economics school for high school students, becoming the training
ground for many skilled craftsmen in future years.

Amid the worst of winter weather, declining economy, and
increasing isolation from the mainland, prospects looked bleaker
every year. By 1905, the population had declined to 2,930, and one
indication of the island's demise was the Nantucket High School
class of 1905; it had one graduate—Vera Sickles.

In the summer of 1905, the little broadside *Sconset Notes* mentioned "We have never seen so many visitors to Sconset this early."
The Nantucket Railroad began its schedule in June and provided
service to Sconset all summer long, although it was often interrupted by equipment failure, accidents, and its precarious roadbed, which
was constantly being reconstructed. On a hot July day in 1909, the
rails spread and the locomotive turned turtle on South Beach—to the
great amusement of the populace, who suggested it be buried on the
spot. The state highway to Sconset—a dusty, muddy, rutted road—
was the first rural road to be paved and was completed in 1910 for a
total cost of $52,983, thus providing more comfortable access to the
island's easternmost village.

The waterfront was the most important feature of Nantucket life in the early years of the century. The colorful vista of catboats, steamships, and sailing dories filled the harbor with many memorable sights and stories. Captain James Andrews brought home a season-high total of twenty-five bluefish, while the dory fishermen landed hundreds of pounds of haddock and cod—pulled in by the traditional hand-line method.

In 1905, the well-known New York yachtsman Paul G. Thebaud, at his own expense, started a venture that would become the Nantucket Yacht Club. He purchased a small building on the steamship wharf that was moved and reconstructed with a new deck and pier built by Holmes & Pease, Contractors. The federal government had spent $525,000 on improvements in the harbor, and knowing that the newly dredged channel would be a great attraction for yachtsmen, Thebaud began to promote Nantucket among his friends and others in the sailing community all along the Atlantic coast. The *Inquirer and Mirror* welcomed the new venture: "Every resident of Nantucket knows that each yacht that enters this harbor means not only increased interest in the island attractions but increased revenue to the town."

When Thebaud sailed into the harbor on his yawl *Normona,* a new sign had appeared on the waterfront: "New York Yacht Club Station," and Nantucket became a port of call for the club's annual cruise.

The Steamship Company changed hands in 1911, when the Nantucket owners sold their shares to the New York, New Haven and Hartford Railroad Co, thereafter linking the fate of the island line to the great New England railroad company, which included Nantucket in its advertising and publicity. A new steamer, *Sankaty,* was put in service in May, and it was announced in August that the schooner *Ariadne,* drawing seventeen feet, had sailed into Nantucket Harbor, the vessel with the deepest draft ever to round Brant Point. The transportation pattern was expanding and improving, slowly but surely.

Beginning in 1912, Nantucket was beginning to show signs of returning prosperity The economy centered around the harbor, where the fishing and shellfish industry showed steady improvement and the newly dredged anchorage providing a safe offshore haven for the New England fleet. During the winter of 1913–14, 7,968 barrels of Nantucket's succulent bay scallops were shipped to the mainland. In the summer, the bluefish returned in abundance, providing great sport fishing and adding to the summer attractions. In a single day, Mitchell Ray hauled seventy-three bluefish from the beach at Surfside, and sold them for 25 cents each. In the winter of 1914–15, the island had daily steamship service to and from New Bedford. The steamer *Sankaty* carried 1,426 barrels of Nantucket fish to the mainland on March 15, the largest such cargo on record for a single shipment. In the same month, it was recorded that 1,140 fishing vessels passed Brant Point, entering or leaving the harbor.

The Cape Cod Canal opened in the summer of 1914, marking a significant change in sea-borne traffic on the Atlantic Coast. It provided an inshore route for vessels that eliminated the passage through the treacherous Nantucket Shoals, known as "the graveyard of the Atlantic."

During the summer of 1916, a telephone cable was laid on the ocean bed between Nantucket and Martha's Vineyard and thence to Cape Cod, and Nantucket finally had its long-awaited telephone connection with the mainland. On a gala occasion—August 29, 1916—a well-dressed crowd of men and women gathered in the Great Hall of the Atheneum to witness the first long-distance call to the mainland. Using the longest submarine cable in America, the island of Nantucket was for the first time in its history in speaking contact with the rest of the country. The historic event was captured in a photograph that still hangs in the Atheneum.

Also in that year, the Nantucket Land Trust was laying out hundreds of house lots in Tom Nevers, where it owned 2,000 acres of land with two miles of ocean frontage. The tract was bisected by the line of the Nantucket Railroad, which figured prominently in the developers' plans. The feature attraction was the rustic Tom Nevers Lodge, a rambling Prairie Style structure surmounted by a five-story tower to view the scenery (it subsequently burned to the ground in 1933.) Building lots were auctioned off each afternoon at $50 to $100 per lot, 5,000 square feet in area. Many tourists rode out to Tom Nevers on the train, stopped to buy a lot, then rode home, secure with their deed to part of Nantucket. However, no houses materialized on the Tom Nevers scene, and the venture faded away like many of Nantucket's early real estate schemes. Much later in the century, a new band of developers would succeed in covering the open vistas of Tom Nevers with hundreds of houses, most of them built as summer rentals.

World War I was presaged by the incursion of German submarines into American waters. The submarine, having no peacetime function, was the one vessel that brought the foreign threat home to the east coast of America. Nantucket was a lonely outpost in the Atlantic and the threat became real in January of 1916, while the United States was still at peace. On January 29, the *Inquirer and Mirror* printed an exclusive story stating that the German submarine *Deutschland* was crossing the Atlantic. The local paper, because it had access to local shipping contacts, scooped the big city press, which widely ridiculed the story, but the story proved true when the sub arrived off Norfolk, as predicted, on July 9. Another submarine sank six foreign ships off Nantucket on October 8, and the clouds of war gathered over the island.

The United States declared war in April 1917, and Nantucket responded to the national mobilization by sending a draft of army candidates to Barnstable. Later, on the Fourth of July, with a huge American flag flying over Main Street, the town also saluted a crowd of boys who had volunteered to help the farmers raise their crops: the Nantucket Agricultural Army, commanded by a summer resident, the playwright Austin Strong.

The war hastened the demise of the Nantucket Railroad, which was a victim of declining patronage because of it. And it was in the last summer of the line's existence, on June 20, that a Nantucket teamster, 61-year-old William Dodge, tried to drive his horse and wagon across the island's only grade crossing, on Lower Orange Street, near Hatch's establishment. He was confident his horse could beat the oncoming locomotive, but he was wrong. William Dodge was killed instantly, becoming Nantucket's only railroad fatality at its only road crossing. The train made its last run on September 23, 1917, and in 1918 the remains of the famous little railroad were sent to France as scrap metal "to aid the war effort." The sole relic of the railroad is the parlor car, which was moved to lower Main Street, where it served for a long time as Allen's Diner and now is the bar of the upscale Club Car.

The U. S. Navy had a large presence in Nantucket during World War I, when the Naval Reserve established a station under the command of Lt. Thomas J. Prindeville. The Navy began its operations with an office in the weather bureau, then shifted headquarters to the Athletic Club (now the Nantucket Yacht Club) on the waterfront; 300 men were billeted in the Springfield House on North Water Street (now part of the Harbor House). A large fleet of small naval craft was anchored in the harbor and used for antisubmarine patrols. The Navy saw no action around Nantucket, but the officers and men contributed greatly to the island's social life and entertainment scene for the two wartime years.

As if to signify the island's involvement in the national effort, President Woodrow Wilson and his wife arrived at the Athletic Club landing aboard the presidential yacht *Mayflower* on September 13. The Navy was in the right place to salute its Commander in Chief, although the visit was not military but personal. The President and First Lady came to Nantucket to visit their daughter, Mrs. Francis Sayre, who was vacationing in Sconset. As there were no motor cars for the cavalcade, the president had the pleasure of a long horse and buggy ride, which he claimed to enjoy.

During World War I, Nantucket sent 192 men and one woman into military service. Four men died in service but only one man, Byron L. Sylvaro, was killed in action, dying from wounds received in France. His body was brought home for burial in the Catholic cemetery, and the American Legion Post was named in his honor.

The war at sea continued into 1918, with German submarines and Atlantic weather continuing to take their toll. The year started with a hard winter, freezing-up the steamer in the harbor for two weeks. The same ice ripped away the moorings of the *Cross Rip Lightship* on February 1, whereupon she was swept out to sea and lost with all of her six-man crew. Several steamers bound for Europe were wrecked on the shoals.

In July, a German submarine sank coal barges and burned a tug off Cape Cod, and in August another sub attacked the fishing fleet on Georges Bank, sinking six fishing boats and a British steamship. Twenty-eight survivors were landed at Nantucket, the first actual victims of the submarine warfare to be seen.

A greater danger faced the island in 1918, when an epidemic of deadly influenza swept the country causing many fatalities in the cities and military camps. The flu struck Nantucket on October 30, quickly filling the hospital facilities, which were taken over by town officials with William Wallace in charge. The epidemic lasted three weeks, but the island survived with 337 reported cases and nine deaths from pneumonia. In the emergency, three doctors and three nurses were provided by the state, and the Nesbitt Inn was used as an emergency hospital, donated without charge by Mrs. George Burgess.

During the last year of the war, a Navy hydroplane flew across the sound from Chatham to Nantucket, landing on South Beach on April 13—the first airplane to come to the island. As there was no landing field, aircraft travel was restricted to seaplanes. The Navy tried it again on April 17, when three pontoon planes landed in the harbor near Brant Point, but a fourth plane hit the flats near Coatue and flipped over: Nantucket's first plane crash; the pilot survived.

On November 11, 1918, the *Inquirer and Mirror* published its "Peace Extra," printing the terms of the peace treaty with Germany and narrating Nantucket's "Peace Jollification and Victory Parade" at length. With the church bells ringing, hundreds of Nantucketers filled the streets, cheering and waving flags. A spontaneous parade assembled, led by Ensign Aldrich, followed by the naval band and Lt. Prindeville and his naval reservists leading Grand Army veterans. Red Cross ladies and Yeomen, Masons, Odd Fellows, Red Men, schoolchildren, fire engines and repair trucks followed, with Captain John Killen riding a runabout and blowing a fog horn. It was an impromptu and highly enjoyable celebration of peace.

At the end of World War I, it was discovered that Nantucket had subscribed a grand total of $1,665,100 for the purchase of U. S. Savings Bonds, known as Liberty Loans, in the course of five fund-raising drives. This amounted to more than the island's quota, and an average of $555 per capita, which made Nantucket the "banner town" of the United States. Substantial purchases of bonds by the summer community undoubtedly contributed to the island's remarkable record.

The wartime year had put a damper on Nantucket's summer seasons; and the submarine threat, the loss of the railroad, and the influenza epidemic had seriously affected the island's attractions to visitors. But Nantucket still had hope for the future. The war introduced many new visitors to the island and the arrival of the first airplanes forecast the transportation of the future. In addition, several real estate ventures were on their way to early success.

The departure of the railroad left a void in the .island's transportation picture, which could only be replaced by one piece of machinery. It was not long in coming.

The mail must go through for Clinton Folger and his "Horsemobile."

THE GREAT AUTOMOBILE FIGHT

THE FIRST AUTOMOBILES TO ARRIVE IN NANTUCKET IN THE EARLY years of the century were greeted with curiosity and amusement. Many islanders who had never been on the mainland viewed the new vehicles as expensive playthings for the summer residents, and were content to leave them alone. The Nantucket horses, however, were terrified by the noisy intruders in the quiet town streets. After the first horses became alarmed and threw their drivers, the town fathers decided to do something. The selectmen met and issued an order setting the automobile speed in town at four miles an hour, which was below the stalling speed of those early vehicles.

Nantucket was proud of its reputation as a quiet and easy-going community. Life moved at a leisurely pace and was expected to remain so; any disturbance of the peace was unseemly and unwelcome. The streets were paved with cobblestones or gravel in town, and were all dirt roads beyond town limits. The town had a substantial number of liverymen, farmers, and wagoneers who depended upon horse-drawn transport, which was an important component of the local economy. A row of livery stables and horse barns at Steamboat Wharf catered to the horse and buggy economy. The town was therefore virtually unanimous in its opposition to the intrusion of the gasoline-powered machines.

In 1905, the selectmen again ordered the restrictive speed limit, which elicited a protest from the newly formed Massachusetts Automobile Association that was signed by fifty state residents and presented to the Massachusetts Highway Commission. The commission came to Nantucket for a hearing. A dozen Nantucket residents spoke vehemently in defense of the selectmen. The venerable Allen Coffin, Nantucket's only lawyer, said, "We challenge the state on both legal and moral grounds!" Two weeks later the commission ruled that the Nantucket regulation violated the liberties of both residents and nonresidents who wished to operate motor vehicles, and declared the Nantucket law null and void.

The unsinkable selectmen simply met again and set the speed limit at five miles an hour in town and ten out of town, limits that remained in effect through 1906, when a new element entered the picture.

Until the year 1906, the Nantucket Railroad had provided summer service to Sconset, but when financial troubles developed in that year the railroad stopped operations and a replacement service by motor bus was offered over the state highway. Four hundred taxpayers quickly contested this attempt to motorize the island, and Allen Coffin stated that the auto should be banned from Nantucket forever to preserve its safety, peace, and quiet. However, several Sconset summer residents and hotel operators claimed the village needed seasonal public transportation. The selectmen responded by calling a special town meeting on May 23, 1906, after which they issued the famous order that made Nantucket history:

"Notice is hereby given that the Board of Selectmen of the Town of Nantucket acting under Chapter 366, Acts of 1905, will hereafter exclude all automobiles and motorcycles from all the highways of Nantucket."

This bold step came as a result of the town's interpretation of a 1905 act of the legislature that empowered selectmen to ban automobiles from "particular streets and ways" of a town. The selectmen figured that if they could ban autos from one street, they could ban them from all streets. They were going all the way in this battle.

No autos ventured out on the sacred streets of Nantucket in 1906, nor in early 1907, when the selectmen renewed their order. Three auto owners in Nantucket, all summer residents, stored their cars in livery stables, and one remarked, "I have found that my auto's use makes me most unpopular here, and I have stopped using it." A public hearing in the summer produced vociferous objection to any relaxation of the automobile ban on Nantucket.

Nantucket's nemesis was the resourceful William A. Thibodeau, an attorney and founder of the Massachusetts Automobile Association, who now joined forces with the Sconset summer residents who wanted to drive their cars on Nantucket's roads. One of them was W. V. Birney, who drove his Maxwell to Sconset, was arrested, and hauled into court. On August 3, 1907, Thibodeau prevailed in his argument before trial justice George E. Mooers, and Birney was found not guilty.

After this victory, Thibodeau argued before another Massachusetts Highway Commission hearing in 1907 that the selectmen could not exclude autos from all Nantucket roadways. Town counsel James Swift declared that no place in the country had the charm of Nantucket and that auto exclusion was necessary to protect its character; the venerable Allen Coffin called the auto an "outlaw on Nantucket." For the third time, the commission ruled against the Nantucket auto law. In October, Superior Court ruled that Nantucket could only exclude autos from *particular* streets and ways, not from all of them.

On the day after this ruling, the selectmen met and issued a new order: autos were banned from Steamboat Wharf, Broad Street, North Water Street, and every other street leading to and from Steamboat Wharf. This closed off the waterfront, and barring an amphibious or airborne vehicle, prevented any invasion of Nantucket by motorized craft. Nantucket was secure for another year.

In March of 1908, thirty Nantucketers went to the State House in Boston. They presented a petition fifty feet long and carrying 684 signatures, seeking a legislative act that would entirely prohibit automobiles on the island. Philip Holmes, chairman of the selectmen, stated that the automobile would ruin the summer business. Civil War veteran James H. Wood said, "All we ask is the right to make the rules to protect us, as the majority wish. That is what those who were in the war fought for—and many died for." Liveryman David Gibbs reminded the legislators, "There are ladies in this town who are afraid of automobiles, and especially those who may be in a delicate condition at this time!"

As a result, an act was passed in 1908, authorizing the selectmen to exclude automobiles from operation in Nantucket during the period from June 15 to September 15—the tourist season, when autos caused the most trouble. This law stood without challenge for four years, with the selectmen also barring autos within the town limits year round, only the the State Road excepted.

Nantucket succeeded in banning all automobiles from 1908 to 1912, the public supporting the auto-exclusion law. However, the island's traditional fear of fire, dating back to 1846, caused the town itself to take the first step to legalize motor vehicles. This came about after a terrible fire that swept the Barnes family's boat house on Commercial Wharf in 1911, taking the lives of four young people, and a midwinter fire in town, caused when sparks from the steam fire engine ignited a fire in a house across the street from the blazing dwelling the company had come to extinguish. The fire wardens recommended the purchase of a motorized chemical fire apparatus, and, after a brief debate, town meeting approved it, at a cost of $5,900, which included 200 feet of hose.

The Knox Chemical Fire Engine, painted a dazzling red with "Nantucket," in gold letters on the running board, arrived on May 29, 1912, and thus became Nantucket's first legal motor vehicle. A great crowd followed it from Steamboat Wharf to its berth at the wooden fire station on Centre Street, where the selectmen proudly posed for pictures. Now the town that banned the automobile owned one. The chemical quickly proved its worth when it extinguished a fire in the residence of Judge Henry Riddell on Centre Street. However, Nantucketers soon began to ask: "If the town can own an auto, why can't I?"

On November 5, 1913, there arrived on Nantucket the most famous outlaw of them all, the Overland touring car that would make Nantucket history. It was owned by Clinton Folger, a Nantucket liveryman who had the contract to deliver the mail to Sconset. Since he was free to drive on the state highway (Milestone Road, over which the selectmen had no control), he felt free to drive from Steamboat Wharf over town streets to his destination. The town rose in wrath, and on November 13 the largest town meeting ever held voted overwhelmingly to support the exclusion of all automobiles, including the Overland. Folger defiantly drove his auto up Main Street, was arrested, and fined fifteen dollars. Despite signs posted against his operation, he persisted, and was fined a total of sixty dollars. Then the resourceful Clint Folger hit upon a foolproof and legal plan for delivering the mail.

On December 19, the townsfolk were startled to see Clinton Folger and his Overland rolling through the streets of the town, running at one horse-power, with his sturdy horse pulling the vehicle.

The reins ran back from the horse through the steering wheel, as Folger drove his "Horsemobile" through town out to the First Milestone. There he unhitched the horse to graze on the Lewis Farm while he cranked up the Overland for its trip to Sconset to deliver the mail. Upon his return, the horse was hitched to the auto and returned to the stable in triumph.

Nantucket followed this action by filing another bill in the legislature, which resulted in a 1914 auto-exclusion act for Nantucket that forbade the operation of automobiles on any public way in the town of Nantucket. That act was approved by the voters 376 to 234.

Another famous Boston lawyer, Franklin E. Smith—credited as the first of the modern land developers on Nantucket and the controlling power behind the development of the Cranberry Company, the Tom Nevers Trust, and other outlying developments—now appeared on the scene. In 1918, he filed a bill in the legislature, seeking repeal of the Nantucket Auto Exclusion Law. Smith claimed to be the third-largest taxpayer on the island, that he owned 8,000 acres of land that required automobile access, and that people in the village of Sconset needed autos because the railroad was terminated.

Two hundred Nantucketers appeared at the State House in opposition to Smith's bill, including the Reverend Samuel Snelling who made a strong plea to preserve the will of the island majority over one landowner, and John J. Gardner who termed Smith's plan a "campaign of imperialism."

The legislature handed the problem back to Nantucket. A bill was passed to present the question on the ballot: "Shall the operation of automobiles be allowed on the island?" The date set for the election was toward the end of World War I, on May 15, 1918. With intense interest in the local issue, 640 of Nantucket's 816 registered voters went to the polls, and when the votes were counted Nantucket had voted to repeal its unique automobile-exclusion law, by vote of 336 to 296, By a margin of forty votes, the automobile came to Nantucket.

It did not take long for the first legal private automobile to arrive. On May 16, a shiny Maxwell rolled off the steamer. More came the next weekend, and by the start of summer vehicles were buzzing around Nantucket. The automobile had come to stay.

Thus did the little island of Nantucket valiantly attempt to stem the tide during the first two decades of the twentieth century, as represented by its most dominant mechanism, Although they could not stop the wheels of progress, those intrepid Nantucket selectmen and other men and women were willing to fight to protect the island and its traditions from powerful economic and political forces. In the end, it was the pressures of the summer community that brought the automobile and all its changes to the island. As one native commented, "They came here to get away from it all, then they brought it with them."

Top: Rescuers were unable to save the victims of the Barnes Boat House fire of 1911.
Bottom: The Surfside Life Saving Station was still in operation in 1911.

An aerial view of Nantucket town taken in the late 1920s.

America adopted Prohibition and started a ten-year celebration that ended with the Wall Street crash of 1929. Americans had their own heroes as they soared with Lindbergh, celebrated with Babe Ruth, and kept cool with Coolidge. Nantucket enjoyed a golden decade, and the boom times of the twenties would later be remembered as "the Good Old Days."

The Good
Old Days

The postwar years brought change and progress to Nantucket in many ways. The island came back to life after the uncertain years of World War I, and the figures from the Steamship Company told the main story: in 1918 the line carried 149,040 passengers; in 1919 the figure was 216,433; and in 1920 it carried 58,236 passengers in the month of July alone. The ships also carried something else, automobiles, with ninety-three vehicles registered to Nantucketers in 1919, and scores arriving for the summer season. With the railroad gone, automobiles became more intrusive every summer.

The summer scene was especially evident in the village of Sconset. Post Office Square was reported "congested" with automobiles, as dozens of summer visitors brought their vehicles and the natives took weekly drives out of town to show off their new machines. The behavior of the summer colony in Sconset was a source of endless fascination and commentary: no one rises before nine, everyone gets a late start; first a stroll to the post office, then to the beach at noon. The afternoon is spent at the Old Sconset Golf Links, where everyone who doesn't play must become a caddy. Then back for a nap and off to the Casino in the evening to watch the actors perform or enjoy the annual masquerade ball at the peak of the season. Most evenings are spent in visiting from cottage to cottage, where the doors are never locked and the hospitality is legendary.

In 1919, the U. S. Congress passed the notorious Volstead Act, which led to the adoption of the Eighteenth Amendment, taking effect in 1920 and prohibiting the manufacture, sale, import, or export of alcoholic beverages; intended to uplift the moral and social character of the nation. Prohibition had a huge impact on the island's social life. As a national movement, it was a dismal failure, and as a social reform, it served only to make lawbreakers of a large segment of the population and promote disrespect for law enforcement at every level of society. Nantucket looked upon national prohibition as a futile exercise by a federal bureaucracy, far removed from the life of the island.

It certainly had an impact on one of the most popular of Sconset's summer residents. Robert Hilliard, a playwright and a matinee idol in the New York theater, owned two cottages, named Sleepy Eye and Wide Awake. When he left Nantucket in the fall of 1919, he left behind his personal stock of pre-Prohibition beverages locked in a brick cellar behind four padlocked doors. Hilliard was at his home on the mainland when he learned the shocking news that his entire stock of choice scotch, bourbon, and wine, valued at $3,400, had been looted, with only a few empty bottles left behind. The valuable collection was not only gone, it was now irreplaceable.

Mr. Hilliard was so incensed by the robbery that he hired his own private investigator and attorney to find the culprit, and the island buzzed with rumors for months. Finally, the local police arrested Larry Welch, who owned a grocery store in Sconset and allegedly sold adult beverages on the side. The town awaited the trial of Larry Welch as the first test of Prohibition enforcement on Nantucket. Then the presiding justice and special justice of the District Court—both alleged patrons of Larry Welch—disqualified themselves, leaving Nantucket perplexed. Judge Paul Swift sailed over from Cape Cod to hear the case, followed by reporters from Boston and New Bedford, and Robert Hilliard made a dramatic appearance in the courtroom. The star witness for the prosecution was old Gus Pitman, a Sconset character who admitted buying a bottle of good scotch from Larry Welch for eight dollars. He drank the contents and then carried the empty bottle around, taking occasional sniffs from it. The empty bottle was offered in evidence, but Judge Swift peered suspiciously and was unimpressed. "There is your evidence!" beamed Robert Hilliard. "There is not," said the judge. "He drank the evidence! I find the defendant not guilty for lack of corroborating evidence." So ended Nantucket's first brush with Prohibition and its consequences.

The town itself was getting busier each summer. By 1920, the island had a year-round population of 2,797 and an assessed valuation of $5,649,990. The summer population was estimated at 12,000. This created a great demand for summer rentals and guest houses, and many old homes were turned into rooming houses for the season, providing a nice source of income for local families. There soon arose a need for more service establishments and restaurants to accommodate the summer visitors. The absence of drinking establishments led to the omnipresent "tea room" business, and many small restaurants sprang up both in and outside of town.

The roads and byways of the town were gradually improved during these years, and in 1921 the county commissioners used the old railroad route leading off Steamboat Wharf to establish convenient access to the south. They couldn't agree on a name for the new way, but the newspaper was calling it "Easy Street," so with public approval the name stuck. This street for many years featured a large willow tree in the middle of the road, a tree that couldn't be removed as it was supposed to have come from a sprig on the grave of Napoleon at St. Helena. When it was finally removed, a cutting from it sprouted elsewhere; it would not die.

One of the most memorable summer establishments of the era was situated at the head of Steamboat Wharf, where it was visible to all arrivals and soon became a waterfront institution. The old two-masted coal schooner *Allen Gurney* made her last voyage to Nantucket in 1920. She was in such bad shape her captain sold her to a pair of local women, Gladys Wood and Margaret Prentice, who had plans for a tea room. The vessel was hauled into the shallow water of Easy Street Basin and named "The Skipper." She was attached to the shore establishment by a wooden catwalk leading to a large old wooden building that had been the print shop of the newspaper—also the site of a laundry and later a carousel—now converted into a dining room and kitchen for the restaurant. The broad wooden deck became a popular spot for lunch and dinner and feeding seagulls. It was the favorite haunt of the artist Tony Sarg, whose shop was next door. He ate most of his meals aboard the ship, and cheerfully obliged tourists by signing autographs and decorating their menus with his clever cartoons. The old *Allen Gurney* gradually lost her masts and salty appearance as she settled into the harbor mud. After several changes in ownership, she was broken up as a waterfront hazard and was sold to the Steamship Authority in 1985, reportedly for a million dollars, and the area was used to enlarge the parking lot. She manages to survive in hundreds of waterfront photographs and thousands of picture postcards.

The steamship line to the mainland was truly the lifeline of the island. New Bedford was the main port for Nantucket in 1920, and the round trip fare was $3.00. The ship left Nantucket at 6:30 A.M., called at Oak Bluffs, Woods Hole, and landed at New Bedford at 11:25. On the return trip, it left the city at 12:40, carrying all the passengers, mail, and freight for the islands. The return boat stopped at Woods Hole, Oak Bluffs, and Vineyard Haven, and arrived at Nantucket at 5:50 P.M. This made a long return trip, and Nantucket complained about the late arrival of the mail. The steamship line responded by saying it was losing money from November to April each year, and could not afford to do better by the island. The two favorite steamers, *Uncatena* and *Sankaty,* were comfortable and popular, however, and the passengers enjoyed the trips. On arrival in Nantucket during the summer, passengers were greeted by a solid line of porters from the local hotels, each shouting out the name of his establishment to attract its patrons. Hearing those names—"Ocean House! Sea Cliff Inn! Point Breeze! White Elephant! The Breakers!"—was one of the happiest memories of a Nantucket vacation.

In September of 1921, an important addition to the island's attractions was the inauguration of Sankaty Head Golf Club, on land donated by David Gray Sr., on the moors west of Sconset. Mr. Gray, an eminent summer resident of Sconset, was given the honor of driving the first ball off the first tee. This gave Nantucket a magnificent 18-hole course, which contributed greatly to Nantucket's future as a summer resort.

The year also saw the celebration of 100 years of island newspapers, as commemorated in a historical centennial issue published by the *Inquirer and Mirror* that contained valuable articles and pictures.

The next year opened with violent storms and almost ten inches of snow. Heavy fog and high winds made the seas hazardous, and two steamships collided in Buzzards Bay. The island fishing fleet remained very active, and Nantucket made a good living from the fishing industry as well as the summer season. The value placed on the fleet was $431,000, and the winter catch alone brought in a total of $835,000 income to the island. The commercial wharves of John Killen and the Island Service Company were always busy places—

fueling, icing, and supplying the vessels; off-loading cargoes; and shipping boxes and barrels of seafood to the mainland packers at New Bedford. During this period, several off-island fishermen brought their families to the island and became permanent residents.

Another arrival came in June via a Nantucket fishing boat. An exhausted male deer that was found swimming several miles out in the sound was rescued, revived, and liberated on the island to make a life for himself. As deer were not native to the island, Old Buck was the sole member of his breed until 1926, when he became the founding father of the entire deer population of Nantucket.

In the summer of 1922, two of Nantucket's popular downtown institutions were enlarged. The Dreamland Theatre, Nantucket's venerable motion picture house, was totally renovated in anticipation of talking pictures. It was enlarged to a capacity of 600, with a sloping floor, new projection room, and modern ventilation. Nearby, the Atheneum library acquired the Cook property at the corner of India and South Water Streets, extending the library property to encompass an entire town block. This land, which then included several small shops and a candy store, later became the site of the children's library and the Atheneum Garden, the only green spot in downtown Nantucket.

During the summer of 1922, it was announced that Sconset would become the site of an intellectual and artistic community known as the "School of Opinion." It was the concept of Frederick C. Howe, a respected legal scholar and progressive reformer from Cleveland. Mr. Howe, who would later become part of the original "Brain Trust" of the Roosevelt New Deal, was a man with far-sighted ideals and national connections. He purchased two buildings on the edge of Sconset and designed a community where liberal thinkers and artists could find an intellectual retreat on the island. Howe's School of Opinion was combined with the Tavern on the Moors to provide social as well as intellectual fodder for the community. Every summer, the school advertised the offerings of its transient faculty, available to the public, to stimulate ideas and promote social exchange. During its early years, the school aroused much comment and controversy, as the community was called the "commies on the moors," but the quality of the speakers and artists gradually won the acceptance of Nantucket and Sconset townspeople.

The good summer seasons and expanding community resulted in a general trend for improvement of Nantucket's industry and infrastructure. These businesslike decisions—some of them far ahead of the Cape Cod communities—served to increase the quality of life and services on the island. During the winter of 1922–23, the electric light service, which had previously terminated at twilight, remained in effect all winter, keeping the streets and homes lighted for the winter nights for the first time. Electric lines gradually extended out of town to Monomoy, and the Polpis Road was finally finished from Polpis to Sconset. The water company began serving the island from artesian wells driven at Wyers Valley, the first time in forty-four years the town did not draw its water directly from Wannacomet Pond.

A new era in steamship service was launched in Maine at the Bath Iron Works on July 19, 1923, when the steamer *Islander* slid into the Kennebeck River. She was the first of three identical steamers built for the company, including the *Nobska* in 1925 and the *New Bedford* in 1928. They were comfortable and reliable ships, serving the line for fifty years or more.

In 1923, another popular vessel appeared on the harbor scene. The Nantucket Boat Works contracted to build four "Rainbow Boats" for the members of the Nantucket Yacht Club. The trim little craft with their colored sails were bright additions to the harbor scene. They were advertised as "loads of fun and safe for children." The cost was $475 each.

By June of 1923, Steamboat Wharf was piled high with freight and building materials for the construction industry, so that "it looks like they are going to build another town," said the newspaper.

During this period so many summer cottages were built it became necessary to import carpenters and other construction workers to the island, many of whom became permanent residents. That month, a new golf course appeared near the north shore on both sides of Cliff Road. Nantucket Golf Links was a par-70 course having spectacular views of Nantucket Sound and was advertised as "more typical of Scotland than any other course."

By midsummer, the increase in summer establishments caused the selectmen to order the chief of police to crack down— that is, to inspect the many new shops and tea rooms to see if they had licenses or were paying taxes on their business. The chief reported that very few were licensed and they were ordered to conform with the law, or else.

Traffic, congestion, and the pace of life were catching up with Nantucket and threatening some of her most cherished institutions. In December, there came the first of many suggestions to move the location of the Soldiers and Sailors Monument on Upper Main Street, at the intersection of Gardner and Milk Streets. It was proposed to move it to the entrance of Prospect Hill Cemetery, as a proper site to remember the Union dead. The proposal provoked a storm of controversy; after all, the monument was placed there so it could be seen, not forgotten. The importance of honoring the Union heroes was more essential than the convenience of transient motorists. Then the question was raised: if we have a monument for the Boys in Blue, how about one for the Boys in Khaki? Certainly the men of World War I deserved equal remembrance with the men of the Civil War. The final and most telling argument came from a writer to the newspaper who asked, "If Nantucketers could navigate whale ships around the Horn, why could not their descendants navigate motor cars around the monument?" The monument remained where it was.

In August 1923, the Main Street Fete, first held in 1921, was repeated and became a biennial event to benefit the Nantucket Cottage Hospital. The street was closed from Fair Street to Pleasant Street and many of the mansions were opened to the public, with costumed figures representing the whalemen and families. Highlight of the show was the appearance of the playright Austin Strong, as a returning whaleship captain, accompanied by his "Chinese wife" and multinational sailors. The midsummer festival was the highlight of the summer season, bringing out an attendance of 4,800 and raising $23,000 for the hospital.

The summer of 1924 started with the tragic loss of the steamer *Sankaty,* which burned at her pier in New Bedford, resulting in a loss of $325,000. She was soon replaced by the *Islander* and the *Nobska.*

The town continued with its program of road improvements, paving the surfaces of Easton, West Chester, Pleasant, and Upper Main Streets, as well as several others. The state highway was rebuilt at a cost of $100,115. The next year, the selectmen voted to pave Hummock Pond, Madaket, and Quidnet Roads, sixteen feet wide and three inches thick. This was a response to the automobile traffic and the increase in out-of-town real estate activity. The construction projects were also vigorously promoted by local contractors, with the solid backing of the voting workmen. Although sometimes criticized as extravagant expenditures for the times, they proved to be far-sighted and necessary public improvements, which held up well during the ensuing years.

By 1925, the population was up to 3,125. Town expenditures had reached the point where they could not be handled by the selectmen alone, and the town thus established its first finance committee to advise on town spending.

One of the constant threats was fire, which had always been a problem in town. In August, the Point Breeze Hotel, a large wooden structure on Easton Street, caught fire in mid-season while full of guests. The old building went up in smoke on August 8, despite a great fire-fighting effort that saved all the customers. As a result of that fire, the town purchased a 750-gallon pump truck from the American La France Company for $12,750. The truck won popular approval when it conducted a demonstration of its power on Main

Street, unwinding its hose to shoot a stream of water over the South Tower. Then the village of Sconset joined in the fire-protection cause by erecting its new standpipe water tower and installing the first fire hydrants in the village.

Among the changes on Main Street was the purchase of the store at Main and Center Streets by J. B. Ashley, who was to conduct a first-class market for over twenty-five years, until the business succumbed to the first supermarkets. Ashley sold prime meat, vegetables, fruit, bakery goods, and liquor, offering easy credit and quick delivery in neat green trucks.

In the fall, the island's attention turned toward its lone male deer, Buck, when summer resident Breckinridge Long offered to purchase some female deer to keep him company. The two females arrived in February 1926, by truck from Michigan. They were liberated in Squam Swamp by the game warden, and soon found happiness in the woods as companions for Buck, who had been awaiting them since 1922, and thus the island's deer herd was created.

By September 1925, Nantucket had become a major port of entry for the "rum running" fleet—swift power boats that were kept close inshore during the days but made nightly visits outside the three-mile limit, where countless vessels from Canada, the Bahamas, and other foreign ports awaited their customers. On September 1, the island was introduced to its first demonstration of federal law enforcement, when eighteen Coast Guard patrol boats were transferred to Nantucket from Long Island and established a base at Straight Wharf. The Nantucket community welcomed the federal effort, but it made little impression on the flow of beverages into the island, where the paper reported, "Prohibition as applied to Nantucket Island has been nothing but a farce. It is common knowledge that liquor has been obtainable here the past summer with little effort." Certainly the small police force of the town, three men plus special officers, was not expected to enforce the federal law.

In October of 1925, a serious fire broke out in the Anastos Block on the south side of Main Street, starting in a small stove in the basement, partially destroying two commercial buildings and damaging a third. Curiously, this fire developed in the same spot where the Great Fire of 1846 started, the fire that destroyed a third of Nantucket town. The buildings were saved by the new Stutz motor pumper and then razed to facilitate the construction of the C. F. Wing Company, the branch of a New Bedford department store, and the Anastos brothers' Spa Cafe, a building still standing at the end of the century.

In February 1926, Nantucket elected its first female selectwoman, the highly respected former school teacher Anne Ring, who served four terms. And in June, Nantucket had its first automobile fatalities, when an open roadster overturned on Madaket Road and killed the driver and passenger.

In July, the real estate boom had reached such proportions that a writer warned Nantucket against the effects of a "Hyannis-style boom," as the Cape town was experiencing, cheap, wooden "developments" and escalating real estate values. Nantucket did not want to see anything of the kind.

That summer, William W. Justice, of Philadelphia, introduced a new sport to the island, bringing hares and hounds together to start the Nantucket Harriers in a stable near Tashama Farm. The riders wore green coats with yellow collars and brass buttons. Extensive stables were planned off Cato Lane.

Mrs. Henry Lang contributed to the burgeoning of the art colony when she opened the Easy Street and Candle House galleries.

One indication of the growth of Nantucket in the twenties was the rise in the school population, a direct result of the influx of contractors, fishermen, and other tradesmen during those years, many of whom had large families. Thus, the town that had graduated only one student in 1905 twenty years later found the school building so crowded it had to bus the eighth grade out to Sconset daily, a grand excursion for the youngsters but a problem for the school committee.

It was recommended that a new school be erected on Academy Hill to replace the old wooden structure. In typical Nantucket fashion, the proposal was defeated, but it was eventually accepted and the new brick Academy Hill School was built in 1929.

Improvements in facilities and transportation continued, with the electric line extended through Polpis to Sconset, which first had its streets lighted on July 1, 1926. A new telephone company office was erected in a brick building on Union Street in 1928, and a larger submarine cable, capable of carrying increased traffic, now extended twenty-four miles from Nantucket to the Vineyard and the mainland.

Meanwhile, the long-awaited dream of air travel soon became a reality. Fred Maglathlin, who had been a principal builder of the cranberry bog, set his crews to working on a barren, windswept plot at Tom Nevers, and soon produced Nantucket's first airfield, a dirt strip with a wind flag. The first air service from Boston to Nantucket was inaugurated on May 17, 1927, three days before Charles Lindbergh flew over the island on his historic flight to Paris. The Boston Air Service offered Nantucket a Stinson biplane, which could carry five passengers to Boston at 100 miles per hour for $30 round trip. The inaugural plane was named Miss Nantucket and was warmly welcomed, but most of her flights were canceled due to fog.

The highlight of the summer season was live theater, provided by Austin Strong, the playwright, with the Nantucket Follies at the Nantucket Yacht Club. This extravaganza of drama and music featured a comic scene in Roger's news store (now the Hub); a "Sailor's Farewell" at the Jetties; Tony Sarg and his marionettes; and the star attraction, Austin Strong, in "The Captain's Return," with a cast of twelve. After that, the annual cattle show and fair of the Nantucket Agricultural Society at the Fairgrounds was a scanty affair, spoiled by rainy weather. The Main Street Fete was again held and netted $18,225 for the hospital.

The defeat of the proposed new school on Academy Hill in 1926 provoked commentary on the Nantucket tradition of skepticism toward any improvement and outright rejection of proposed projects when first presented to the town, after which they were accepted, embraced, and pointed to with pride. The editor of the *Inquirer and Mirror* expressed it as follows:

Nantucket voters turn down new school building. . . . History repeats itself. In 1878, there was opposition to a proposed water system in town. Water could not be made to run uphill. Moses Joy, the promoter, was refused the use of the town's pumper and fire hose to demonstrate his new water system. Impossible! Water could never be brought to town from Wannacomet Pond and put over the Congregational Church. He's crazy! Mr. Joy went to New Bedford and borrowed their fire hose from the city, and on October 14, 1880, he brought the water to town and fired a stream over the Congregational Church. Look at our water system today.

In 1884, the town was opposed to a sewer system. Today both Nantucket and Sconset are sewered, and there is not a village on Cape Cod or the Vineyard that has a sewer system.

When the first telephone line was installed, many Nantucketers refused to believe the human voice could be carried through a wire, or that people could carry on a conversation at a greater distance than possible by hollering. Yet today Nantucket has more telephone lines than any other town in New England and talks through a submarine cable with America.

Some years later, there was opposition to establishing an electric light system. People would be shocked; it would be dangerous to walk on the streets with the wires overhead; the birds would all be killed. Yet on August 17, 1889, people went to the Congregational Church and the Hotels Springfield and Nantucket to see the lights turned on, lights coming through wires. Today both Nantucket and Sconset are enjoying electric service day and night. No one has been shocked and the birds are still flying around.

Now the same opposition is manifested to the new school, the same kind of reception the other projects received; the same attitude as was held out to water, sewer, electricity, telephone, and other improvements. The new school will come, too.

In spite of the poor weather, 1927 was hailed as a good season, with more steamship passengers, freight, and telephone business than any other summer. Nantucket was doing better every season, and the business outlook was optimistic. Already people were making hotel and auto reservations a year in advance, and the real estate market was booming.

One figure was missing from the waterfront. Captain John Killen, who was born in Ireland, died in Nantucket on December 24, 1927, at the age of 80.

By 1928, there was a new steamship, the *New Bedford,* built in Quincy to replace the old paddle-wheeled *Uncatena* with a modern screw-propeller vessel. Together with the *Nantucket* and the *Nobska,* the steamship line now had three almost identical white steamers for its island fleet.

Many promising movements started in 1928. The Nantucket Historical Association began the project of providing a Whaling Museum in the old Hadwen and Barney candle factory on Broad Street. The association also acquired the Jethro Coffin House, the Oldest House, on Sunset Hill, and set about restoring it to proper condition for display. The town received a deed to Altar Rock from the Coffin family, and the Hospital Fete was moved from Main Street to Easy Street and Old North Wharf, where it became the Waterfront Carnival. It featured a visit to Austin Strong's house by Governor Frank Allen and his wife, and it netted $25,584.

The availability of open buses saw the commencement of the first genuine Nantucket tours, as J. B. Folger launched his open-sided buses in front of the Atheneum, advertising "40 miles around the island," which the natives translated to "40 miles in 40 minutes." Buses also served Sconset and the bathing beaches.

The popular Tavern on the Moors suffered a devastating fire on August 5, which hastened the demise of that institution.

In November, Nantucket voted 865 for Hoover and 395 for Al Smith. If 1928 was good, 1929 had to be better.

Early in 1929, the editor of the *Inquirer and Mirror* reflected the optimism of the nation in his front-page column on the wave of prosperity promising a good year for Nantucket: "The public is in the stock market to stay. . . . It seems as though there is going to be a terrible crash, yet the country is more prosperous than ever and no crash is in sight this year." The town was looking forward to continued growth in the summer season, and the improvements in road construction and public facilities gave the town a prosperous appearance. The fire department now boasted two motor-pumpers and a ladder truck, which called for the construction of a new brick Central Fire Station on South Water Street. This building, seventy years later, after substantial improvements, is headquarters for the Police Department. In May, the Sconset telephone exchange opened, giving that village a connection with the outside world. The first call between Nantucket Town and Sconset was made by the eldest citizens of each community: Levi Coffin, 85, calling his old friend John W. Cook, 95, who was told, "Speak up, I'm hard of hearing!"

The greatest symbol of the island's prosperity was the launching of the new steamship *Naushon* from the Fore River Shipyard in Quincy. On June 4, she made her maiden trip to the island where a large crowd met her with honking horns and whistles. The *Naushon* was much larger than her sister ships and featured a comfortable saloon deck with cocktail lounge. She was soon acclaimed as the Queen of the Line and became everyone's favorite ship for her comfort and amenities.

But progress also meant change. The summer of 1929 saw Nantucket meeting four boats a day. This made the Steamboat Wharf so busy it needed to expand, and one of the casualties was the old catboat basin on the south side of the wharf, which was filled in to expand the parking and freight area. With the basin went the Adams Boat House, a sixty-five-year-old shanty that had been the headquarters for the old salts who loved to sit and enjoy the waterfront. The late summer saw a renewal of the waterfront fete on Old North Wharf as the high point of the summer season.

One dramatic event occurred when a huge fire swept across the moors in mid-August, burning 6,000 acres in its path. Although no lives or homes were lost, the fire, which crossed both the Milestone and Polpis Roads, was unprecedented in its scope and brought out hundreds of men and women volunteers to aid the local firemen and auxiliaries.

In the last year of the decade the stock market crash was hardly noticed, but was to have long-term consequences for Nantucket.

The good times of the twenties ended with the dark days of October in 1929, when the stock market crashed and started a world-wide depression. As Nantucket had been enjoying booming tourist seasons, little attention was paid to the impending calamity, which eventually brought dismal years to the island and the nation.

After 1929, there was an abrupt decline in vacation travel as the public restricted its spending habits. Hotels and restaurants were the first to feel the dispiriting drop in businesss. Many boarding houses closed permanently. Nantucket's out-of-town establishments ceased operations, and only the Beach House in Sconset and the Wauwinet House continued in business.

The reduction in private spending due to the Depression curtailed plans for several ambitious real estate developments that were not resumed for several decades. There was no market for vacation homes or proposals for building on vacant land. One of the most unlikely speculations was for the huge, four-story Broadview Hotel, sprawling across the Cliff area at Lincoln Circle, proposed to contain 150 rooms and a dining room seating 300 people. The plans never left the drawing board.

Spectators and photographers await Nantucket's first commercial flight, 1927.

FROM FARM PASTURE TO MODERN AIRPORT

WHEN CHARLES LINDBERGH LAUNCHED HIS FAMOUS FLIGHT across the Atlantic in 1927, his course from Long Island to Paris took him close to Nantucket. On the island, a quiet, genial farmer named Leslie Holm was working his large farm near Nobadeer on the south shore, when he was startled to see a private plane come soaring in for a landing in his pasture. The pilot was a summer resident from Chicago who owned one of the first private planes to visit the island. He suggested to Les Holm that he convert his pasture into a landing strip for the planes that would come to the island, and the genial Holm agreed to do it.

In the early thirties, a handsome young flier named David Raub settled in Nantucket and eventually married a local beauty. Dave Raub was one of those pioneers who could fly anything, and his first plane in Nantucket was an old Fairchild, in which he gave many islanders their first thrilling ride.

The next Nantucket aerial pioneer was Parker Gray, a former Navy lieutenant who had already had his share of adventures in the service. He also settled on the island and married a local woman. He and Raub flew the Fairchild on all sorts of missions, emergency medical flights, hauling freight during the many harbor freeze-ups, and rescuing people stranded on Tuckernuck and Muskeget. They flew in all sorts of weather, landed on dirt strips, and made their way to the ground without instruments or landing lights.

Both men went into the air service during World War II. There Captain David Raub lost his life in the crash of a training plane in Delaware. His comrade, Captain Parker Gray, flew transports and ferried planes across the Atlantic throughout the war, retiring to Nantucket to open his roadhouse restaurant, Knotty Pines, a popular watering place that has seen several reincarnations since Gray died in 1979.

World War II brought many changes to the island, but none so important and far-reaching as the transformation of the old Nobadeer Airport into Nantucket Memorial Airport. In 1942, the U. S. Navy took over the field, installing new runways and building several Quonset huts for materiel and personnel. When the airport was returned to the town in 1946, it was a modern facility, to be named in memory of the Nantucket men who died in the war.

Rebuilt in 1992 with a greatly improved terminal and state-of-the-art landing facilities, Nantucket's airport is now one of the busiest in New England, second only to Logan Airport in number of landings. Essential to the island's year-round economy, it has served the town and the nation and greatly enhanced the life of the island, thanks to those early pioneer fliers and a genial farmer who let them land in his pasture.

Like many streets in town, Union Street once had a pastoral flavor.

Top: A heavy sleet storm felled utility poles on March 26, 1933.
Bottom: Tony Sarg's light-hearted sea monster was towed ashore on South Beach in 1937.

Worldwide economic malaise, the Great Depression, and the rise of foreign dictatorships around the world spread dark clouds over the nation, relieved only by the messages of hope and help from the new President. Slow to respond to the changes on the economic and political scene, Nantucket continued to indulge in its seasonal pursuit of pleasure, hoping for one more good season before the impending crisis.

Hard Times

The population reached 3,678 by 1930, but began a steady decline that would not be reversed for many years. Although private construction projects were not resumed, several of the worthwhile public projects started in the twenties were carried to completion in the first year of the decade. The veterans opened the doors of American Legion Hall in April; and in July the Nantucket Historical Association's Whaling Museum opened. Nantucket artists launched the first Sidewalk Art Show alongside the Atheneum on Federal Street. The Old Mill, newly restored to working condition, began grinding corn in August. From all appearances, unlike the rest of the country, Nantucket was still having a good tourist season and looking forward to its continuance.

The highlight of 1930 was the Massachusetts Tercentenary Celebration, to commemorate the landing of the Puritans in Massachusetts Bay in 1630. Like other Bay State towns, Nantucket was asked to participate in promoting the event as a stimulus to local business. The event was widely promoted on the island with Old Home Week in July, featuring a parade, a formal testimonial in the Congregational Church, theatrical productions, and baseball games. The long and colorful parade featured whalemen, craftsmen, working women, and Native Americans. The place of honor was held by the three surviving veterans of the Civil War, riding in a horse-drawn surrey: James H. Barrett, Josiah F. Murphey, and James H. Wood Sr. It was the last roll call for those three Nantucket heroes.

Nineteen-thirty also saw the beginning of one project that had important implications for the island. Although a few islanders had flown in private airplanes from the primitive airstrip at Tom Nevers, the idea of a municipal airport had not taken hold. It was a controversial subject and a dubious public enterprise for an island so connected to the sea and so dependent on the steamship service. Navy Lt. Parker W. Gray wrote a long article for the newspaper proclaiming the need for an airport and its importance to Nantucket, an article that started a long and eventually successful movement for the town to acquire the land to build its own airport. Like many innovations on Nantucket, it met with early opposition from islanders, but they began to appreciate the convenience of regular air service and were more willing to accept the need for the airport.

Other municipal amenities and public services were promoted with great enthusiasm. Although the tourist business was declining, the island had not yet felt the long-range impact of the Depression and continued to hope for a return to the prosperity of the twenties. The town was treated to a full schedule of summer theater, with the Nantucket Players performing at the American Legion Hall (where hard times lowered the admission price to one dollar). The New York playwright, Austin Strong, produced his annual variety show at the Nantucket Yacht Club, and several Broadway stars, including Burgess Meredith, appeared in island theatricals as a new organization, the Nantucket Theatre, took over Legion Hall the next summer.

For sheer curiosity value, Nantucket scored another achievement in the summer of 1931 when men working in a home known as the Gardner house on Upper Main Street discovered a live toad imbedded in a cement wall. The native appeared to have been imbedded in the cement for twenty-one years, but when released from his captivity and exposed to a little fresh air and some sunlight, he emerged somewhat bug-eyed from his imprisonment. He was taken to the newspaper for an interview, after which he had his picture taken at Boyer's Studio and was released.

The old Orange Street school building, the original South School, was used as the courthouse until the last sitting of the Superior Court in October 1931, when it was torn down to be succeeded by the Cyrus Peirce School on Atlantic Avenue, built by John C. Ring Jr. and dedicated on November 30, 1931.

The Nantucket Civic League sponsored an informal social institution called Nantucket Neighbors in 1932, holding weekly gatherings in the Old North Vestry, where anyone was welcome to come and hear an informal talk on a local subject. The first meeting on July 11 saw 150 persons in attendance to hear a talk on "Why I Like Nantucket," and to hear Civil War veteran James A. Wood's few words of wisdom. At their second meeting, the Neighbors heard the artist Edgar Jenney and the decorator Mrs. Fred Ackerman speak on the historic architecture of Nantucket. The warm and casual Neighbors attracted many visitors each summer and became a feature of island life throughout the thirties, lasting beyond the wartime years.

Livelier entertainment was in store for Nantucket when the American Legion post announced its plans to bring professional wrestling events to the island. Placing a wrestling ring in the center of the racetrack at the Fairgrounds and advertising with colorful posters and widespread ballyhoo, the promoters got the first event under way on July 2, 1932, under the lights on a summer evening enlivened by recorded music and steamed hot dogs. The contenders in the first event were Manuel Souza, a local lad, pitted against Young Cassidy of New Bedford. To no one's surprise, the local boy won the contest. Four more bouts ensued. The imported gladiators repaired to celebrate, and for weeks the natives talked over the spectacle of real professional contests on the island. In later years, the promotions were taken over by Bob Hardy and Doc Ryder, and came to feature such well-known names in professional wrestling as Killer Kowalski, Man-Mountain Dean, Steve "Crusher" Casey, and the famous Frenchman with the homely face known as "The Angel." It was all good fun and a popular attraction while it lasted.

Near the end of the Prohibition era, Nantucket police discovered a clandestine still on the island, located in the Mooney Pines west of the Polpis Road. The still was elaborately constructed and fully functional, obviously the product of many workers, but only one man was found on the scene. He was arrested and convicted of violating Prohibition laws.

In October, there occurred the first and last successful escape from the jail on Vestal Street. Charles Freeman, incarcerated for sexual crimes, managed to coax the aged jailer, Edgar Ellis, into his cell, where he was assaulted and overpowered. Freeman ran down the street to the town laundry, where he was hidden by an accomplice and smuggled off the island in a laundry cart. He remained at large until 1937, when he was found in California and returned to Massachusetts for a long sentence in state prison.

In March of 1933, the Roosevelt administration took office, and one of its first official actions was to close all the banks in the country. With the two local banks closed, the people of Nantucket came to rely on barter and credit for dealing in necessities, but the crisis soon passed and the newspaper advised the populace to have confidence in their neighbors and continue to trade with the friends who had helped them in time of need. As if to accentuate the dismal business climate, a fierce storm of snow and sleet swept the island on March 26, ripping down fifty telephone poles on the Milestone Road. The island, taking action to help the many unemployed workmen in town, appropriated $10,000 for a program to improve the dirt roads on the island. Three hundred men applied for the available jobs, which paid $4.00 per day, a sum that attracted many carpenters and fishermen who needed work.

On June 19, President Franklin D. Roosevelt sailed into Nantucket Harbor on his private yacht *Amberjack II*. He didn't come ashore, but with his jaunty air and beaming smile welcomed a boatload of local officials; he was photographed at the wheel of his yacht and was inducted into the Wharf Rat Club.

During the summer, the Nantucket Neighbors featured talks by the historian William F. Macy and the noted attorney Morris L. Ernst, one of the early members of Roosevelt's Brain Trust.

An interesting feature of the summer was the "Picnic of the Intercollegians," at Tom Nevers Head, where young men and women out of college for the summer enjoyed refreshments, cigarettes, and each other well into the evening hours.

Despite the occasional bright spots of the summer, 1933 was a dismal year for Nantucket. The Nantucket Savings Bank foreclosed on three of the largest hotels: the Sea Cliff, the Point Breeze, and the Ocean House. With the decline in the tourist business, none could meet their mortgage payments. The big hotels were in trouble even in good times, and now they could not be sold for any price, so they remained closed.

Bringing the year to a grim close, a December freeze sent temperatures down below zero and the frozen harbor trapped the steamboats at their berths. The frigid weather continued into January and February, the ice stretching out as far as Cross Rip in the middle of Nantucket Sound. The island came to rely on squadrons of airplanes, which flew food and other necessities into the field at Nobadeer, where on February 14 a record thirty-three planes landed on one day. The mail arrived by open planes sent by the War Department. When the freeze finally ended in March and the boats resumed service, the island was hit with ten inches of snow.

The year 1934 started as one of the bleakest in history. Almost universal unemployment and the resulting hardships of life on the island had depressing effects on the population, which saw an increase in alcoholism and several suicides during those hard times. Men who could not support their families lost their self respect, and many working-class families were held together by public welfare or church charities. The national calamity also affected summer residents in a curious development; many of them retreated to the island as an economically prudent move. Experiencing Nantucket off season for the first time, they found themselves enjoying the experience. As a direct result, they formed the Winter Club, a group of men who gathered monthly for companionship and intellectual stimulation.

The Depression evidently didn't affect everyone negatively, for at the beginning of the 1934 season James A. Backus opened his newly remodeled Wauwinet House. With rooms for sixty guests, it was the most up-to-date hotel on the island.

Another venerable institution ended in 1934 when August saw the last of the Nantucket County Fair, the annual cattle and farm show of the Nantucket Agricultural Society, a victim of modern times and a dying interest in agriculture. The old fairgrounds were kept as an exhibition area for wrestling and other events, but the acreage was eventually sold off and finally became the location of the Nantucket Electric Company.

The New Deal did not find much favor on Nantucket, and the population remained heavily Republican in its politics. Perhaps for this reason, there was spirited opposition to the idea of taking money from Washington. When the federal government proposed building a new post office in downtown Nantucket, it was controversial for several reasons. The chosen site on Federal Street was occupied by the venerable Joseph B. Macy mansion, but the house was in such poor condition that the town finally voted to demolish it but wrangled over ownership of the sidewalks. Finally, the project was approved, and in May of 1935 hundreds of Nantucketers gathered to watch the huge steam shovel excavating for the foundation at low tide (at high tide the hole would have been filled with sea water). The post office was completed in 1936 at a cost of $50,000, and was still in service at the end of the century. To the chagrin of the Republican town, a bronze plaque was installed bearing the names of President Franklin D. Roosevelt and Postmaster General James G. Farley.

The administration of Massachusetts Governor James Michael Curley gave Nantucket much to talk about in 1935. Upon the death of the beloved Judge Reginald T. Fitzrandolph, Governor Curley appointed to the Nantucket District Court the first female judge in Massachusetts, Ethel E. Mackiernan. She lasted on the bench six months, resigning after hearing the facts in several lurid cases of sexual misbehavior. Her replacement was Judge Caroline Leveen of Boston, who came to the island every week for thirty years. In August, Governor Curley himself visited the island accompanied by several friends on a private yacht. He traveled to Sankaty Golf Club to demonstrate his putting skills, freely posed for photographs with his Nantucket friends, and hosted a lively party at the White Elephant. The jovial governor and his entourage, attempting to navigate their yacht from the White Elephant, ran aground in Nantucket Harbor and had to be towed to sea by the Coast Guard. The Boston newspapers recorded the Nantucket adventure in great detail.

The summer Main Street Fete and Waterfront Carnival netted $13,000 for the Nantucket Cottage Hospital, but there were indications of falling revenues from tourist dollars on the island. The steamship service to New Bedford offered a round-trip ticket for $2.50, while Parker Gray's new Mayflower Airlines began service to

Boston for $7.50. Mayflower Airlines operated from a dirt strip newly constructed north of the fourth milestone, less than two miles from Nobadeer Airport, but largely free of the coastal fog.

December of 1935 was marked by the first hunting fatality on the island, as one man was killed and another wounded by deer hunters. Since the arrival of Old Buck and his companions, the deer herd had grown so large (1,922 bucks, 1,926 does) that Nantucket had its first open season. The fatality caused Governor Curley to order the shooting stopped, but that was impossible to enforce, so the shooting resumed with over sixty deer taken.

By the end of the year, the population stood at 3,491. The year ended with three heavy snowfalls at Christmas time, and ten days of subfreezing weather, permitting Nantucket to enjoy a white Christmas, followed by horse-drawn sleighing through the streets on New Year's Day.

The new post office opened on January 7, 1936, with Miss Alice Roberts, one of three sisters who owned the Roberts House, as postmistress. Cold weather and the ice-bound harbor kept the steamships at their berths for two weeks, while airplanes brought the mail and provisions to the island. Unemployment figures continued to rise, and perhaps for that reason there were twenty-one candidates for the Board of Selectmen, ensuring a lively election. In November, the presidential election brought out 1,580 voters, who went against the national tide.

Atop Beacon Hill on Centre Street, the Congregational Church built a church hall, a multipurpose building half submerged in the hillside beside the church. The project was promoted by the popular minister of the church, Fred D. Bennett, who thought Nantucket needed a public hall for recreational and social events. The hall was completed on December 16 and opened with a turkey dinner for 245 people. It was named Bennett Hall and became the location for athletic and public events, serving as the high school basketball court and housing many wartime activities in World War II. Rev. Bennett left the island in 1938, served as a Navy chaplain during the war, and returned to retire on Nantucket.

Nantucket was reminded that its economic future lay with the tourism industry when, in September, a writer for the *Inquirer and Mirror* declared: "Nantucket is dependent almost entirely on its summer business for a livelihood, and on the employment which summer residents give to many of the islanders during other seasons of the year. The island must cater to the summer visitor. . . ." This would be the theme of the Nantucket economy for years to come.

In 1937 ownership of the bathing beach at the Jetties provoked great controversy among the townsfolk. The public beach and bathhouses had been leased to Leon M. Royal, a former bank teller, who added to the property and established a night club called Club Royale, the legality of which was disputed because it served beer and ale at a time when Nantucket had no night clubs. The selectmen sent Chief Mooney down to collect the liquor license and haul Royal into court. Royal refused to pay the town any rent under his lease because he claimed the Jetties land was "not owned by the town but belonged to Franklin E. Smith." Smith thereupon offered to sell the land to the town for $6,000, and to put it through the Land Court for a legal fee of $500. This provoked a violent controversy, which was resolved when the legislature passed a bathing beach bill authorizing the purchase, and the town bought the Jetties for $6,000.

The island was still suffering from unemployment, and when the selectmen applied for additional federal assistance they were informed that the town limit was set at seventy jobs with the WPA, the federal agency that was providing jobs for the millions of unemployed across the country. The big hotels were open for business, and proudly listed their patrons in the weekly Hotel column in the newspaper. The Nantucket Neighbors held a Siasconset. Night at the Casino, featuring William O. Stevens, author of the new book about Nantucket, *The Far-Away Island*.

The biggest sensation of the summer was provided by Tony Sarg, the artist and illustrator who had for several years designed the colorful balloons and floats for the Thanksgiving Day Macy Parade in New York. In the summer of 1937, Sarg designed a 200-foot rubber sea serpent, destined to become St. George's Dragon in November. In midsummer the veteran prankster decided to launch his dragon by starting an elaborate hoax, which eventually gained Nantucket much mainland publicity. A Nantucket fisherman reported a large animal at sea, heading toward the island; then some huge footprints were found on the beach; finally a weird creature was reported ashore on Coatue. In mid-August, the great sea serpent was towed ashore on Washington Street's South Beach where hundreds came to ogle and photograph it. Tony Sarg himself posed in the forty-foot mouth of the creature, surrounded by eighty Nantucket youngsters (the author was one of them).

In September, the Nobadeer Airport, formerly the farm of Les Holm, was purchased by a summer resident named Alexander Hagner, who promptly offered it to the town for a public airport. The town disapproved of the location because it would cause planes to fly over the houses in town. The pioneer fliers, led by David Raub, wrote letters and lobbied for a public airport, a vital need on the island. It took four years, but the town finally approved the airport in July 1941. The next year, the airport was taken over by the U. S. Navy for wartime use, to be returned in 1946.

Nantucketers were intrigued by the biggest news story of the year when Edward VIII, the King of England, renounced his throne and became the Duke of Windsor, marrying the woman he loved and moving to Paris. Nantucketer Bassett Jones sent the Windsors a telegram inviting them to settle in Nantucket, where they would be insured peace and privacy, thirty miles at sea.

As 1938 began, better times seemed ahead. The town valuation was up to $13 million, a tremendous increase over the past twenty years. There were 500 more houses on the island than in 1917, and although construction had slowed during the thirties, the prospects looked good. An interesting development was that the 387 horses on the island in 1917 had dwindled to 45, and the island now had 1,300 registered automobiles.

At a special election to fill the office of State Representative, Bob Backus of Wauwinet won with 1,080 Republican votes against 99 Democratic votes.

In February, the town turned out to honor the Reverend Joseph M. Griffin, pastor of St. Mary's Church, on the twenty-fifth anniversary of his pastorate. A crowd of hundreds filled the auditorium at the Cyrus Peirce School to hear tributes to the saintly priest delivered by all the ministers on the island—the selectmen and the Masons joining in. The editor of the *Inquirer and Mirror* wrote: "Respected by all denominations—a man among men—Father Griffin has built for himself a monument in the hearts of the people of Nantucket." It was a memorable occasion.

In May, the first air mail service was launched from Nobadeer Airport, giving Nantucket faster postal contact with the mainland. This was a formal occasion, with Postmistress Alice Roberts delivering the first bag of mail to pilot Parker Gray, who was then sworn to the performance of his postal duty. That summer, the steamship schedule connected in New Bedford with the steamers of the Coastal Line, offering overnight service to New York. At the time, many travelers preferred the leisurely cruise to the jarring journey on the New Haven Railroad: and the boat fare was $5.00 per person, $5.00 per auto, which made the boat trip a pleasure, while it lasted.

The end of summer saw the end of another Nantucket hotel as Tom Nevers Lodge, situated on the south bluff in Sconset, went up in smoke. The old building had often been the target of vandals and the site of many evening adventures. The cause of the fire was not accidental, but the town wrote it off as the final bursting of the Tom Nevers bubble.

In September the hotel owners and businessmen of Nantucket gathered at the Breakers to discuss the future of Nantucket as a summer resort. They listened to an advertising man who recommended that they encourage more long-term guests, extend the season with golf and tennis tournaments, and advertise widely in the New York papers to attract visitors from the forthcoming World Fair, in 1939.

The question of public advertising had come up before, but the existing state laws severely restricted the use of public money for such commercial purposes. Representative Backus filed a bill in the legislature to authorize the town to spend up to $6,500 on advertising, but the Senate cut the figure down to $3,000, which was approved and spent. The next year, the island was featured in a brochure produced by the New Haven Railroad that was a colorful description of the island and its attractions. To make the island even more attractive, the Civic League started a campaign to eliminate ragweed, a serious health hazard to people with respiratory problems, and induced Nantucket youngsters to pull out 37,000 pounds of ragweed, paying them forty cents per hundred pounds. At that rate, tons of ragweed were brought to the town lot on Silver and Pleasant Streets in bags, wagons, wheelbarrows, and baby carriages, on Ragweed Day, August 1.

The year saw the appearance of a new byline in the *Inquirer and Mirror*, as young Edouard A. Stackpole began to include the first of his whaling histories in the columns of the paper. Stackpole worked at the newspaper in every capacity over the years. Beginning with youth adventure stories, he expanded his writing into the history of island whaling, specializing in the international aspects of the industry. Always friendly and popular, his growing reputation never detracted from his island roots, and he became the island historian of the twentieth century.

Nantucket's last jail-breaker, Charles Freeman, who had escaped in 1932, was arrested in California and brought home for trial. Freeman was dangerous but not too bright, as he answered an advertisement to redeem his Nantucket home for unpaid taxes. As soon as he sent his address to the tax collector, the police were knocking on his door, and in Nantucket Superior Court he was sentenced to fifteen years in state prison.

The year 1938 is remembered for the great hurricane that struck New England on September 21. Coming without warning in the days before modern weather forecasting, the storm sent a tidal surge of deadly proportions into the New England coastal communities, ripping down bridges and houses in southeastern Massachusetts and drowning people in the streets of Providence. By good fortune, the storm swept inland west of Nantucket, flooding the south shore but doing no major damage on the island. It was later claimed that the storm swept past Nantucket on both sides, sparing the vulnerable island.

The end of the thirties was a time for uncertainty in Nantucket. Like a final scene from the past, one of the great old sailing schooners, the *Laura Annie Barnes,* was wrecked on Tuckernuck Shoal and went to pieces on January 18, 1939. The *Barnes* had been built in 1921 at the Bowker Boatyard in Phippsburg, Maine, and was the last of the four-masted wooden schooners to pass from the island scene. Several Nantucketers visited the wreck to salvage part of her cargo and others photographed her final hours before she slipped into Nantucket Sound.

Despite the darkening clouds spreading across the Old World, the island optimistically laid plans for the summer of 1939. The New Haven Railroad ran a special excursion train from Boston to Woods Hole on the weekends, offering 500 people a round trip at bargain rates on the train and steamer. Whereas the islanders had originally demanded rail service to the Cape towns, it now appeared that Cape Codders had given up on the trains and relied upon the automobile for their Boston trips. The combination of the rail and steamship service was a major incentive for island travelers.

One of the most spectacular events of the season was the first Nantucket Air Meet, sponsored by David Raub at the Nantucket

Nobadeer Airport. This became an invitational event for private pilots to visit the island and to demonstrate to the island residents the potential of a modern airport. The day featured sightseeing rides, stunt pilots, and parachute jumps, providing Nantucketers with an exciting view of aircraft in action over the island.

The highlight of the summer of 1939 was the Fourth of July celebration. Nantucket made a strenuous effort to provide the town with a great variety of entertainment for residents and visitors. The night before the Fourth was the occasion for a great bonfire, fueled by rubber tires and plenty of gasoline, at the town dump on Madaket Road. The next morning, sports races and pie-eating contests were held on Federal Street, with a tug-of-war and baby-carriage parade. This was followed by the Big Parade in the afternoon, featuring the most elaborate floats ever seen on the island. They provided live portrayals of Nantucket history and local business enterprises, some of which were very well done. They included the Island Service Company fish shanty on a truck with Dick Barrett mending nets, the American Legion float with Charlie Brown manning the machine gun, the huge milk bottle of Somerset Farm surrounded by the three pretty Jaeckle sisters, and the shining copy of the New Bedford whaleman's statue with a gilded Arthur Parker poised with the harpoon. The parade scene was preserved for history, in a special supplement of the *Inquirer and Mirror* with several pages of pictures.

The island continued to provide a lively summer season with the expansion of the summer theatre business. There were performances at the Siasconset Casino, the Nantucket Yacht Club, and at a new theatre on Commercial Wharf, providing live shows to be seen and heard every night. Following the death of the popular actor-manager George Fawcett, his memory was preserved by the Fawcett Players, a theater company founded by his daughter Margaret Fawcett Wilson and her husband Robert. They produced a repertory of Nantucket historical plays, first on Commercial Wharf and later on Straight Wharf. The latter location became the Straight Wharf

Theatre, which after remodeling in 1940 seated 185 people in snug fashion. This location became a permanent fixture on the Nantucket theatrical scene for thirty-five years, lasting until the old wooden building and all its sets went up in smoke one windy evening in April of 1975.

The island continued to advertise its advantages and hope for one more good season. Increased railroad advertising brought one last summer of carefree relaxation, and it was claimed the day of August 17 was the busiest travel day in Nantucket history. People were emerging from the Depression and hoping the country could avoid war with Nazi Germany, but the war clouds were forming and Nantucket faced an uncertain future.

The decade of the thirties was remembered as the last of the "good old days," before the traumatic events of World War II and the rapid changes wrought in the postwar years. The pace of life was slow and congenial. There was no sense of competition for steamboat reservations or parking spaces. Traffic moved lazily on two-way streets and everyone parked where most convenient. It was a casual and unregulated life, centered upon Main Street square and the downtown stores.

Nantucket life still depended on the waterfront, and the arrival of the steamboat each afternoon was the big event of the day, when all the mail and passengers arrived. It was the custom of many natives to walk down to "meet the boat" and talk about the new arrivals, amid the colorful chatter of the porters for the local hotels. On the other wharves, grizzled veterans of the waterfront met every day to talk about the fishing fleet, now reduced to a handful of deep-sea draggers, and watch the scallopers, catboats, and rainbow fleet, which still filled the harbor.

Nantucket was a town of talkers and walkers. Almost anyone could tell a good story or remember some piece of a story that would keep the conversation going for hours. Most of the population lived in town, within a few minutes' walk of Main Street, and many families did not own automobiles. As a result, during those years most of the people went to work on foot or occasionally by bicycle. In the Depression, even a bicycle was a luxury, and many families could not afford them, so Nantucketers walked everywhere.

People living in the outlying villages or on the farms usually owned automobiles, but came to town only when necessary. Most schoolchildren walked to Academy Hill School, a mile or more, twice each day. The outlying villages had school bus service, but if the children from Sconset missed the last bus, they faced a seven-mile hike to get home for dinner.

Business was done in small, personal transactions, among friends and on a face-to-face basis. At a time when the banks were not noted for their generosity, many personal loans kept the economy alive, while many families were struggling to make ends meet. The farmers and fishermen could produce enough to feed their families, in a good year, but there was no money to spare. Life in the tourist business was the riskiest of all, for it depended on the weather and the uncertain economy of a very short season, beginning on the Fourth of July and ending on Labor Day. The good old days were not all that good.

The young people on the island could enjoy the natural attractions and activities that were open to everyone: swimming, boating, and picnicking in the summer; sliding and ice skating in the winter. When there was a good heavy snowfall, the police department closed Main Street so the sleds could coast down Orange Street hill all the way down to Straight Wharf. Most recreation was self-directed, without formal organization or facilities, except for the newly constructed basketball court at Bennett Hall.

Trips to the mainland were usually confined to preschool shopping trips on the boat to New Bedford, where islanders shopped at the Star Store and stayed at the Mansion House or the New Bedford Hotel. Most families tried to save up for one trip each fall, but many spent years without leaving the island. Boston was a long trip by boat and train and took most of a day, leaving the traveler too exhausted to go shopping.

During this decade, the town fathers, particularly the selectmen and the assessors, controlled the town finances with a steady eye on the tax rate and a firm hand on expenditures. Town government was small and unintrusive. The island was fortunate to obtain most of its municipal services—its roads, sewers, and utilities—during the heady twenties, but it continued to pave roads and complete other projects to provide employment in the thirties. The town was run by veteran officeholders who kept their positions by remembering they were public servants. The telephone directory listed not only the numbers for the Police Department and the Fire Department, but the home numbers for the police chief and the fire chief. During the Depression, those who held steady jobs were fortunate, and grateful.

Nantucket ended the thirties with continued hope for the future, a future that was clouded by the threat of war. War always brought changes, and the island was to be tested and changed as never before.

During these years, Nantucketers remained optimistic that the good times would return. They did not. It became apparent in later years that Nantucket did not recover from the Depression until after World War II.

Police chiefs Howes (left) and Mooney served a total of seventy-eight years.

Two Chiefs

WENDELL H. HOWES AND LAWRENCE F. MOONEY

THE LAW-ABIDING TOWN OF NANTUCKET DID NOT HAVE much crime to worry about in the early days, and was content to entrust its law enforcement to a five-man police force working from a tiny one-room office on Washington Street. The town expected to see the Chief of Police on Main Street, every day, where he heard complaints, answered questions, and generally kept a close watch on the island and its people.

Lawrence F. Mooney started life as a farmer on Polpis Road, but took a night job with the police department in 1912, where he remained for thirty-nine years, seventeen as chief. With no formal police training, he had a native brand of common sense and good humor that enabled him to handle most of the town's problems. He lived through the era of the horse and buggy days, through the years of expanding tourism, the Prohibition era, the Great Depression and

World War II. His favorite spot for many years was the corner of Main and Federal Streets, where he became the most familiar figure in town. He seldom left the island, but made it to his son's college graduation, and even after his retirement in 1951 he returned daily to a seat on Main Street.

Wendell H. Howes came from a seafaring family and joined the police department shortly after his high school graduation in 1936. The popular young officer married one of the local beauties and quickly developed a talent for personal friendships, which aided his police duties and added to his knowledge of the island and its people. He seldom lost a case in District Court. When Chief Mooney retired, Howes was the popular favorite to succeed him. He soon displayed his own brand of law enforcement, hustling undesirable characters back to the boat, arresting homeless hippies, and refusing to uphold the Massachusetts "Blue Laws" against Sunday business. His favorite location was the rail in front of the Pacific Club, where he surveyed the Main Street scene each day. When Howes retired in 1975, he too had thirty-nine years of service. The two overlapping careers of the two chiefs totaled seventy-eight years of service to the town.

In 1952, the Police Department moved from its antique location to a new wooden building on Chestnut Street, which soon became overcrowded with men and equipment, so the police took over the renovated fire station on South Water Street in 1980. The moves gave Nantucket a more modern department and far more manpower, but many islanders remembered the days when one man could control everything in downtown Nantucket, and the time it was all done by two super chiefs.

Rev. Joseph M. Griffin
PATRIARCH OF THE ISLAND

REV. JOSEPH M. GRIFFIN ARRIVED IN NANTUCKET IN 1913 and remained as pastor of St. Mary's Church for the next thirty-four years. Nantucket and its church were his entire life from the moment he arrived. He always declined promotion to higher office and larger parishes. The public believed he remained because of his love for the ocean, but that was not so.

As the only priest on a remote island, Father Griffin set the standard for the faithful, raised the island's opinion of the Catholic community, and practiced his own brand of religion, "with malice toward none; with charity for all." His charity became legendary, and since he came from a family of means, it was often assumed he purchased some church property, including the rectory at 6 Orange Street and part of the cemetery, with his own funds. His charity was not limited to his own parishioners.

His practice was to take long walks about town, always

dressed in his clerical garb and Chesterfield coat and carrying his walking stick, speaking to everyone and chatting with people from all walks of life. These contacts enabled him to learn the needs of the townspeople. During the Depression when everyone was having a hard time, Father Griffin's stroll took him by the Baptist Church where he met the minister out front. The church had started a project to paint the building, but ran out of money and had to lay off the men, the minister told him. "You finish the job," said Father Griffin, "I will take care of it."

During one period the parish was enjoying a steady income from the weekly Bingo games in the parish hall, until the attorney general ruled these games illegal under the state gaming laws. The bishop ordered all parishes to stop playing Bingo. Father Griffin faithfully read the bishop's message on Sunday, then announced, "Canon law stops at Woods Hole. The parish will hold its usual card party on Thursday night."

On his twenty-fifth anniversary as pastor in 1938, Father Griffin was honored by a community testimonial of over 300 people, including all the civic leaders, every Protestant minister, and representatives of the Masons and Odd Fellows.

When Father Griffin died in 1947 the Church of St. Mary had to hold two funeral masses to accommodate the crowds who attended. The bishop delivered his eulogy and revealed why this holy man chose to remain on Nantucket; repeating Father Griffin's secret: "I did not stay on the island because I like to listen to the roar of the wind and sea. I stayed there because I could love God there and perchance teach others to love Him better than I could elsewhere."

Top: Troops driving on Main Street, 1942.
Bottom: The mid-island fire as seen from Jetties Beach in July 1949.

The overwhelming events of World War II swept prior history into insignificance: Blitzkreig, Dunkirk, the Battle of Britain, Pearl Harbor, the Holocaust, Casablanca, Normandy, D-Day, Yalta, V-E Day, Hiroshima, V-J Day. Then peace, followed by Soviet expansion and the Iron Curtain drawn across Europe. Isolated in the Atlantic, Nantucket lived out the war years with fortitude and patriotism, then looked forward to a brighter future.

Wartime
&
Peacetime

NANTUCKET AT WAR: 1941-1945

The wartime years brought many changes to America. Although Nantucket was isolated from the mainland, it was not insulated from the grim reality of the world war, and the island felt the impact of the events that shook the world.

Hundreds of young men, many of whom had never left the island, suddenly found themselves in military service and traveling to foreign lands they never knew existed. Many men volunteered for the navy and marine corps, while several women went into the military and nurse corps. Governor Saltonstall appointed a Nantucket Draft Board, three men who had the responsibility for choosing from their friends and neighbors who would march down to take the steamboat to the army camps. By the end of the war, 499 men and women had served in uniform, and of these, eleven lost their lives in service.

The harsh reality of the human contribution to the war effort was relieved by an overwhelming spirit of support for the cause and patriotic pride in the nation. On the anniversary of Pearl Harbor, the town gathered on Federal Street to witness the unveiling of its first honor roll, a wooden structure with painted names, on the grounds of the Sanford house. The Sanford house (now the site of the town building) was the town headquarters for the civil defense program and the selective service office—in effect, the wartime headquarters for the island. In addition to the public memorial, hundreds of homes displayed in their windows pennants with one or more blue stars to indicate their children in the service. When the servicemen and women wrote home, their letters and adventures were often reprinted in the newspaper.

The greatest threat to Nantucket came from the sea. Early in 1940, the Nazi submarine fleet ranged across the Atlantic and began to threaten the sea lanes from America to Europe, bringing Nantucket dangerously close to the war zone. The islanders were well aware of their isolated location and the peril they faced when the country was finally involved, as was anticipated, in the war with Germany.

It came as a surprise when the radio broadcast the terrible news of the Japanese attack on Pearl Harbor, Sunday, December 7, 1941— "A date which will live in infamy." It was a surprise attack and it came from the wrong direction. Nantucket was stunned, because it considered the real enemy to be Nazi Germany. Now the Pacific Fleet was crippled, the Pacific Coast was in danger, and America was at war on two oceans.

Two days later, Nantucket had its first war scare when the radio broadcast a false report that enemy bombers were approaching the Atlantic Coast. Children were sent home from school and families huddled around the radio. General Daniel Needham of the Massachusetts Committee on Public Safety mentioned "the possibility there may be bombings here before the first of the year." Nantucket was a lonely place during the dark days of 1941. The town called an emergency town meeting, which voted $10,000 for defense measures in the record time of ten minutes. A Public Safety Committee was appointed with an office and telephone in the Sanford house. Air raid wardens were appointed, with authority to advise the public on proper action to take in the event of an airborne invasion ("Stay Calm") and additional powers to enforce the blackout rules. The town distributed sandbags on strategic street corners, and householders were advised to put pails in front of homes, where trucks would fill them with sand. Townspeople were reminded "…a single plane can release over 2000 bombs, and the Town of Nantucket has exactly five pieces of fire apparatus."

The most visible impact on the island was the blackout of the entire east coast. No outdoor lights could shine from houses, streetlights were shaded with hoods, and automobile lights were painted over halfway. Blackout curtains were installed on home windows and air raid wardens patrolled the streets, carrying flashlights and wearing blue civil defense armbands. Millie Jewett patrolled Madaket on horseback, and her blackout was total. As a safety measure, Police Chief Lawrence F. Mooney banned the parking of autos at night on all streets and highways of the town. The police department was issued eight new .38 revolvers, and the force was supplemented by fifty auxiliary police armed with nightsticks and flashlights.

The actual defense of the island was in the hands of the U.S. Coast Guard, which at one time had six manned stations on the island. Brant Point Station commanded stations at Madaket, Surfside, Sankaty Head, Coskata, Great Point, and the Nesbitt Inn on Broad Street, which was taken over and used as an office and sickbay for servicemen until 1944. The Coast Guard also maintained a foot patrol of the island beaches with trained patrol dogs. It maintained a fleet of patrol boats operating out of the harbor, and local fishermen were restricted from leaving port without Coast Guard permission.

The public lived on war news and everyone relied upon the radio for current news. Most homes had one radio in a prominent place in the living room, and during the news broadcast, the family gathered and looked at the radio, as they now watch television. Daily newspapers came on the afternoon boat and the famous weekly magazines— *Life, Look,* and *Time*—were eagerly awaited for their vivid pictures of the war scenes.

Amid the real news came rumors. Mysterious sightings of German submarines, flashing lights off-shore, and actual landings of U-boats to pick up supplies, were part of the rumor mill. Wartime secrecy regulations added to the atmosphere, and some measures went to unbelievable extremes. The steamships of the Nantucket line were painted battleship gray for protection from submarines, the boat schedules were not published for reasons of secrecy, and the passengers were forbidden to carry cameras on deck. Such measures led to the biggest rumor of all: that Nantucket would be closed for the summer of 1942!

Lacking any other form of air defense, the town erected an observation tower in the field east of the Old Mill, where two people were stationed day and night, equipped with binoculars and recognition books for reporting every sighting of aircraft. The tower was faithfully manned and the skies were scanned. The observers reported many friendly fliers and several seagulls, but so far as known, no Nazi bombers ever dared approach Nantucket.

The United States Navy was the great benefactor of Nantucket during the war years, when it took over the grass-strip runways of Nobadeer Airport and developed it into a strategic modern facility. On June 22, 1942, a barge loaded with heavy construction equipment arrived, and the Bianchi Construction Company began work on the runways, storage bunkers, and Quonset huts, some of which remain at the end of the century. The airport was used as a training field for aviators from Quonset Point Naval Air Station, for antisubmarine patrols, and for bombing of Gravelly Island as target practice.

The Nantucket Airport had a curious history. Despite vigorous promotion by early Nantucket aviation pioneers like Parker Gray and David Raub, the town refused to take over the airport as a public facility, since the citizens objected to the noise and worried about the danger of aircraft flying over the town. The town finally accepted ownership of the airport in 1941, then leased it to the Navy in 1942 until it was totally taken over by the Navy in 1943. With the end of the wartime need, the Navy returned the airport, with all its new facilities, to the town on June 20, 1946.

As the Battle of the Atlantic was fought out in 1942, the shoreline of Nantucket became a picture of wartime reality. Wreckage, debris, and oil from sunken tankers and other targets of the U-boats were found along the shores and many souvenirs were carried home by beachcombers. The beaches were closed after sunset.

The first human casualties of the war arrived in Nantucket on May 24, 1942. Two boatloads of survivors of a British ship torpedoed off Bermuda were brought into Nantucket after drifting at sea for several days. A total of forty-two survivors, of which thirteen were Chinese seamen, were lodged at Bennett Hall as a temporary hospital. The Red Cross called for volunteers, and scores of nurses and volunteers responded to help out. All the men survived and left the island in a few days. This was Nantucket's first experience with wartime victims and it left a lasting memory with all who attended them.

Patriotism was strongly displayed in Nantucket. The traditional Memorial Day celebration in 1942 was superseded by celebration of War Bonds Day, with a holiday declared and Main Street closed. Led by the American Legion color guard, the parade featured the High School band, Boy Scouts, Girl Scouts, and a detachment from the Coast Guard. Speakers on the steps of the Pacific Bank included the chairman of the Board of Selectmen, the Reverend Claude Bond, and Robert Ray, a Nantucket High School junior, who delivered the Gettysburg Address. The impressive occasion featured, for the final time, the appearance of Commander James H. Wood; he was the last surviving Nantucket man to serve in the Grand Army of the Republic, attending his last patriotic ceremony at the age of ninety-six. The occasion also included Nantucket veterans of the Spanish-American War, World War I, and active servicemen of World War II, thus representing Nantucket's service to the nation in four wars over the past eighty years.

The summer of 1942 was one of change and uncertainty. Rumors swept the mainland that there was no boat service, that the beaches were not fit for swimming, and the island was to be evacuated. The newspaper hit back that the rumors were false and the island was expecting its usual tourist season. Summer residents like Bassett Jones, Gardner Russell, and Morris Ernst wrote to assure the public that Nantucket was still their favorite summer place. Wartime travel was limited to a few people, servicemen, and those on essential business. The wartime slogan was: "Is this trip necessary?" Gasoline rationing, the coastal blackout, and national worry over the war took their toll on the vacation business.

In the middle of the year, the steamers *Naushon* and *New Bedford* were taken by the government; the former became a hospital ship for the invasion of Europe and the latter became a freight carrier. The *Naushon,* the comfortable favorite ship of the island line, never returned. With these popular ships gone and the remaining steamboats painted dull gray, the islanders were missing part of their traditional lifeline, but it was part of the war effort.

In August of 1942, the U.S. Army arrived on Nantucket for the first time in history, as a company of military police took over the old Crest Hall Hotel on North Water Street, a building which is now the rear of the Harbor House Hotel. Their function in guarding Nantucket was somewhat obscure, but they were sent from Camp

Edwards on Cape Cod in the belief that Nantucket beaches would provide good training for the African desert. They made a fine appearance as they marched through the streets out to Madaket and back. They also proved popular with the young women of Nantucket. There were many broken hearts when the soldiers departed Nantucket in the spring of 1943, and the newpaper commented, "Some of the girls took advantage of the opportunity and gathered in farewell kisses all too promiscuously." Some of the soldiers returned to Nantucket and married their wartime sweethearts.

Meanwhile, the island made several attempts to keep its economy alive. Some of the large hotels closed due to shortages of help and food supplies. The island advertised itself as "An Oasis of Peace in a World at War," citing the many advantages still available even under wartime conditions. The *Inquirer and Mirror* did its best by producing the largest edition in history, 11,000 copies of eight pages each, printed on June 12, 1942, and mailed free to all servicemen. In addition, the island opened a Servicemen's Club on South Water Street, staffed by local women, and continued the full schedule of movies at Dreamland Theatre throughout the war. In 1944, Preston Manchester opened his bowling alley on the south side of Main Street, which proved a popular activity for a few years.

Inevitably, Nantucket began to receive the tragic news of local boys killed in the service. The messages came by telegraph, and the local manager of the Western Union office, John F. McLaughlin Sr., had the responsibility for delivering the dreaded telegrams to the families. It was a grim responsibility he remembered all his life.

The hard aspect of wartime life on the island was emphasized by the severe winter weather during the winter of 1942–43, when the temperature hit 2 degrees below zero on December 17 and plunged to 8 degrees below zero on February 15, with a bitter northwest wind.

As if to compensate for the harsh winter, the summer of 1943 was unusually fine, without a stormy day from June 25 to September 13. Tourists returned, Nantucket boomed, the beaches were crowded, and the streets full of bicycles. Nantucket was the perfect escape from the reality of war. The darkest days were over, and patriotism ran high. There were many successful war bond drives and many collections for "essential war material," including newspapers, rubber tires, and scrap iron, all of which was hauled to Steamboat Wharf and sent away to aid the war effort. Wartime rationing extended to gasoline, meat, and other foods, and wartime ration books were part of daily life, but nobody went hungry on Nantucket.

One surprising result of the war years was the almost total disappearance of crime from Nantucket. The island adhered to the old British tradition of awarding a pair of white gloves—the symbol of purity—to the presiding justice of the Superior Court when there were no crimes to prosecute, and this special ceremony was held in both 1943 and 1944. Nantucket was on its best behavior.

In early 1944, Nantucketers traveling by train from Woods Hole to Boston were stopped at the Bourne railroad bridge, which was raised to permit the passage of ships through the Cape Cod Canal. There was an endless convoy of vessels of all types, steaming through the canal, headed into the North Atlantic: destroyers, escorts, freighters, fleet tugs, oilers, troop transports, ships of every size and description. It was a mighty display of Allied shipping headed for the invasion of Europe. It passed in silence and the passengers watched in silence for two or three hours. Amazingly, none were disturbed by the long delay of the train. This was war, and they were doing their part, even if it involved watching and waiting as the men went to war. Nobody complained about the delay.

On April 12, 1945, President Franklin D. Roosevelt died. The town fell into grief, the schoolchildren marched to Bennett Hall for a memorial service, and Nantucket mourned the president it had last seen smiling on his yacht in Nantucket Harbor.

On a sunny afternoon in August of 1945, Nantucket heard the first news of the atomic bomb blast at Hiroshima. The news came by a radio broadcast from President Harry Truman, who announced, "It is an atomic bomb. It is a harnessing of the basic power of the universe." The war would soon be over and the boys would be coming home. A few days later, President Truman announced that Japan had surrendered.

The date was August 14, 1945, forever after known as VJ Day. In the early evening, the bells of Nantucket began ringing. The town bell-ringer, Jay Gibbs, climbed the South Tower to ring 250 strokes of the town bell by hand. "It was some pull on the rope," he said, "but I was mighty glad to do it." People knew what had happened without being told and everyone in Nantucket headed for Main Street. There Nantucket erupted into a wild celebration never seen before. Crowds, veterans, sailors, civilians, girls, tourists, and islanders joined in a happy swirl of celebration. The Electric Company blew its whistle for two hours, church bells pealed, and firecrackers saved for years were exploded. Tons of newspapers were shredded and scattered to create a wild background for the cheering crowds. The local police wisely decided to let the party wear itself out, and the drinking and revelry continued until midnight. Later in the evening, the crowd assembled to hear the popular blind accordionist, Herby Brownell, play a memorable version of "God Bless America."

Despite the crowds, the drinking, and the revelry, there was no damage done, no injuries, and no arrests. That was one of the interesting results of the war years: with patriotism running high and many men in uniform, crime almost disappeared.

By midnight, most of the crowd had worn itself out and drifted home, leaving Main Street knee-deep in newspapers, and the island with the memory of its greatest celebration—the end of World War II.

POSTWAR:

When the war ended, Nantucket servicemen returned home by the hundreds. The island was hardly prepared for them. Although the families were happy to have their boys home from the war, the island did not offer enough job opportunities for the sudden influx of man-power. However, several possibilities were open to the Nantucket vets. Some chose to marry their hometown sweethearts and start work in the local construction or retail businesses. Others took advantage of the GI Bill to obtain academic or technical education on the mainland. Those who could not find work received benefits from the "52–20 Club," which provided unemployed veterans with twenty dollars a week for fifty-two weeks. Many of the vets went to work as apprentices to older contractors and thus learned valuable trades that would be useful in the new economy.

With the availability of building materials that had been scarce during the war, a demand for housing launched the first postwar building boom. Nantucketers built their own homes in record num-bers, as the town gradually expanded beyond its traditional limits. The town responded to the demand for housing by financing its first housing development on Old South Road/Gold Star Drive, near the Rotary, where eight cottages were built and sold to local veterans with liberal GI mortgage loans of $5,000.

One of the first postwar businesses with a Nantucket character was started on Lower Orange Street in 1947 by a returning veteran from Sconset, Albert F. "Bud" Egan Jr. After trying his hand at the family construction business, Egan decided to settle in town and start his own lumber company employing local men and women, some of whom were still working for Marine Home Center fifty years later, when Egan was the largest private employer on the island.

An exciting offshoot of the postwar years was the island's fasci-nation with aviation and great interest in the new airport, which the town had resisted for so many years. Nantucketers flocked to the air-port and took flying lessons, which were cheap and often paid for with GI benefits. Soon the island had more licensed pilots than any other town in New England. Several high school boys won their pilot's wings after school and were licensed at sixteen.

The economy still revolved around the summer season and the

reliability of transportation by steamship. Here, problems were on the horizon. By the end of 1945, the steamship company, after running wartime deficits, announced its intention to sell the line. The winter schedule was cut to one boat a day, arriving at two o'clock in the afternoon and departing just fifteen minutes later—a most unsatisfactory arrangement. The steamships were repainted white for the 1946 season, which was welcome, but the line would not recover its most elegant ship, the original *Naushon*, which never returned from the war after serving as a hospital ship in the European Theater. To add to the boatline's woes, a September strike—part of a national strike by the International Brotherhood of Longshoremen and the Teamsters Union—shut down operations for a few critical days, which directly imperiled the island and provoked public doubt about the future of the line. It also produced some ingenious innovations as the public scrambled to get off the island using private motor boats, catboats, and a decommissioned landing craft, 144 feet long, which hauled automobiles from the Washington Street Beach.

The summer of 1946 witnessed an outburst of activity at the airport, which was soon named the Nantucket Memorial Airport in honor of the eleven men who lost their lives in World War II: Theron Coffin, Harry Gorman, Robert Henderson, Mason Stevens, David Raub, Frank Hanlon, William F. Jones, Ralph DeGraw, Sidney F. Henderson, John F. Walling, and Robert Cartwright. The only buildings available were the Navy's Quonset huts, which soon became the offices for a half dozen small airlines and charter services, offering flights to Boston, Cape Cod, and New York. The major airline was Northeast Airlines, with eight daily flights to Boston and Newark on DC-3s holding twenty-four passengers. It was a season for free enterprise, and Allen Holdgate, a former Navy pilot, combined a charter service, flight instruction, and coffee shop in one Quonset building.

Modern technology became more visible on the island in January 1946, when the first microwave tower was erected on the Madaket

Road to send telephone messages through the air to the mainland, thirty years after the first long-distance call was made from the Atheneum to New Bedford. Mounted on a tower at the intersection of Eel Point Road, the antenna beamed waves to a similar tower on Clay Hill in Barnstable, providing a signal "virtually absent from static and man-made interference." On Low Beach in Sconset, a series of towers and low-lying huts constructed during the war, which were secret for years, were disclosed to be the Loran station—a long-range aid to navigation.

The island got some free publicity in the form of articles by Boston columnists Earl Banner in the *Globe* and Lawrence Dame in the *Herald,* who called the summer of 1946 "the greatest summer invasion in its history." They reported 2,146 air passengers in one week of July and full planes for Northeast Airlines in August. Earl Banner called the new Loran station the "first cousin to radar," and predicted it would provide faster and more accurate navigation for vessels at sea. Dame loved the fact that Nantucket was unspoiled, despite the influx of visitors, with room for all to do just about what they pleased, within decent bounds. Everyone remarked about the wonderful evening sing-a-long on Main Street, where Herby Brownell, the blind accordionist, provided the music for two hours of spontaneous and free entertainment, "like something out of Stephen Foster." Those evenings were memorable for bringing together Nantucketers, tourists, and celebrities for mutual enjoyment on summer nights.

Nantucket's first genuine night club was Preston Manchester's Upper Deck on Main Street, where the tireless Gus Bentley played his piano for cocktail music and dancing. Next came the Knotty Pines on Fairgrounds Road, where Capt. Parker Gray established the first roadhouse restaurant. Also that summer, Gwen and Harold Gaillard opened the Opera House, which became a Nantucket institution with its continental cuisine, sophisticated decor, and intimate seating in the famous red building on South Water Street—much favored by such visiting celebrities as Elizabeth Taylor and Frank Sinatra.

Amid all the postwar activity, the old institutions continued to hold their own in Nantucket social life. The Nantucket Cottage Hospital held its annual fete, the Nantucket Yacht Club was at the center of the summer scene, and the venerable Wharf Rat Club had a well-established clientele on Old North Wharf, where its cannon boomed a salute to incoming members arriving on the steamboat. The Artists' Association, newly founded in 1945, restored the annual Sidewalk Art Show, and the museums and historic properties of the Nantucket Historical Association were popular attractions.

In September, the waterfront awakened with a chorus of horns and bells to greet Nantucket's newest fishing dragger, the 77-foot, 175-ton dragger *Carl Henry*, named for the son of Captain Rolf Sjolund. She was the pride of the Nantucket fishing fleet, and destined to be one of the last fishing vessels based in Nantucket. Her crew list reads like a roster of the last of the Nantucket deep-sea fishermen: Leendert Block, Leif Olsen, Karsten Reinemo (cook), Ralph DeGraw, James Worth, Richard and Stephen Ledwell.

Nantucket turned out in November to support the Republican ticket by a large majority, as it had since the days of Lincoln. It was reported that the highest vote for a Democrat leader was the 624 votes for Franklin D. Roosevelt in 1940, against 1,015 for Wendell Wilkie. Nantucket customarily went Republican by over 400 votes in state and national elections.

The annual Boston meeting of the Sons and Daughters of Nantucket drew a crowd of 170 people on the fiftieth anniversary of this most unusual organization. Organized in 1894, when a group of winter-bound Nantucket natives met in Boston to socialize and talk about their island home, the tradition continued as an annual dinner with speeches and entertainment. This year, the popular president was Billy Fitzgerald, the secretary was Catherine T. Flanagan, and the soloist was young Charles E. Flanagan. The tradition of the Sons and Daughters was later extended to other cities and other members, including in the reunions both Nantucketers and summer residents.

During the year, the federal government began construction of five high towers on ninety-eight acres of land in the Head of the Plains area at the western end of the island. The four towers were part of a new aerial navigational system under control of the Civil Aeronautics Administration. Each tower had a cement base and was bolted down with eleven-foot bolts weighing 125 pounds apiece. The size of the towers was impressive, for each one stood three times the height of the 109-foot tower of the Old South Church. A violent gale in November snapped the insulation joints of the towers and brought them crashing to the ground, exactly one day after their completion and shortly after they had been pronounced ready for service.

The Massachusetts Steamship Company reported some 10,000 automobiles transported to the island in the summer of 1946, and planned another vessel to bring more in the future. The town was now aware of its traffic problem but did not wish to impose any hardships on residents or visitors, so nothing was done. The road to the airport was surfaced and the paving of other dirt roads continued. The summer of 1947 brought more and more people, by air and sea, aided by a beautiful August that was the driest in history.

In July of 1947, a new weekly paper appeared on the scene. Sporting a banner masthead featuring the legendary Billy Clark, the *Town Crier* was the creation of newspaperman Joseph Indio and his Nantucket wife Constance Heighton Indio. The paper featured well-written news articles and dynamic editorials that were often controversial but never dull, as the editors took forceful stands on many local issues.

The most pressing issue for the islands was the deteriorating steamship service, which was the cause of an emergency message to the legislature from Governor Robert Bradford, which resulted in a study by a legislative commission later in the year.

The summer season brought a great revival in summer theater on the island, with the Straight Wharf Theater producing "Moby Dick" and the Siasconset Casino and Yacht Club producing their popular shows. The Nantucket Neighbors added to their lecture series a number of new events for visitors including a fishing trip, sailing cruises, and nature walks. The summer also witnessed the Nantucket Policemen's Ball at the Casino in Sconset, a night when all the local policemen attended in uniform, leaving the town in the hands of volunteers from the American Legion. A long-time summer resident, Clement Penrose, produced a moving description of old Sconset and its many legendary characters and activities, told with warmth and wit.

The Nantucket Neighbors heard another great tale of the past, when David Sarnoff, the famous founder of RCA, returned to tell about his days at the old Marconi Wireless Station in Sconset, adding many details about the wonderful world of radio and his role in 1912, when he manned the New York station to bring the news of the *Titanic* to the rest of the world.

Nantucket author and native son Edouard A. Stackpole announced the news that he had found the ship's log of the *Huntress,* a Nantucket ship under Captain Christopher Burdick, which affirmed the American discovery of the continent of Antarctica in 1821. Stackpole presented a research paper to the government that proved this long-disputed American claim of discovery.

The new airport was proving to be a goldmine for the town, as all the Quonset huts were rented to various air services. The large hangar was used for a Nantucket Flying Club ball in November, with parachutes draping the walls. The only complaint was the high price of airplane fuel at the airport—thirty-five cents a gallon. The prospect of receiving federal funds was eagerly awaited.

The building boom continued on the island and the employment situation was good. One interesting development on the Cliff was the renovation of the Kimball House on Lincoln Avenue, a summer cottage that had been gradually enlarged by successive owners until it contained twenty-eight rooms and nine baths. The house was dismembered and the parts moved around the property until it became three separate houses, each of which was still a good size. The transformation of one trophy house into three livable domiciles was widely admired. It may happen again!

In February of 1949, Gus Lake, chairman of the airport commission and a member of the town's transportation commission, announced that prospects for improving the steamship service were gloomy: "The line hasn't got boats enough to handle the summer traffic, and if it had not been for the plane service we would have had a pretty dull season last year." He had a vision of an airport administration building, financed by town, state, and federal money, that would cost $200,000 but would be justified by the increased revenues from many businesses that benefited from the airport. The airport manager, Jean Cook, reported that the previous year's air traffic brought $40,000 to the island.

One of Nantucket's most visible but unheralded assets, the shade trees of the town, came under study, with a recommendation for establishment of a tree commission and full-time tree warden. The Police Department was operating on a budget of $18,702, for the entire police force, and the Fire Department, under Chief Archibald Cartwright, presented a budget of $18,000, which included a raise for the volunteer firemen from $11.50 to $25.00 a *year*.

One of the peculiar accidents of island life occurred in March 1948, when a slight list of the steamboat sent a full trailer-load of mail overboard as the steamer approached the jetties. The steamer *Martha's Vineyard* lost the 600-pound trailer and almost lost its electric tow motor in the accident. The Coast Guard responded with alacrity, bringing ashore fifteen sacks of mail and several loose packages. Coast Guard patrols found three sacks of mail on Smith's Point and Chester Williams found the Sconset mail pouch on Madaket Beach. Finally, the last sack of mail was found by two men on the shore at Monomoy. Ten individual packages were lost, but, amazingly, every sack of mail was recovered and sorted out in a soggy scene at the post office.

In January of 1948, the federal government officially turned over the airport to the Town of Nantucket. The installation was valued at $680,564 for the land and $261,500 for the buildings. The figures for the previous year showed 46,641 passengers passing through the airport. There were now seventy-eight privately licensed pilots soaring over the island. The importance and popularity of the airport continued to increase every year, and in the summer of 1948 a giant air meet was scheduled with 1,000 private planes expected to land. That number did not materialize because of bad weekend weather, but a total of 252 planes did arrive and the aviators were treated to a clambake at the Wauwinet House.

More transportation was added to the Nantucket travel scene this summer as the Hyannis Boat Line began to run daily excursion service using two 100-passenger vessels, the *Iyanough* and the *Nautican,* two former Coast Guard cutters converted to passenger use. It was reported that the Hyannis line carried 15,000 passengers in 1946 and 25,000 in 1947. Although Nantucketers were slow to make use of the Hyannis line, it proved very popular with tourists, and the downtown streets, which used to be empty at midday, were soon filled with wandering crowds of shoppers and sightseers. The islanders joked about the "day-trippers," but they welcomed the business.

The Steamship Company responded by promising Nantucket three boats a day for the summer season, with one round trip to New Bedford and good train connections to Boston and New York. It was proudly announced that the new schedule would increase the line's capacity for carrying cars to Nantucket by a hundred percent.

The summer of 1948 was a big year for baseball in Boston, with both the Red Sox and the Braves involved in close races for the pennant. Many Nantucketers took their first plane rides to see the games, with Northeast Airlines flying special weekend flights to the doubleheaders. Representative Cyrus Barnes and John F. McLaughlin Sr. made the arrangements. Robert F. Mooney, a senior at Nantucket High School, built a scale model of Fenway Park from Balsa wood and pool-table cloth, which was put on display on Main Street.

During the summer, the Barnes boathouse at the end of Commercial Wharf was sold at auction to Eben Hutchinson Jr. The Boathouse was a popular restaurant and night spot for many years until it was acquired by Sherburne Associates and became part of the Nantucket Boat Basin.

The most important event of 1948 was the establishment of the Steamship Authority, which came about after a study of the operation by the Massachusetts legislature. The legislature concluded that the existing company was on the verge of failure due to increasing costs and decreasing revenues. A public transportation authority was enacted into law with a mandate to provide service to the islands and to issue tax-exempt bonds to finance its operation. It was named the New Bedford, Woods Hole, Martha's Vineyard, and Nantucket Steamship Authority, and in December it paid $1,375,000 for the assets of the Massachusetts Steamship Company. The authority was organized with a five-person board, one from each port, and a chairman appointed by the governor. Nantucket's first representative was the highly regarded businessman Lawrence Miller.

November 1948 witnessed the passing of a notable Nantucketer, Harry B. Turner, editor and publisher of the *Inquirer and Mirror* for forty-two years. Born in Nantucket in 1877, Turner began his newspaper career at the age of fifteen. He became an island institution, not only for producing his weekly paper but for serving as writer, photographer, editor, and historian. He was succeeded in office by his son, Gordon Turner, and daughter, Merle Turner Orleans.

At the end of the year, the first television sets made their appearance on the island at the Marine Appliance Store, which operated out of John Stackpole's home on West Chester Street. They were not immediately popular because the reception from the Boston stations was poor and subject to weather conditions. Stackpole promised the reception would improve with warmer weather and possibly closer stations at New Bedford and Providence. In the meantime, John

Stackpole left his set on all day and often came home to find his living room full of people who just wanted to come and stare at the TV screen. The early days of television were confined to the cities of the east coast, and the daily programs were limited. It was announced that within the year there would be television coverage from the east coast to the Mississippi River, but that would not mean much to Nantucket. The island would continue to rely on the radio for its news.

The Nantucket Agricultural Society, which had operated the annual county fair since 1856, went out of business in 1949 and offered its Fairgrounds Road property for sale. Thus ended another venerable Nantucket institution, once the pride of the island's farming community and a memorable part of the social fabric on the island. The farms were declining in number and size and the farmers were moving to town. Most of the farms would become house-lot developments, and the Fairgrounds Road property was destined to become the new site of the Nantucket Electric Company.

A long dry spell during the summer fed the flames of a major forest fire in July, when a thoughtless visitor started a picnic fire in the woods off Fairgrounds Road. The fire soon blazed out of control, burning 1,500 acres and cutting off Sconset and the airport from town. Hundreds of volunteers turned out with brooms and shovels, and ninety soldiers were flown in from Camp Edwards on Cape Cod before the fire was stopped on the Polpis Road.

It was another good summer at the airport, showing a twenty percent increase in traffic. A federal grant of $34,000 was received, which promised runway lights for the airport and made additional night landings possible. Both Northeast and Massachusetts Airlines were running shuttle service to Boston.

Disaster befell the cabin cruiser *Constance*, taking nine lives in waters within sight of the island. The twenty-eight-foot *Constance*, skippered by Russell Palmer, left Falmouth carrying the Allenby family and several young couples for a day cruise and picnic on Nantucket. When the vessel left the island at about eight o'clock on

September 9, it ran into a thunderstorm and heavy seas over Tuckernuck Shoal, which swamped the vessel and forced the passengers into the water wearing life jackets. As night came on, they were within sight of land and saw many vessels passing but couldn't attract their attention. When the *Constance* didn't return to Falmouth, the alarm was sounded and the Coast Guard alerted. It was not until mid-morning the next day that the survivors were sighted from the air by Nantucket pilot Allen Holdgate, and several rescue boats were launched. It proved too little and too late. Nine people drowned and only two survived. An official investigation later found fault with the local Coast Guard station for inadequate training and equipment. They had failed to alert local mariners who knew the waters and could have made the rescue.

So, with its victories and tragedies, the dramatic decade of the forties ended, and worldwide events would have their impact on the future of the island community.

OPPOSITE PAGE:

A fifty-year-old photograph brings back memories of World War II in Nantucket. With most of the island manpower gone to war, the island relied on volunteers to defend the home front. In the north end of town, a small but dedicated force of lads, some as young as ten, gathered near the crossroads of North Liberty and West Chester Streets to guard the strategic heights of Sunset Hill, where the Oldest House was considered a likely target for enemy attack. Although short of weapons and uniforms, they fashioned their own wooden guns of realistic quality, and cleverly camouflaged themselves in casual outfits designed to blend into the scenery. Born too late to get into real uniforms, we were eager to take part in this, the last "Good War," and our memories of those years in Nantucket remain fresh and unforgettable.

Defending Nantucket in 1943: Photo taken by David Gardner in field off West Chester Street, showing rear of Lamb home on North Liberty Street. L to R: Sidney Thurston, Robert Mooney, Leslie Martin, Richard Gardner, Michael Lamb (rear), Neil Lamb, James Patterson, Leonard Chase, Charles Ellis. Photo enhanced by Terry Pommett, 1993.

WORLD WAR II: A MEMOIR

THE NEWS OF PEARL HARBOR CAME TO NANTUCKET ON SUNDAY, December 7, 1941, shortly after the arrival of the steamboat with the Sunday newspapers. My Sunday job was to deliver the paper to an elderly woman on High Street. I had just returned to Federal Street when I met Edward (Tony) Ruley, flying down the street on his bicycle, yelling, "They bombed it, they bombed it! . . . That place in the Pacific . . . they bombed it!" It was Pearl Harbor.

We returned home to listen to the radio. The news was confusing, because the attack had come from the wrong direction. We were in the Atlantic, and our enemy was Nazi Germany. The Pacific coast may have been in peril, but what would happen to us?

I was in the sixth-grade class of Mrs. Elizabeth Chase at the Academy Hill School. Within a couple of days, there was an air raid warning and all the children were sent home at noontime. This war was hitting home. The large brick building on Academy Hill was considered a prime target for German bombers, so the plans called for evacuating the children at the outset; later in the war this procedure was changed from going home to simply gathering in the schoolyard for a few minutes.

The town quickly organized a Civil Defense Service Unit, with headquarters in the Sanford House on Federal Street, where the selectmen met and appointed local officials to organize the defense of the island. Because the entire east coast was subjected to a wartime blackout and no outdoor lights could be shown, the streetlights were hooded and the auto lights were shaded by painted eyelids. Most important, no home could show any light, and blackout curtains became standard on the windows. Air raid wardens were appointed to patrol the streets, carrying flashlights and wearing blue triangular civil defense armbands. Some wardens rode bicycles, and Millie Jewett patrolled Madaket on horseback. There were some colorful clashes between the new wardens and the local citizens, but most people accepted the regulations.

One of the most visible of the wartime outposts was an observation tower, erected in a vacant field atop Mill Hill, just east of the Old Mill. Here two people were stationed day and night, equipped with binoculars, radio telephones, and recognition books, for the purpose of reporting every sighting of aircraft. We manned the tower faithfully, and scanned the skies for enemy aircraft, reporting many friendly fliers and several seagulls, but no Nazi bombers ever dared approach Nantucket.

Around the town, the Civil Defense forces set out generous piles of sandbags on strategic street corners, intended for use against incendiary bombs. The fire department and police department recruited reserves to help in any emergency. Volunteer Coast Guard auxiliaries were recruited from the local seamen as local fishermen were banned from the high seas.

The real defense of the island was in the hands of the U. S. Coast Guard, which at one time maintained as many as six manned stations on the island. Brant Point headquarters had command of smaller stations at Madaket, Surfside, Sankaty, Coskata, Great Point, and finally the Nesbitt Inn property on Broad Street, which was used as a medical station for island servicemen. The Coast Guard had the vessels and men with primary responsibility for the island, and during the early years of the war they maintained foot patrol of the beaches with trained patrol dogs. In 1942, the government required identification cards for civilians in strategic occupations, and people rushed to be photographed, then showed their pictures to amused friends.

The Nantucket airport was the great benefactor of the defense establishment in 1942, when the U. S. Navy discovered the strategic importance of the island's grass-strip runways. A barge loaded with construction equipment arrived on June 22, 1942, and the Bianchi Construction Company began its heavy construction of runways, Quonset huts, and storage bunkers, some of which remain fifty years later.

The Nantucket airport, originally known as Nobadeer Airport, had a curious history. Despite vigorous promotion by early Nantucket aviation pioneers like David Raub and Parker Gray, the Town of Nantucket refused to take over the airport as a public facility because it was thought that it would disturb the town with noisy and dangerous aircraft. The town finally accepted ownership of the airport on June 13, 1941, leased it to the government in 1942, and saw it taken over by the Navy in August of 1943, after which it was used as a training field during the war. Navy fliers from Quonset Point staged antisubmarine operations from the island and used the shoals of Gravelly Island for target practice. The boom and rumble from the shoreline continued for many months, until the end of the war, when the Navy turned the airport, with all its improvements, back to the Town on June 20, 1946.

Throughout the early years of the war, the island's shoreline brought home the reality of the Battle of the Atlantic. All along the shore could be found oil and debris from sunken ships and even personal belongings—grim souvenirs of war that were lugged home by island youths. On May 24, 1942, two boatloads of survivors from a vessel torpedoed off Bermuda were brought into Nantucket and lodged at Bennett Hall, which was pressed into use as a temporary field hospital. Nurses and other volunteers across the island responded to the call of the Red Cross and helped care for the forty-two victims, thirteen of whom were Chinese. It was a unique experience for Nantucketers, and those who tended the survivors never forgot the event.

The U. S. Army arrived on Nantucket August 26, 1942, for the first time in history, and took over the old Crest Hall Hotel on North Water Street, a site that is now a wing of the Harbor House Hotel. It was a company of military police, and no one was exactly sure of its function on the island. As a boy, I watched some of them peel potatoes on the porch of Crest Hall, polish their rifles, and march out to Madaket and back. They were a fine body of men.

Steamship service to the island was somewhat interrupted by the wartime restrictions, and there were many changes. In 1942, the familiar white ships were painted a dreary battleship gray as a measure of camouflage against submarine attack. Frequent fire and abandon-ship drills were held. In the middle of 1942, the steamers *Naushon* and *New Bedford* were taken over by the government and refitted for service in Europe. The *New Bedford* became a freight carrier, and the *Naushon*, the luxury liner of the fleet, lost its cocktail lounge and became a hospital ship, never to return to Nantucket.

As the bombs fell on London, Nantucketers were called to support British War Relief and the American Red Cross, giving food, medicine, and supplies to the beleaguered Britons. The seriousness of the European situation had an effect on the island, resulting in the suspension of the hospital fete and curtailing yacht club festivities, as the participants engaged themselves in more urgent causes.

The men of Nantucket rapidly went to war, along with several women volunteers for different branches of the service. The first local draft board was appointed by Governor Leverett Saltonstall, consisting of three eminent men: William E. Gardner, Eugene M. Perry, and Harry B. Turner. They heard the cases of men appealing the draft calls, and made the hard decisions of who went to war. The early draftees left in groups, marching to Steamboat Wharf for photographs and public farewells. Many volunteers left for service in the navy, coast guard and merchant marine. As the numbers mounted, the island rapidly lost its able-bodied men. Beginning in 1942, the news of men killed in the service began to arrive, as eleven Nantucket men lost their lives during the war. John McLaughlin Sr., manager of the Western Union office on Main Street, had the sad responsibility of delivering the telegrams to their families, a task he remembered all his life.

The grim aspect of island life was emphasized by the severity of the weather during the winter of 1942–43, when the temperature went to 2° below zero on December 17, and plunged to 8° below zero on February 15, with bitter northwest winds. On February 16, I remember trying to chop ice for a birthday party, with the hatchet bouncing off ice that was like a rock.

Many attempts were made to keep the island economy alive during the years from 1942 through 1945, when wartime restrictions on travel, rationing of gasoline, and the coastal dim-out were in effect. Perhaps the hardest hit were the big hotels; the Sea Cliff closed in 1943, Crest Hall was taken over by the army, and the Nesbitt Inn was used as a Coast Guard office and sick bay.

The *Inquirer and Mirror* did its best to promote the island and cheer the servicemen with its largest edition ever: 11,600 copies of eight pages each, printed on June 12, 1942. The large commercial building on South Water Street was converted into a servicemen's club, operating a local USO on the site later occupied by Hardy's hardware store. In May 1944, Preston Manchester opened his bowling alley on the south side of Main Street, which became a popular spot for a few years. Dreamland Theater remained in operation, and wartime movies were crowded with servicemen and their dates. The restaurants and food establishments were struggling to operate with limited food supplies and constant shortages. The drug stores were always running out of ice cream, cigarettes, and candy and instituted their own rationing systems. In those years, people who worked in drug stores and food stores were considered lucky.

As if in answer to the previous hard winter, the summer of 1944 was unusually fine, without a stormy day from June 25 to September 13. For those tourists able to get to Nantucket, it was a beautiful summer, with crowds at the beaches, many bicycles and no traffic problems. I spent that summer working at the Galley on Cliffside Beach, delivering lunch to the patrons on the beach. It was a wonderful summer to be on Nantucket. One of my memories is of the day I heard the announcement on a portable radio at the beach that Harry Truman had been nominated for the vice presidency at the Democratic National Convention, and the almost universal question, "Who's Truman?"

In the early summer of 1944 I took one trip that gave me an unforgettable picture of the war effort. My father had some police business in Boston and agreed to take me along for a taste of adventure on the mainland. We were lucky to get one trip a year off island; some children never left the island unless school events took them. On that occasion, my father and I took the steamboat to Woods Hole; at that time the train for Boston was right there at the dock, and it was usually a two-hour trip. We got as far as the railroad bridge at Bourne, where we came to a stop because the bridge was up.

As we sat there, we saw an endless convoy of ships passing through the Cape Cod Canal, headed north and into the Atlantic. Destroyers, escorts, fleet tugs, freighters, oilers, troopships; ships of every size and description seemed to pass before us for two or three hours. It was a mighty display of Allied shipping, and it was all headed for Europe. As I remember it, the battleship-gray ships passed in silence. The passengers in the train also watched in silence, and, amazingly, none seemed disturbed by the long delay on the train. This was war, and we all had to do our part, even if it meant waiting and watching the men going to war. When the last ship passed, the bridge came down and we went on our way to Boston.

We lived by the radio during the war. It was the primary source of news and we treated it with respect. Most homes had one radio, and it held a prominent place in the living room. At news time, the family gathered around and looked at the radio, as we today watch television. We knew all the famous radio commentators and personalities, their voices and their schedules. Perhaps because they were invisible, they seemed more real and important than today's television personalities.

The other great sources of news were the weekly magazines, then in great popularity: *Life, Look, Time,* and also *Collier's* and *The Saturday Evening Post.* The picture magazines brought the most vivid portrayals of the wartime scenes and were eagerly awaited each week. There were daily newspapers, but they arrived in the afternoon on the steamboat and were not as entertaining as the magazines and the radio, especially to someone my age.

The national program of rationing wartime scarcities was followed on Nantucket as everywhere else, with gasoline, meat, and various foods restricted to limited weekly amounts. Each auto carried a windshield sticker to announce its category, A for personal, B for business, and C for other vehicles. These restrictions were not very onerous on Nantucket where travel was limited, but they did inhibit mainland trips. Rationing stamps, tokens, and stickers were a large part of daily life for the shoppers, with various numbers of stamps needed to buy sugar, butter, meat, and other items. With ready access to family farms and local seafood, few people in Nantucket missed any meals, and food rationing was a minor nuisance. The only thing we missed was red meat, as beef and lamb were in short supply; in those days such meats were a virtual requirement for a large family meal. Only because items where in short supply did they become necessities. We had never heard of calories or cholesterol. Cigarettes, always scarce during the war, were considered positively beneficial for the nerves and social life, and were widely advertised by athletes and motion picture stars.

Patriotism was the watchword in World War II—"The Good War" —and Nantucket was no exception. Wartime slogans called for everyone to aid the war effort, and there were many opportunities for volunteer work. In addition to manning the aircraft watchtower on Mill Hill, we marched in parades with the Boy Scouts, collected war stamps to buy savings bonds, and took part in dozens of collection drives for "essential war material." As the war went on, this seemed to include almost everything, for we collected huge piles of newspapers, rubber tires, tin cans, and scrap iron. All of this junk was collected across the island and hauled down to Steamboat Wharf, where it departed to "aid the war effort." It may have been dumped overboard once out of sight of land, but we had done our duty.

With public spirit running high, and so many young men gone to war, there was one interesting result of the war years: crime almost disappeared from Nantucket. Nantucket held to the old British tradition of presenting a pair of white gloves—the symbol of purity—to the presiding justice of the Superior Court at those sessions where there were no crimes to prosecute, and this special ceremony was held in Nantucket in both 1943 and 1944. With only a small police department of five men—two on days, three on nights—the local police were fortunate to have a well-behaved population, winter and summer. The Army, Navy, and Coast Guard supplied their own military police and shore patrol to control their forces, but no serious crimes ever took place.

Nantucket schoolchildren in the 1940s had three school locations: a one-room school in Siasconset for the first four grades, the Cyrus Peirce School on Atlantic Avenue for the first six grades, and the Academy Hill School, where I attended all twelve grades. The big brick building on the hill was the focus of most school activities during the war.

Since Academy Hill had no gymnasium, the schools used the recently built hall of the Congregational Church, known as Bennett Hall, for high school assemblies and sporting events. During the war the boys drilled with wooden guns, and basketball was played under the peculiar groundrules set by the undersized court and low ceiling of the hall. Still it was a place for great times in Nantucket. Bill Toner can remember many humorous events inspired while playing basketball in Bennett Hall. At Academy Hill, the air raid warnings diminished as the war moved away from Nantucket, but the eager students often rushed to the windows to watch low-flying planes as the war continued to have its effect. Boys could leave school to enlist at the age of sixteen, and many seniors left for the service before graduation, receiving wartime diplomas from the school.

On April 13, 1945, we were all marched to Bennett Hall for a sad event, a memorial service for President Franklin D. Roosevelt, the only president most of us had ever known, and certainly the only one we ever remembered. There was no way he could be replaced, and we knew nothing about Harry Truman.

Although far removed from the battlefields, minor incidents occurred on Nantucket during the war and are vividly remembered. A medium bomber of the Royal Canadian Air Force, headed for Nova Scotia, went wildly off course and crashed on the old golf course off Cliff Road. Since the plane was disabled, it was towed to the wharf and shipped back to Canada on a barge. Local fishermen and yachtsmen were enlisted in the Coast Guard Auxiliary and did patrol work about the island, a useful service since private boating was severely curtailed. Although the Coast Guard had a station at Madaket, the legendary Millie Jewett maintained her private patrol of the harbor and beaches, raising and training her own watch dogs. She also collected a memorable assortment of salvage from the beaches to decorate her Madaket property.

For the youth of Nantucket during the war, there was little organized recreational activity; we were pretty much on our own. The high school fielded a basketball team, and both boys and girls played in Bennett Hall, but that was the only school sport. Consequently, the boys played a lot of touch football after school and weekends, using any available field: the Sanford House yard, the fields around Cyrus Peirce School, and the Harbor House area on South Beach Street. The football in those days was not sharp and smooth, but a blunt oval leather bag that became soggy and heavy with hard use. We played our own baseball games on any available lot, in season, and many basketball hoops were erected on family garages and barns to provide primitive basketball facilities for half-court games. Of course, there were no automobiles for joy-riding, and nobody could have afforded them if available; we were lucky to have bicycles.

The Coffin School on Winter Street was the home of the industrial arts program of the high school, a valuable training ground for many future Nantucket contractors, although we did not appreciate it at the time. On the first floor, the boys were taught carpentry and woodworking by instructors like Leroy True, while in the basement they learned metalwork and plumbing under Tom McAuley. The young women of the school were taught cooking and sewing in a home economics course under stern taskmistresses like Sarah Packard and Mrs. Earl Ray.

From this institution, much maligned and often ridiculed, came many of the finest contractors and craftsmen on the island, some of whom are still in business.

Wartime life consumed the thoughts of many young men and women on Nantucket. We lived, worked, and played with the war on our minds. The young women were much in demand for parties and dances with the visiting servicemen, and as the older girls flocked to the Servicemen's Club, the high school boys began dating younger girls in school. There developed many long-term romances, many of which led to permanent marriages. Several local girls married servicemen who returned to live on Nantucket. It was all very exciting and romantic.

As the war went on, there were permanent symbols of Nantucket's contribution to the national effort. A war memorial, listing the names of Nantucket's servicemen and women, was erected on the grounds of the Sanford House on Federal Street. The Nantucket Airport, growing in size and importance during the war, became the permanent memorial to Nantucket's war dead later in 1946, but was a constant reminder of the island's importance in the war. The security forces along the waterfront, and the armed military patrols in the streets, reminded us we were still subject to national emergency conditions, and wartime rationing was a constant reminder of the war. Closest to home were the many houses displaying the famous wartime servicemen's stars: one blue star for each man in the service, with an occasional gold star for a son lost in combat. We can remember the tiny one-room cottage of Oscar Hamblin on the Madaket Road, which displayed a four-star flag for the four sons he had sent to the war.

On a sunny Sunday afternoon in August of 1945, I was riding my bicycle back from Cisco Beach with my friend Bob Flanagan. A man was parked beside the edge of Hummock Pond Road in a convertible car, with the top down, listening to the radio. He called us over to hear the news. President Harry Truman was announcing the news of the bomb. "It is an atomic bomb. It is a harnessing of the basic power of the universe. . . ." We had unleashed the power of the sun. The war would be over very soon; we would not have to invade Japan. We hurried home to listen to the radio. A few days later, on August 14, 1945, President Truman announced that Japan had surrendered.

We were playing tag football at the Cyrus Peirce School early in the evening when the news broke. All the bells of Nantucket began ringing. It could mean only one thing. The war was over. We had to get to Main Street, where all the action was. Everyone erupted into a wild celebration never before seen on Main Street. Crowds, sailors, girls, civilians, veterans, tourists and islanders—everyone was happy, drinking, celebrating in a great swirl of happiness. Jay Gibbs climbed the South Tower and rang 250 strokes of the bell by hand. "It was some pull on the rope," he said, "but I was mighty glad to do it." The Electric Company blew its whistle for two hours; firecrackers saved for years exploded. Tons of newspaper was shredded and scattered to create a wild background for the cheering crowds. Later in the evening, the crowd assembled to hear the popular blind accordionist Herby Brownell play a memorable version of "God Bless America."

The local police wisely decided to let the party wear itself out, and the drinking and revelry continued until midnight, when the crowd drifted home.

World War II was over.

—R. F. M.

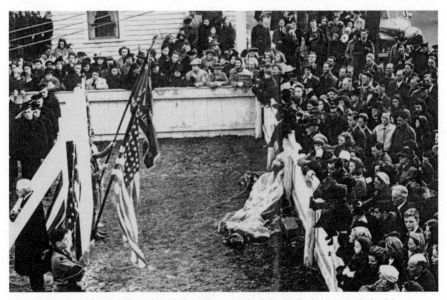

A war memorial was dedicated in 1942 on the grounds of the Sanford House on Federal Street.

Charlie Sayle was an accomplished builder of ship models.

Charles F. Sayle Sr.
WATERFRONT PHILOSOPHER

CHARLIE SAYLE WAS NANTUCKET'S MAN OF THE SEA FOR almost fifty years. He never learned to drive a car. He walked to the waterfront daily, surveying the fishing boats, the scallopers, and the other working boats that crowded the wharves, before they were crowded out by luxury sport vessels. He was in his element as Commodore of the Wharf Rat Club, with his mate's cap, his famous beard, and his wealth of good conversation.

Charlie was born in Cleveland and left school to sail on Great Lakes steamers, but that water was not deep enough, so he moved on to Gloucester and its fishing fleet, which eventually brought him to Nantucket. Here he dropped anchor for good, fixing up an old cottage on Union Street and making it his shop and home for life. He met and married young Muriel "Mickey" Stafford, a Nantucket woman, and they raised two sons. He built his own famous green sloop, the *Argonaut,* and made a career of building ship models, carving scrimshawed whales, and studying the lore of the sea.

After World War II, Charlie teamed up with Jose Reyes, who was then making open lightship baskets that sold for modest prices. Mickey Sayle one day suggested that she'd like a lid for the basket Jose had made for her. Jose obliged, and Charlie decorated it with his trademark, the ivory whale. The rest is history.

Charlie Sayle was more than a skilled craftsman and waterfront character. He was also a serious scholar of the sea and a lively natural speaker and writer on Nantucket history. His "Waterfront News" column was for years a popular feature of the local newspaper, because he wrote as he spoke, in straight and simple language. He was often called to appear at mainland museums, to resolve questions of historic and maritime importance, and to identify old ships and photographs for the Nantucket Historical Association. Over the years, Charlie welcomed many friends from all walks of life who enjoyed his good stories and good fellowship.

When he died in 1994, Charlie left a legacy of waterfront lore and many happy memories. His sons, Charles Jr., who became a fisherman and seafood dealer, and William, who continued the scrimshaw and lightship basket tradition, carried on their father's lifetime interests. Charlie Sayle's rare talents and personal qualities will be long remembered in Nantucket.

This image of Reyes hung on the wall of his basket shop for years.

José Formoso Reyes

BASKET MAN

"YOU MUST BE FROM NANTUCKET—I CAN TELL BY YOUR basket!"—words that have been heard all over the world by travelers from Nantucket, as someone sights the distinctive Nantucket Lightship basket. The originals were made by bored sailors weaving straw baskets on the lonely lightships, but the tremendous popularity of the modern product may be attributed to one man: José F. Reyes.

Born in the Philippine Islands, Reyes obtained an education at Harvard College and returned to teach at the university in Manila. During the war, he served with General MacArthur's forces, and after the war he arrived in Nantucket with a distinguished war record but no job. He had a Harvard education but could not get a job in the Nantucket school system. With a wife and three children to support, he was willing to work at anything. Having made a few baskets in his youth, he learned the craft of the Nantucket basket from old Mitchy Ray, who made hundreds of baskets—none of them signed.

José set out his baskets on the lawn of his home on York Street, where the public bought them for $22 to $45 each. He called them "Friendship Baskets," useful for shopping and household storage. His handles were made of white oak for strength, and each basket was handmade and signed, which adds to their value today. Next he developed the cover, and with this improvement the basket became a fashion accessory. He worked from dawn to almost midnight, and could not keep up with the demand.

One day, Muriel Sayle looked at her Reyes basket with its blank top and asked her husband, Charlie Sayle, to carve a sperm whale to decorate the basket, where it looked right at home. Soon everyone wanted a whale or another piece of scrimshaw on her basket. Local artists like Charlie Sayle, Aletha Macy, and Nancy Chase were hard at work decorating Reyes baskets. He worked hard and fast, turning out about 200 baskets a year, but there was always a backlog of orders.

José Reyes lived out his career on Nantucket as a successful and popular man, a respected member of the Rotary Club and the owner of a beautiful estate in Polpis. It is too bad he never had the opportunity to teach the school children of Nantucket; they might have learned something from him.

Top: A bright spot during the summer of 1941, the Sidewalk Art Show.
Bottom: WAVEs helped put a bright face on the Nantucket war effort.

Top: The *Andrea Doria* sinks after being struck by the *Stockholm* on July 25, 1956.
Bottom: The hour strikes at Stone Alley, a well-used route to the Unitarian Church.

The heady years of postwar prosperity were interrupted by the outbreak of the Korean War, reminding Americans of their responsibility to keep peace in the world. American education confronted the challenges of segregation in the schools and Soviet satellites in the sky. Nantucket faced its own challenges from a new brand of tourist and new patterns of transportation, and looming problems with the island's steamship service.

Starting
to
Move

The decade of the fifties marked a turning point from the long tradition of shared interests and close relationships within the Nantucket community. Prior to those years, the center of town was the place both residents and summer visitors mingled for shopping and recreational pursuits, typified by the evening sing-a-longs on Main Street, after which everyone went home at ten o'clock.

In the fifties, many things contributed to change this life style as a new breed of people discovered Nantucket. The influx of tourists from the Hyannis boats turned Main Street into a daytime shopping center, while the direct air service from Boston and New York brought a younger and livelier crowd to enjoy the weekends. They gathered at Jetties and Surfside Beaches during the day and flooded to the in-town cafes and bars at night. Nantucket catered to their needs with cheap rentals and tolerance of casual life styles. Members of the traditional establishment wrote resentful letters to the newspapers, depicting the newcomers as "that cheap New York crowd" and barely concealed their antipathy to the newcomers; they were anti-hippie, anti-homosexual, and anti-Semitic.

For the first time, Nantucket seemed to be facing problems beyond community control. As the downtown area shifted toward more businesses catering to the transients, Main Street lost its year-round appeal. Nantucketers began to take advantage of low land values and low taxes to move into outlying neighborhoods where they had more space and more modern homes. The old Nantucket was fading away, and nobody seemed to know what to do about it.

In February of 1950, the town began the first of many attempts to plan for the future development of the island when the newly formed Zoning Committee made its report to the Board of Selectmen. Designed to protect the integrity of the island community and regulate the spread of commercial establishments in residential areas, it was a sensible start but it went nowhere. It would be twenty-two years before Nantucket would accept any kind of zoning legislation.

The first of several maritime tradegies struck the island on April 7, 1950, when a sudden northeast snowstorm coming on Easter weekend caught the fishing dragger *William J. Landry* on Pollock Rip, about twenty miles northeast of Nantucket. As the vessel was driving for home against 63 MPH winds, the men on board were in radio-telephone contact with their families and seemed homeward bound. Suddenly, the fishing boat went down in mountainous seas and three Nantucket men were lost: Arne Hansen, Earl Blount, and Ted Polosky, leaving wives and children to mourn them on the saddest of Easter Sundays.

Nantucket was making concessions to progress. The town clock needed repair, and it was recommended that the works be electrified, but for another seven years the great Portuguese bell in the South Tower continued to be struck by the wonderful brass mechanism provided by William Hadwen Starbuck in 1881.

One Nantucket institution did pass, however, when R. G. Coffin's drugstore at the corner of Main and Federal Streets went out of business after forty-three years. This was more than a drugstore, for it had long been a favorite meeting place for the men on Main Street and a place where schoolchildren could warm up over the big hot-air register in the floor. It was eventually replaced by an upscale antiques store.

The summer saw a burst of theater activity. Margaret Fawcett Wilson continued her Nantucket repertory at the Straight Wharf Theater, and Vincent Bowditch opened the novel theater-in-the-round at Barn Stages on North Liberty Street.

Another pleasant summer season was starting in June of 1950, when the world was shocked by events on the remote Korean peninsula. North Korean forces invaded the Republic of Korea to the south, and the United Nations responded with an allied force led by American troops from the army of occupation in Japan. Reserve soldiers and sailors were recalled and a peace-time draft began to call up men for active service. Nantucket was far removed from the war scene, but its men were soon back in uniform.

The national crisis did not greatly affect the local economy, and business continued apace. The newspaper continued to publish its "Notes" from the airport, the waterfront, the hospital, and the outlying villages. The hotels listed their guests' names and the hospital reported on the patient list—a practice that was part of the island's charm, until in the interest of personal privacy the practice was discontinued. One distinguished guest was Eleanor Roosevelt, the president's widow, who visited with the former secretary of the treasury Henry Morgenthau Jr. The HyLine Cruises out of Hyannis reported more business than ever in its fifth year of operating the summer line for passengers only—no cars allowed.

In the fall, the Nantucket Rotary Club was established with the popular Henry B. Coleman as its first president. The town completed construction of the veterans housing development off Old South Road, which proved a valuable and successful project. In December, a committee report suggested a zoning bylaw be placed on the next town ballot, but it did not happen.

A legendary Nantucket figure, Chief of Police Lawrence F. Mooney, retired from the police department in February of 1951, after thirty-nine years of service. He was succeeded by his protégé, Wendell H. Howes, who served as chief until his retirement in 1975, also serving thirty-nine years on the force.

Perhaps the most notable Nantucketer of the modern day, the local newspaperman and historian Edouard A. Stackpole, achieved national recognition in April of 1951 when it was announced that he had been awarded a Guggenheim Fellowship to pursue his research on the Nantucket whalemen and their contributions to maritime history. Stackpole's remarkable ability and his thirst for knowledge overcame his lack of a college education; his personal popularity stemmed from twenty-seven years of hard work at the *Inquirer and Mirror*. The Guggenheim grant enabled Stackpole to conduct his research in many places, including England and Ireland (where the venerable Irish names of Stack and Poole had helped produce this "hybrid Irishman"). The award was applauded by the community and by the Boston *Globe*, which noted that it came on the anniversary of the publication of Melville's *Moby-Dick* in 1851. Ever reliable, Stackpole produced his great history of the whalemen, *The Sea Hunters*, which was published to great acclaim in 1953.

Transportation problems arose in May when a two-week strike suspended steamship operations and again reminded the island of its frail connections with the mainland. Fortunately, the planes were flying, but islanders again worried about the future of their lifeline.

A new passengers-only vessel, the *Kateri-Tek*, offered summer service out of Hyannis, and Northeast Airlines was running four flights a day to Boston and New York. An airport administration building was opened at the end of the year, supplanting the old wooden buildings and Quonset huts. Progress was also evident in town with the opening of Preston Manchester's 5&10 on Main Street and Waine's Appliance Store on India Street. Nantucket was picking up speed. It was, however, paying a price for progress, as both the Steamship Authority and the Wannacomet Water Company announced an increase in rates.

The island was hit by several major blows in 1952, beginning with the weather. In January, a three-day northeaster struck with 72-MPH winds, knocking out electric and telephone service. In February, two large oil tankers, the *Fort Pierce* and the *Pendleton,* were wrecked in a heavy storm off Pollock Rip and the local Coast Guard participated in the rescue of seventy men, of whom sixty-three survived. Then, on February 27, came a record-breaking blizzard with twenty inches of snow and howling winds that caused over $10,000 damage to electric and telephone lines. The Brant Point area and the waterfront were flooded with twenty inches of water. The huge Loran tower at Low Beach and many TV antennas fell. It was the biggest winter storm on record, and to add to the disaster the Nantucket fishing dragger *Anna C. Perry* went down with all hands. It was truly a hard winter.

Once the winter season was over, the selectmen began to contemplate what provisions should be made for the 1952 summer population, which they estimated would be around 22,500. Selectman George Burgess Jr. was quoted as saying that "half of them will be sleeping on the sidewalks," as controversy swirled around the number of liquor licenses to be granted.

In midsummer, Nantucket town was beginning to feel the impact of its growing tourist business. A long hot summer brought an influx of complaints about the growing problem of noisy crowds, after-hours drinking establishments, and a newly perceived threat to the island—homosexuals. In August, the Board of Selectmen adopted regulations aimed at preventing "homosexuals or other persons of immoral character" from gaining a foothold in Nantucket. Although Chief Wendell Howes said that no overt acts had been reported to his department, he vowed there would be no replication of Provincetown's problems. The police promptly rounded up six defendants and charged them with indecent exposure on a north shore beach. Judge Caroline Leveen found each of them guilty, imposed a fine of $100 each, and ordered them to leave the island on the next boat or plane. The district attorney joined the crusade by sending two plainclothes officers down to the island to scout the bars and restaurants for possible solicitations. Their undercover work paid off with enough indecent proposals to find another six men who were tried, convicted, sentenced, and deported.

The town continued to promote its attractions with an advertising budget of $20,000, although some were beginning to question the wisdom of mass advertising for the island. The Chamber of Commerce, whose origins went back to 1912, was reorganized and incorporated with the official motto "To promote the prosperity and preserve the traditions of Nantucket." According to the newspapers' front pages, summer theater was flourishing and an air tour of ninety-two planes was scheduled for the fall.

The fifties saw problems for the Steamship Authority continuing and being compounded. Organized as a public authority in 1948, the authority had a mandate to provide service for the islands of Martha's Vineyard and Nantucket from the mainland ports of New Bedford and Falmouth (Woods Hole), with one member appointed by the municipal government of each port and a chair appointed by the governor. The authority could issue bonds and set its own rates, but any deficit in its operations was to be paid by the four communities in various percentages.

As the line began operations, it was beset by labor disputes, scheduling problems, and increasing conflict between the mainland

and island communities. Furthermore, operational costs continued to be higher than revenues, and annual deficits grew higher. Several short strikes had been settled in favor of union demands that called for full-time, year-round employment, despite seasonal declines in service. The islands responded by calling for the cessation of winter service to New Bedford, an issue that the Supreme Judicial Court decided was within the power of the majority of authority members. The authority made plans to stop winter service to the city in January and February and discussed plans to eventually move the headquarters of the line to Woods Hole. This provoked a new series of proposals in the legislature, whereby New Bedford sought to ensure year-round service to the city and the islands proposed to maintain control of the line. The legislative response was to form an investigative committee that would survey the situation in 1953.

The legislative recess commission, signed into law by Governor Christian Herter, soon found the Steamship Authority problem a "hopeless muddle." It was apparent that the city of New Bedford viewed the service as a source of employment and a traditional element of its economy, which it was loath to lose. The mounting deficit, which amounted to $95,000 in 1952, was a relatively small price for the city to pay, but it threatened to add several dollars to islanders' tax rates. The islands based their claims on the waste of time and the expense of the run to New Bedford (five hours for the Nantucket run), and the need for a shorter, more efficient route to the nearest mainland point. Furthermore, the old steamships with their side-loading, dolly-freight operations were quaint but outmoded; both islands looked forward to faster ferry service, attuned to modern trucking systems. The city had the power of the Longshoremen's and Teamsters unions behind it and the hefty political clout of the New Bedford *Standard Times,* the only daily paper in the area. The islands claimed to have reason and necessity on their side, but the political problems seemed insurmountable.

The battle was carried on through legislative hearings, court trials, public forums, and Supreme Court decisions. Most visible were the battles fought by the newspapers—with the Nantucket *Town Crier* and its editor Joseph Indio the most outspoken proponent for the islands and the *Standard Times* firing its broadsides for the city and its political supporters. Soon everyone had heard about the islands and their "steamboat problem."

The island economy continued to grow, with a year-round population of 3,600 and real estate valuation up to $13,953,130. Nantucket had ten hotels and eleven inns, and new restaurants opened every year. The energetic superintendent of streets, Matthew Jaeckle, proposed and won approval for paving lower Pleasant Street, Sparks Avenue, Cliff Road, and Milk Street Extension. In 1954, the selectmen made the momentous decision to make Main Street and Centre Street one way for the first time in history, changing the driving and parking habits of the island in the name of traffic control. Letters complained about the crowds, the traffic "bedlam," and the cheap stores full of "cheap people and half-naked men." The sight of "skimpy attire" on Main Street was a common source of irritation to some, but not all citizens. The police were given credit for keeping the street crowds under control. The Hyannis excursion vessels were reported to bring $100,000 into the local economy, but the sight of all those day-trippers with their ice cream cones and shopping bags was too much for many. Among the better news of the summer of 1954 was the founding of the Nantucket Garden Club, an organization that was to promote and display the more attractive sights of the island.

The fall of 1954 brought two named hurricanes smashing down on Nantucket: Hurricane Carol passed west of the island on August 31 but caused heavy damage to the heavily foliaged trees of the town; then, on September 11, Hurricane Edna hit the island directly, with the eye of the storm showing blue skies and calm air before the tail end struck in full fury, filling the air with debris and flying shingles. The major damage was to the south shore and Madaket, where the wind-driven surf filled the Long Pond area and the pounding seas cut off the end of Smith's Point to create Edna Island. The barometer reading dropped to 28.165, setting a record for the lowest glass in Nantucket history.

Yet another ongoing controversy made the news in 1954. Two Nantucket boys were charged with the crime of fishing in local ponds without a state fishing license, provoking the old question of "who owns the ponds?" Under Massachusetts law, any pond over ten acres in area is a "great pond" and under the sole jurisdiction of the state, whereas smaller ponds may be privately owned. Nantucket based its claim on the colonial ordinance of 1686, which preserved to the inhabitants of the town their traditional rights in the ponds and shoreline. Thus, Nantucket fishermen had never bothered to obtain state fishing licenses, and the state in return had never stocked the fish in the ponds. This year the two local boys were arrested by state officials in an attempt to force Nantucket to comply with the state law. The case came to trial in Nantucket District Court, where the boys were ably represented by attorney George M. Poland, who sought a binding decision on the question. He did not get it, because Judge Caroline Leveen found the boys not guilty. The state's attorney asked for an appeal to a higher court, but did not get it and the matter remained unresolved, except that the boys did not need a state license to fish in the Nantucket ponds.

At the end of the year, the airport reported that passenger traffic had reached 75,000 persons coming and going by plane, with Northeast Airlines alone carrying 51,335 people. In addition, Hyannis carriers had handled 430,000 pounds of freight, and the airport had carried more air mail and freight than ever before. The steamships may have had their problems, but the airplanes had become an important part of the island economy.

In January of 1955, the U. S. Navy returned to Nantucket in force. Islanders flocked to Steamboat Wharf, where a 327-foot LST (Landing Ship, Tank) began to unload heavy equipment and a battalion of SeaBees. The ship was described as "the largest vessel ever to enter Nantucket Harbor," and it was followed by more landing ships, which hit the beach at Sconset during the winter. The Navy had come to build a facility on the bluff at Tom Nevers Head, and although the purpose of the installation was considered secret, it soon became known as a land-based system to detect Soviet submarines, which were considered a major threat during the years of the Cold War. On Nantucket, the SeaBees lived in tents while they constructed the base, some of whose cement buildings and Quonset huts still remain on the property.

The population of Nantucket was recorded at 3,642, and was soon to be enlarged by several hundred Navy men and their families, which helped stimulate the local economy and fill up the schoolrooms. The new high school building was used for its first graduation on June 9, and the U. S. Naval Facility was commissioned on August 1.

As the command of the Police Department had changed in 1953, the year 1955 was the time for change in the Fire Department, when the colorful Archibald H. Cartwright resigned as chief, to be replaced by Irving Bartlett. Archy Cartwright, the last Nantucketer to have gone whaling, was immediately appointed curator of the Nantucket Whaling Museum, a post for which he was eminently qualified with his local background and salty stories.

Other Nantucket institutions were experiencing growing pains in 1955. The Nantucket Atheneum, the venerable public library, announced that it was intending to renovate and improve its facilities and would mount a campaign to raise $65,000. Ground was broken on South Prospect Street for the new Nantucket Cottage Hospital, a badly needed modern building to replace the old facility on West Chester Street with its cluster of wooden "cottages." The newly organized Chamber of Commerce got under way with a good cross-section of local business members that included twenty-one guest houses and three real estate brokers. A "Courtesy Town Meeting" for summer residents was held to hear the comments of seasonal residents on problems that centered around the increased traffic and congestion in the streets. Northeast Airlines announced the purchase of a fleet of ten new four-engine DC-6 airplanes to add service to the island, provided the runways were extended.

On Beacon Hill in Boston, two similar legislative bills were pending to establish the first historic districts in the Commonwealth, one on Beacon Hill and one on Nantucket. The concept of treating an entire town as a historic district was new but intriguing; the Nantucket Historical Association and other civic groups sponsored the local legislation, which would preserve the exterior appearance of buildings in specific areas of Nantucket and Sconset. Future construction or changes were to be regulated by a local commission and permits would be necessary for any exterior alterations. Both bills survived a test before the Supreme Judicial Court, and the Nantucket bill emerged to be signed first by Governor Christian Herter, making Nantucket only the second historic district in the nation—Newport, Rhode Island, was the first.

By the end of the year, several notable figures had passed from the island scene. The last blacksmith, Aquila Cormie, closed his shop on Lower Main Street and retired, a victim of age and progress. The popular commodore of the Wharf Rat Club, Herbert H. Coffin, a waterfront figure for most of his eighty-four years, died in December, followed by the veteran craftsman and lightship basketmaker Clinton "Mitchy" Ray, at eighty-six, in February. Miss Clara Parker, librarian of the Atheneum, retired in January after fifty years of service. Her predecessor Sarah Barnard having served fifty years, the Atheneum had had only two librarians in a century.

On the waterfront, a new figure emerged when Lawrence Miller announced the purchase of Straight Wharf, which he intended to completely restore from its dilapidated condition at a cost estimated at $50,000. The old wharf, built in 1723, had been part of the Killen estate for years and was sinking into the harbor. Miller proposed to install new facilities, build up the bulkheads, and create a landing for small boats and the Hyannis excursion boats. Improvements would include shingling all commercial buildings and construction of a new restaurant to be known as Captain Tobey's.

In the closing days of 1955, the Steamship Authority announced its decision to suspend winter service to the city of New Bedford in an attempt to cut expenses and reduce the annual deficit—a decision that was to have far-reaching economic and political consequences. With the decision of the authority to stop winter service, the city of New Bedford turned to the legislature for help, and it was not long in coming. A special act of 1956 required the Steamship Authority to provide year-round service to the city in return for the city's paying half of the line's deficit.

The Steamship Authority and the islands resisted the New Bedford legislation and appealed to the Supreme Judicial Court, which upheld the act, and the U. S. Supreme Court, which refused to hear the case. The city and the islands were now bound by law to operate the boatline despite rising deficits and rising levels of bitterness and controversy.

The first winter months of 1956 reserved their heaviest hit for March, when a St. Patrick's Day storm hit with a combination of snow, wind, and high tides. Flooding forced the evacuation of Brant Point and Washington Street, where seventy-three people were taken from their homes to emergency shelters. Snow returned a week later, when 24.5 inches of snow fell on March 24, setting a record but doing little real damage.

A fairly uneventful spring led into a season heralded by a published "Declaration of Courtesy and Consideration," underscoring the need for mutual respect between Nantucketers and summer visitors. On July 10, speaking at the Friends Meeting House, Doctor Will Gardner, president of the Nantucket Historical Association, proposed that the island hold a 300th birthday celebration in July 1959 to commemorate the settlement of the island in 1659. The proposal was warmly received, and plans for the celebration began immediately.

The worst maritime disaster since the sinking of the *Titanic* took place forty-five miles southeast of Nantucket on July 25. The Italian luxury liner *Andrea Doria*, with 1,706 people on board, passed the Nantucket Lightship, bound for New York at full speed. At the same time, the smaller Swedish liner *Stockholm*, with 534 passengers, was headed east from New York to Stockholm. Although a heavy fog covered the waters, both vessels were operating at full speed, relying on radar and lookouts for safety. They were on a collision course, and neither took timely action to escape the inevitable. At about 11 P.M., the heavy, ice-breaker bow of the *Stockholm* sliced into the starboard side of the *Andrea Doria*, inflicting a fatal wound in the 29,000-ton luxury liner. Wireless messages immediately alerted ships and stations all over the Atlantic coast, and Nantucket became the center of the rescue efforts. Planes, helicopters, and rescue vessels rushed to the island. Many of the injured were flown to Nantucket Cottage Hospital, where dozens of vacationing doctors and nurses volunteered for duty. Forty-three people died on the *Andrea Doria*, but with 1,662 survivors it was the most successful rescue operation in maritime history—the *Titanic* story in reverse.

Two more local institutions passed from view this year: On August 5 fire totally destroyed the Moby Dick restaurant and lounge on the south bluff at Sconset, where it had been one of the most popular gathering places for the summer crowd. In October, the old steamer *Martha's Vineyard* (formerly the *Islander*) retired from the line after thirty years of service. She was to return a few years later in another role. The old vessel would be replaced the next year by a new ship intended to handle a new generation of vehicles and passengers.

It was in the election year of 1956 that the author began to play a part in the political life of the island. Nantucket had been a traditionally Republican stronghold since the days of Lincoln, never showing more than a few hundred Democratic voters at the polls.

The town had always elected Republicans to its seat in the Massachusetts House of Representatives, and the incumbent, Cyrus Barnes, at seventy, was a strong prospect for reelection. The sole Democrat to place his name on the ballot was Robert F. Mooney, then a twenty-five-year-old student at Harvard Law School. Howard U. Chase, a former member of the Steamship Authority, was the other Republican contender. Little interest was shown in the contest until August 1, when Representative Barnes died in office—after the deadline for filing nomination papers. This created turmoil in the Republican party on Nantucket, because another popular candidate, John L Hardy, a veteran selectman, decided to run as a write-in, creating a three-man race.

It was remembered as one of the liveliest campaigns in Nantucket history, with weekly battles of words in the two newspapers, each candidate vying for space while their supporters worked to gather votes for their favorite candidates. Nantucket was straining between its traditional voting patterns and its new candidates for office.

When the votes were counted on November 6, Nantucket held to its Republican roots in the Presidential election, casting 1,582 votes for Dwight Eisenhower and only 317 for Adlai Stevenson. But the voters of Nantucket made history by electing as their state representative the first Democrat to hold any office—state or federal. The final ballot count was Mooney, 763; Hardy, 600; and Chase 531.

The new representative announced he would dedicate himself to being "a Nantucketer first and a Democrat second." Several bills were filed for the 1957 session of the General Court and regular reports were sent to the hometown newspapers. The first legislative achievement was enactment of a special law to provide for state funding of a bicycle path beside the state highway to Sconset, at a cost not to exceed $7,000 per mile. It was the first bicycle path in Massachusetts and represented the first such use of gasoline taxes in the state's highway fund. When the path was finished, it was opened by Doctor Paul Dudley White, the eminent Boston cardiologist who had gained national fame while treating President Eisenhower after his heart attack. Other towns followed Nantucket's lead in opening a happy new era for the pedaling public.

The year 1957 featured the new and the old on the Nantucket Scene. In the spring, the island witnessed the promised arrival of the *Nantucket,* a newly designed ferry that featured front-end loading and large open deck spaces. Built at a cost of $2.45 million, the *Nantucket* utilized the new transfer bridge on the north side of Steamboat Wharf to accommodate her 229-foot length. It was argued whether she was the largest vessel ever to serve the islands; the old *Naushon,* at 250 feet, was longer but had less deck space.

The passing of a great tradition took place on July 8, when the clock in the South Tower was electrified and town bellringer Jay Gibbs climbed the tower to ring the bell for the last time. Thus ended a tradition of 107 years, with the bell rung by hand fifty-two strokes, three times a day, at 7 A.M., noon, and 9 P.M. As his father James had done before him, Jay Gibbs did the job for thirty years, never missing a stroke until the twenty-seven-inch snowfall of 1952 frustrated him for one evening. Electrification of the clock was delayed until Gibbs announced his retirement from the job he had so faithfully performed for the town, which paid him $830 a year. There were no immediate applicants for his position.

A major construction project was undertaken this year when the U.S. Navy built a residential complex on Vesper Lane to accommodate the many young naval families on the island. Nineteen units were built at a cost to the federal government of $16,500 each. When completed, the project was named Gouin Village in honor of Nantucket native Vice Admiral Marcel E. Gouin, a hero of World War II.

Two years into the planning stage, Nantucket's 300th birthday celebration was being promoted by the Nantucket Historical Association in cooperation with the Board of Selectmen and other civic groups. It would emphasize the island's historic position as a microcosm of America and help promote the economic development of the island.

Concern over the steamship service and utilization of the new *Nantucket* brought more conflict between the islands and the city of New Bedford, resulting in a Supreme Judicial Court decision that endorsed the authority's intention to terminate winter service to the city. Bills were filed in the General Court to alter the authority's function, to establish new private operations, and to use the state's gasoline-tax revenues to eliminate the deficits. None of the bills passed, but the problems of the line attracted much attention. The authority then announced that it was going into the tour business by contracting for buses to compete with the successful tour-bus service being offered on Nantucket by the Hyannis-based HyLine. The authority's proposal was not well received by Nantucketers.

In 1958, the Steamship Authority reported a deficit of $615,000 for the previous year, and, as mandated, Nantucket was asked to pay its share—$123,000—a bitter pill for the island. The problems with the authority slightly dampened spirits, but with the spotlight on summer theater and the improved quality of Nantucket's night life, spirits began to rise. The director of the Theatre Workshop, Joseph "Mac" Dixon, was honored for his contributions to the cultural life of the island. The newly refurbished Harbor House lounge presented the world-renowned flamenco guitarist Carlos Montoya in July and the brilliant pianist George Feyer in August. Life looked a little brighter on the island.

The bright summer season was suddenly overshadowed by the darkest of tragedies. On Friday evening, August 15, while attempting to land in steadily lowering fog conditions, a Northeast Airlines Convair crashed 1,400 feet short of the runway at Nantucket Airport. The crash left twenty-four dead, including the pilot and copilot, and eleven injured. Police and fire services sped to the rescue and pulled the survivors from the smoking wreckage.

Nantucket Cottage Hospital experienced its finest hour in

responding to the crisis, aided by dozens of volunteer doctors, nurses, and medical students who left their island vacations to assist in the emergency. Hospital trustees arrived to help out. Even the patients took part in the effort. One of them was the author's mother, Ethel Mooney, a retired nurse who was in the hospital awaiting an operation; she jumped out of bed and spent the night dispensing medications and handling telephone calls.

There were many stories connected with the Northeast plane crash, but the most touching was that of little Cindy Lou Young, eighteen months old, who was returning to her island home with her mother, eighteen-year-old Jacqueline Young, after an unsuccessful journey to attempt a reconciliation with the baby's father. The mother was killed in the crash, but the baby went flying out of the plane and landed safely under a tree. New York attorney John Shea heard the mother's last words, "Take the baby," before she died. The little girl was miraculously uninjured, with only bruises and pine needles to show for her ordeal. She was soon resting in the hospital where she was treated like a lucky little princess.

This was Nantucket's worst disaster in terms of lives lost. A report of the Civil Aeronautics Board placed the blame for the Northeast Airlines crash on pilot error—for attempting to land in low-visibility conditions. Fortunately it was never repeated, because local, state, and federal authorities awakened to the importance of the local airport, and work soon began on an instrument-landing system that has helped prevent further tragedies.

In September, Representative Mooney won both the Democratic and Republican nominations for representative, which assured his reelection in November. The problems of the Steamship Authority were still uppermost in the minds of the islanders, and the legislator called for a study of a new transportation system for the islands. In a speech to the House he declared: "Although it is impossible to change the transportation picture overnight, the failure of the authority during its ten-year history and the change in the economic picture of this area justify a full study of all possible alternatives. The potential of Hyannis as a year-round port for Nantucket and the possible separation of the present authority into independent and flexible operations should be fully explored and presented."

In 1959, the two major issues on Nantucketers' minds were the Steamship Authority and the school system.

A legislative recess commission recommended repeal of the mandatory New Bedford winter service and bills were filed to accomplish that. Airport traffic dropped in 1958 by 23,538, a severe decline that was blamed on poor weather and the Northeast plane crash. The island was satisfied that its airport situation was improving when the Federal Aviation Administration announced that the island was scheduled to receive an instrument-landing system and control tower for improving flight conditions.

William Voorneveld, the town tree warden, delivered the sad news that the stately elm trees that graced the downtown streets were inflicted with the deadly Dutch elm disease and their days were numbered.

Two venerable Nantucket businesses changed hands in January, when Philip C. Murray succeeded his father Philip Murray at Murray's Toggery Shop and Franklin Bartlett took over his father's business at Bartlett Plumbing.

Even more devastating was the conflict that developed around the Nantucket School Committee. On the national level, as a result of Russian advances in science and space technology, these years were filled with controversy over education. Amid conflicts over progressive versus traditional education, conservative versus liberal, and the politics of the John Birch Society in its crusade against left-wing policies, the tide of modern politics swept over Nantucket. The School Committee commissioned a survey of the local schools from the Harvard School of Education, which immediately provoked controversy. The superintendent of schools announced the difficulty of obtaining teachers, and the committee proposed a merit-pay schedule to attract teachers, with salaries beginning at $4,100 to a maximum of $6,000, which met with heavy opposition. Nantucket divided over this issue and many leading citizens involved themselves in the dispute, which lasted for years.

On February 7, Nantucket Memorial Airport became an international airport, if only for one flight, when an Iberia Airlines Constellation made an emergency landing after fog closed Boston and New York airports.

On the good side of the news, the spring concert of the Nantucket Community Orchestra was a great success, and the musicians were soon in demand for public events. Five Nantucketers took ownership of the old Nantucket Cranberry Company and promised to revive the traditional Nantucket crop, while the Civic League vowed to eradicate poison ivy and ragweed. Young Charles F. Sayle Jr., fifteen, won a medal from the Massachusetts Humane Society for saving the life of seven-year-old Edward Chambers after he fell into Nantucket Harbor. Nantucket found a friend in Boston when state treasurer John F. Kennedy (no relation to the Kennedy clan), announced that he would not demand from the islands payment of the Steamship Authority deficit until the situation was clarified.

In June, the town began its 300th birthday celebration with the arrival of the first reunion group, the Macy family. They were followed by the Boston Symphony Orchestra, the Nantucket Community Orchestra, and the Otis Air Force Band. Then came reunions of the Coffin clan, the Folgers, the Swains, the Husseys, and the Bunkers. It seemed like everyone was coming to Nantucket in 1959.

The actual birthday, on July 2, was swallowed up by a pea-soup fog that grounded all flights and delayed the steamboats. The town did manage to hold a clambake at Children's Beach for visiting dignitaries including U. S. Congressman Hastings Keith and former Speaker of the House Joseph Martin, but no governor. A ribbon was cut on Main Street to open the parade of antique cars and a later

Main Street fete, while a crowd of 5,000 watched the fireworks through the fog.

The 300th Birthday Celebration was the biggest public event in island history to date, and undoubtedly gained the island much publicity. Although the day was somewhat spoiled by bad weather, it did bring dozens of state politicians to the island for the first time, many of whom turned out to become supporters of the island in the boatline controversy.

In a controversial move, the Steamship Authority sold the thirty-three-year-old steamboat *Martha's Vineyard* to the Rhode Island Steamship Lines for $25,000, the best price offered. That purchaser subsequently sold the ship to Island Steamship Lines, which began operating the vessel for excursions between Hyannis and Nantucket, and defiantly sailed her into direct competition with her former owners, which produced more lawsuits and injunctions.

The Massachusetts legislature took up the islands' petition to repeal the law calling for year-round service to New Bedford, and in August the House of Representatives voted in favor of the island bill by a healthy margin of 136 to 73. For a while, it appeared the islands might be on the way to victory in their long struggle against the city politicians. But heavy lobbying in the Massachusetts Senate snatched defeat from the jaws of victory, as the Senate defeated the island bill by the narrow margin of 18 to 14, with several senators disappearing from the scene rather than be counted. The islands seemed destined to lose this political game. However, a group of good citizens under the leadership of the eminent businessman Edwin F. Chinlund organized on Martha's Vineyard to study and take positive action on the steamship problem. They hired a professional consulting firm to prepare a study of the boatline and make recommendations. They also retained a public relations firm to broadcast the islands' story across the state, especially to win the support of legislators from other areas of the Commonwealth. The Chinlund Committee was soon joined by Nantucket members and proposed a thorough program to put the boatline back on a "break-even basis," with legislative support.

The summer of 1959 was a good summer season for local theater, with Thornton Wilder himself visiting the Theatre Workshop, where Gwen Gaillard and Norman Wilson starred in *The Matchmaker*. Five hundred music lovers enjoyed the Community Orchestra and paintings bedecked the Sanford House at the Annual Sidewalk Art Show in August. The Sanford House itself, the stately Greek Revival mansion on Federal and Broad Streets, was still in heavy use for town offices, but was scheduled for demolition as the site for a proposed town hall and court house. A long debate over its value ensued for several years.

Nantucket was still embroiled in the school controversy, the steamship problems, and its plans for the future. The pace of life was increasing, and after an eventful decade for Nantucket no one could foresee the future, but all could join in the old-fashioned pleasures of the island when the year 1959 ended with a seven-inch snowstorm and a White Christmas.

The new Nantucket Cottage Hospital was erected in the 1950s to meet increased demands.

THE NEW NANTUCKET, 1955

IN A FAR-SIGHTED EDITORIAL CALLED "FOUNDATION FOR TOMOR-row," the *Town Crier* (published 1947 to 1963) noted a big change in Nantucket's summer season of 1955: the trend toward more short-term vacationers and a decline in the traditional season-long vacationing families.

Traditionally, Nantucket summer visitors owned or rented houses for the ten- or twelve-week season, returning year after year, and often bringing household help with them. They enjoyed the island beaches and waters, joined the social clubs, and provided their own quiet pleasures with little need for public entertainment. Islanders respected the summer visitors and their way of life, and they lamented any change in this seasonal life style. The summer people fit gracefully into the local life style and generously supported the local economy.

Now, Nantucket was experiencing a change; aided by direct flights from Boston and New York and frequent excursion boat service, more short-term visitors were coming to Nantucket for shorter and livelier vacations. The town reacted unfavorably to the change.

The editorial mentioned the factors contributing to the changes on the Nantucket scene: the ease of transportation, the changing attitudes of the younger generation, the booming economy in the country, the lure of other vacation destinations, and the wider interests of the vacationing public. Nantucket, it said, should look forward to accepting this new generation, rather than deploring the demise of its traditional way of life. In reality, the short-term visitor often becomes the potential long-term visitor and retiree, when family and financial situation permit. This prediction often came true in future years.

Edouard Stackpole gave the island a sense of its history.

Edouard A. Stackpole

NANTUCKET'S HISTORIAN

EDOUARD STACKPOLE WAS THE MAN WHO EDUCATED THE island to its place in history and awakened the world to the importance of Nantucket in the maritime world. Born in Boston to a Nantucket family, he was raised on the waterfront, listened to the old mariners, and began to love the sea. Graduating from Nantucket High School in 1922, he was inspired by Margaret Harwood, the legendary astronomer at the Maria Mitchell Association, to attend Roxbury Latin School. He was largely self-educated, and although unable to afford college, he won honorary degrees from the University of Massachusetts and Yale University for his scholarship.

Stackpole went to work as a young man for the *Inquirer*

and Mirror, where he labored as reporter, printer, and associate editor for twenty-seven years, using his columns to explore Nantucket history. This led to his first works, a series of boys' adventure books set in Nantucket. His expertise and reputation developed to the point where the small-town reporter won a prestigious Guggenheim Fellowship to pursue his favorite subject—American whaling, which resulted in the 1953 publication of his leading book on the subject, *The Sea Hunters.* This led to a second fellowship, enabling him to travel and publish the great work on the international business of the whalemen, *Whales and Destiny,* in 1972.

In 1953, Ed Stackpole was appointed curator of the Mystic Seaport Museum in Connecticut, where he remained for fifteen years, developing the marine collection and continuing his research and writing on the sea. His pioneering study of the Nantucket sealer, *Huntress,* Christopher Burdick, master, helped establish the claim of the United States for the discovery of Antarctica. During his long career, he produced twenty-eight books and monographs.

Upon his return to Nantucket in 1967, Ed was appointed or elected to almost every position in town that suited his many interests, serving the Nantucket Historical Association, Nantucket Atheneum, Chamber of Commerce, Maria Mitchell Association, and becoming the director of the Peter Foulger Museum and its library, which was named in his honor.

When he passed away in 1993, the island realized it had lost a great man, a gentleman, and a good citizen. Ed Stackpole gave Nantucket more than books and articles: he gave the island a sense of its history.

Collecting Nantucket art was one of Bud Egan's passions in life.

Albert F. "Bud" Egan Jr.
AN ISLAND ORIGINAL

FROM HIS ROOFTOP OFFICE ABOVE HIS SPRAWLING MARINE Home Center on Lower Orange Street, Bud Egan, with his independent outlook on the life of the island, enjoyed a stunning panoramic view of Nantucket Harbor. Here he worked every day, running the largest private company on the island, handling all its many problems, paying the biggest payroll, pursuing his multiple charitable and artistic interests, and loving every minute of it. He was always on the job, pausing only for his daily round of golf at Sankaty Head or lunch with his beloved wife, Dorothy.

Bud was his nickname from his birth in 1916. He went to work at an early age, like a true son of Sconset, and after high school went into the building trade with his father, who had built twenty-five houses in Sconset. He was always busy and full of ideas. After he and Dorothy married in 1940, he built their first house with his own hands and $2,000 of borrowed money. When the war came, he went off to serve and built barracks for the U.S. Army. After returning to Nantucket he started his own Island Building Company, offering to build houses for a firm price, a Nantucket innovation.

In 1944, Lawrence Miller offered the twenty-seven-year-old Egan the management of his lumber yard, the first Marine Lumber Company. Bud was bursting with ideas to expand the business into a home center, selling more than lumber. In 1950, he built his first model home on West Creek Road and advertised it for a fixed price: $12,000.

When Miller went into partnership with Walter Beinecke Jr. in the sixties, Bud Egan contributed his ideas for the proposed downtown development, and in 1965 when Beinecke sold off some operating companies to concentrate on real estate, Egan purchased the Marine Home Center. With the growth of the building industry, the home-furnishings business flourished, and Egan's company grew in all directions, with new shops, an expanded truck fleet, and, for a while, giant transport planes.

Bud Egan always had a serious interest in Nantucket history, and he developed into a patron of the arts, publishing works with his Mill Hill Press imprint and preserving Nantucket history via the Egan Foundation, located in the historic Coffin School on Winter Street. Bud will be best remembered for his energy and dedication to Nantucket: a native son who made good, but also did good in return.

Top: The Nantucket Conservation Foundation, incorporated in 1964, found willing leaders like Alfred F. Sanford. Bottom: The Steamship Authority strike of 1960 brought assorted vessels into service.

The decade of the sixties had a permanent impact on all aspects of American life. Within its ten years, Americans faced the challenges of the Cold War, the Cuban missile crisis, the space race, the civil rights movement, and the seemingly endless ordeal of the Vietnam war. The people were inspired by the birth of a new administration, then were in despair with the deaths of its brightest young leaders. The nation wallowed in Southeast Asia, rioted in the streets, reveled at Woodstock, and rocketed to the moon. Rachel Carson's Silent Spring *was published in 1962, launching the environmental revolution.*

Meanwhile, the old island of Nantucket was brought, however reluctantly, into the mainstream of American life, undergoing many changes—to become the New Nantucket.

The New Nantucket

The beginning of the sixties saw many changes in the downtown business area. In February, the old bakery and the real estate office on Lower India Street were acquired and razed by the Nantucket Atheneum in order to extend the landscaping of Atheneum Park, the only green spot in downtown Nantucket. The work was performed by Edward Backus and his son (who found an 1868 half dollar in the process) and the new garden was designed by the Nantucket Garden Club. The venerable Roberts House hostelry was sold at auction for $24,000, and Island Service Company purchased the Boathouse and what remained of Commercial Wharf for $30,000. Such prices were common to the times. The *Inquirer and Mirror* published a feature article urging the visiting public to settle down and purchase or build homes on several choice sites on the island, stating, "We are glad they come, for it is our sole source of revenue. . . . Why not look around the island and see if there isn't a house just meant for you?"

Nineteen sixty would be remembered for the significant events overtaking the Steamship Authority. On April 15, the simmering conflicts with the Teamsters Union boiled over into a wildcat strike over the size of the crew to man each vessel; soon the strike affected the entire line, officers and men, and the service was shut down. The strike lasted seventy-seven days, during which Nantucket and Martha's Vineyard were without public steamship service, which meant no automobiles or heavy freight to or from the islands. The effect on business and transportation—at the start of the summer season—was enormous. The airlines carried the load with increased service and a heavy volume of passengers, but many seasonal residents refused to come without their automobiles. The crisis was met in part by private ingenuity, with small vessels and landing craft pressed into service to provide emergency transport to and from private wharves on the mainland and the Washington Street beach. Daily reports of the islands' plight appeared in the mainland newspapers with photographs of the impromptu rescue fleet, and crowds gathered to watch the landings.

As disastrous as the steamship strike had been, it had a beneficial effect on the islands' political fortunes. In the legislature, the islands' bill to reorganize the Steamship Authority and eliminate the port of New Bedford received a great deal of publicity during the course of the strike and won the support of many legislators. The House approved the Sylvia-Mooney bill in May by a vote of 149 to 71. The focus then was on the state Senate, where the battle was fought by Senator Edward C. Stone of the Cape and islands against the powerful city and labor forces, The tide had turned against the city during the boat strike, and the Senate passed the islands bill by a vote of 24 to 7 in September.

Settlement of the boat strike on July 2 brought the boats back into service for the Fourth of July weekend, but the real invasion over the holiday came from the air. Weekend traffic at Nantucket Memorial Airport saw 552 landings and 3,239 passengers in and out of the facility, breaking all records. The strike had made a big dent in Nantucket's summer season, but for the rest of the summer things were back to normal.

First National Stores opened the first true supermarket on the island at the Sparks Avenue location on July 20, and thus started the trend to the suburbs. Preston Manchester announced plans to build a bowling alley on a vacant lot at Washington and Coffin Streets, provoking a flurry of petitions pro and con, with the islanders generally favoring the idea and the abuttors objecting to it as a threat to their peace and quiet. The Nantucket School Committee continued to be a source of controversy, with conflicting theories of education that divided the town. In March, six candidates ran for two positions on the committee, and only seventeen votes separated the top three candidates. A shift to a conservative majority resulted in the dismissal of a school counselor despite much public protest, and she was immediately hired by the Nantucket Civic League to initiate the Family Counseling Service. The school controversy smoldered beneath the surface for several years, resulting in the termination or resignation of several professionals and making the School Committee the most controversial of public boards.

In November, Nantucket went to the polls, driven by the hotly contested Presidential election. The town voted for Nixon with 1,219 votes, but gave the Massachusetts candidate, John F. Kennedy, a surprising 698 votes.

The year closed with two major storms: Hurricane Donna, on September 12, caused heavy seas and 73 MPH winds that washed out Broad Creek; and on December 10 a northeast storm brought sixteen inches of snow. In the latter storm, the New Bedford fishing dragger *Sharon Louise* was smashed on the tip of the western jetty, and the Coast Guard patrol boat almost sank making the rescue. The eleven survivors managed to get ashore at Dionis and found shelter at the Tupancy house after a grim struggle in the icy waters.

More harsh weather came with the new year. On January 19, another northeast storm brought sixteen inches of snow and forced the evacuation of Brant Point. Then sixteen days of subfreezing weather broke a record for winter freezes that had stood for sixty-eight years. Ice as thick as eighteen inches covered the harbor and out of sight into Nantucket Sound, halting all steamship service for several days. By the time the freeze ended, another storm dropped fourteen inches of snow on February 4, and Nantucket had reason to remember this season as a real old-fashioned winter.

The new Steamship Authority got under way the first of the year, with a three-man board consisting of Tell Berna from Nantucket, Robert Love from Martha's Vineyard, and Frank McLean from Falmouth, in charge of administration. The previous year's deficit for Nantucket was $112,188, but within two years that deficit would disappear. The cost of the 1960 boat strike was set at $326,700 to the boat line, with additional losses to island businesses unknown. However, the authority made its first positive move to institute direct service from Hyannis to Nantucket in 1962. Pending automobile reservations made it look like the islands would be busier than ever.

Another Nantucket landmark passed from view in April. The huge Victorian mansion Sea Crest, atop the Cliff at Step Beach, was torn down to make way for something more modern, the owner claiming the old house was beyond repair. The mansion had been built in 1881 by the famous New York lawyer Charles O'Conor as his retirement home. An adjacent brick building housing his private law library of 18,000 volumes was also demolished, the books having been returned to New York. The last owner of the old landmark was Breckinridge Long, former ambassador to Italy, who summered in Nantucket for the rest of his life.

As the old order passed, new technologies arrived. The first direct-dial telephone system went into operation on June 18, the honor of making the first call going to the chairman of the Board of Selectmen Sidney H. Killen, who called his brother in California. Thus ended the days of the tireless telephone operators, who for decades had rendered many personal services to local customers and knew many of them by the sound of their voices.

Nantucket Memorial Airport instituted its new instrument-landing system in June, a direct result of the 1958 Northeast crash. The new control tower went into service on July 2, and within eleven hours handled 515 takeoffs and landings. The new tower building cost $247,000 and its equipment $150,000, bringing the total value of the airport to $4 million.

During the summer of 1961, Nantucket became embroiled in a dispute with the state over enforcement of the famous Sunday "Blue Laws," which prohibited the conduct of nonessential business on the Lord's day. The laws were a holdover from the Puritan era but strongly endorsed by the modern church hierarchy. On Nantucket, they were widely ignored and the chief of police described them as "just plain silly." The governor and attorney general ordered Chief Wendell Howes to enforce the law or resign. He did neither, and business continued as usual all summer long. A few years later, Governor Michael Dukakis recommended repeal of the Sunday closing laws as detrimental to the state's economy, and they quickly vanished into history.

The year 1961 was remembered as one of the dark years of the Cold War, with the Berlin Wall erected in August and Americans warned to prepare for possible nuclear attack. The first bomb shelter on the island was built at a private home on the north shore. At the Tom Nevers naval facility, a secret underground shelter was prepared for possible use by President Kennedy, but was never put to use. The civil defense forces of the island were reorganized, but never utilized.

The impetus to the revitalization of the island's lagging economy took place this year with the purchase of the old Ocean House hotel by the Nantucket Historical Trust, which also bought the Marshall Gardiner building at Main and Washington Streets. This trust, dedicated to preservation and renovation of historic properties, marked the first venture by Walter Beinecke Jr. into the development of the New Nantucket. The movement was closely watched and hailed as a great benefit to the island, the prospect of a first-class, year-round hotel making a tremendous contribution toward the future economy. Within the year, contractors were swarming over the old Ocean House and renovating it into a classic hostelry, and Frank Sylvia's antiques gave the new building a tone of elegance and dignity. The Gardiner building became the site of Nantucket Looms, which sold fine handwoven goods and other articles produced by local artisans.

September brought the annual hurricane season; this time it was Hurricane Esther that did the damage, cutting off Smith's Point to create Esther Island and isolating the few cottages on that strip of sand. Esther eventually resumed her proper place and reattached herself to Nantucket in the nineties.

In 1961, two groups concerned themselves with the development of the Nantucket waterfront. The Nantucket Fishermen's Association, worried about the sagging scallop industry, proposed an advertising campaign to promote the superior quality of the Nantucket bay scallop. The low price of local scallops ($5 a gallon) and the invasion in northern markets of Florida "calico" scallops were seen as threats to the future of the local industry. The planning board and selectmen recommended that the town meeting take a forty-five-acre portion of the Creeks at Washington and Union Streets for a waterfront development that would encompass fishing, boating, bathing, and other recreational uses. The proposal met with opposition, and the project was soon taken over by private enterprise.

Early in 1962, a newspaper editorial extolled the promise of the new President, rendering the opinion that Mr. Kennedy "has rallied the united nation to a tremendous challenge and an undertaking as have few predecessors so early in their administration and gives great promise." The new administration was certainly a benefactor of the Nantucket airport, which received a million dollars' worth of improvements, including the control tower, the new instrument-landing system, and a modern weather-forecasting system. Additional federal money was pouring into the naval facility, with new buildings and equipment, dormitory, and recreational facilities. In addition to the President's interest in the area, Nantucket had become the summer home of U. S. Senators Mike Monroney of Oklahoma and Stuart Symington of Missouri, who became good friends of the Nantucket community.

The Nantucket Police Department became the subject of some merriment when it was learned that one of its most popular patrolmen, George Rezendes, at five feet, six inches, was one inch too short to comply with civil service requirements for police officers. A bill was introduced in the state legislature to waive the requirement for the Nantucket Police Department and evoked some humorous reports in the Boston papers about the "Short Cop Bill." It did became law and George Rezendes went on to a long and distinguished career.

In May of 1962, another transition in the local economy arose as the famous waterfront hotel, the White Elephant, was purchased by Walter Beinecke Jr. for a reported figure of $150,000. The new owner announced plans to reconstruct the hotel with modern facilities and a swimming pool, and the work began under local contractor Michael Lamb. Meanwhile, the old Ocean House was being renovated by Richard Corkish and his crew at a reported cost of $300,000, in addition to the $85,000 purchase price. Beinecke's wife Marianne, who had started Nantucket Looms, enlisted a group of Nantucket women to weave the fabrics for the new hotel, which would hereafter be known as the Jared Coffin House after the man who had built it in 1842. Nantucket was witnessing an energetic and creative spirit of enterprise this year.

The new Steamship Authority reported increased business for

the year with reduced deficits for the island ports. Traffic and parking problems were developing at Woods Hole, the only port serving the two islands, and the need for a Hyannis terminal was becoming evident. Nevertheless, the move to Hyannis was contested in court by Falmouth, which didn't want to lose the business derived from the steamship operation, despite the traffic. The situation was somewhat relieved when the Supreme Judicial Court issued a decision in May that the authority could not operate from Hyannis but could contract for other parties to do so. This resulted in the return of the derelict steamer *Martha's Vineyard,* which the authority had sold to Capt. Joseph Gelinas for $25,000. The highly optimistic Gelinas had the steamer overhauled, painted afresh, and equipped with surplus diesel engines. Under license from the authority, she began service from Hyannis to Nantucket in June.

It was a year of turnover in operation for many local businesses. On Main Street, Philip C, Murray bought the Coffin Block and Albert G. Brock Insurance Company bought the Reed Hardware Store, formerly Coffin's Hardware. The Nantucket Historical Trust bought the old Spa Cafe and Restaurant on Main Street and obtained a year-round liquor license for the Jared Coffin House. The Cliffside Bathing Beach was sold to Robert T. Currie and became Cliffside Beach Club, and the old Wauwinet House was sold to a group of fourteen summer residents who sold it again in 1965 to Mrs. J. Allen Backus, a member of its founding family. Finally, the old island paper, the *Inquirer and Mirror,* was sold to George W. Morgan of New York.

Two fine public servants retired this year: Richard J. Porter, who had taught and been superintendent of schools for twenty-nine years, retired in August. F. Stuart Chadwick, sergeant of the Nantucket Police Deptartment, retired in June after thirty-two years' service; three candidates scrambled for his $4,750 annual salary.

In July, the *Town Crier* editorialized on Nantucket's condition and asked "Where is Nantucket heading—as a resort, a year-round community, or a combination of the two?" Conceding that the island must preserve its historic charm and that its natural beauty should not be marred by resort development, the paper called for the formation of a group to consider the future of the island. Among important points for discussion would be harbor and beach development, recreational facilities, and traffic congestion. The editorial also called for long-term summer visitors to build and buy more homes and contribute to the economic, governmental, and cultural aspects of the island community. It was an uncanny glimpse into Nantucket's future.

On the death in August of Stephen Peabody, owner of a ninety-acre estate in Quaise, the property was bequeathed to the University of Massachusetts for a research and conservation station. The transfer of ownership in 1963 was to have a significant impact on the island's conservation efforts.

One man's blueprint for Nantucket was outlined when Walter Beinecke Jr. described in a speech to the Rotary Club his vision for the Nantucket Historical Trust's role in preserving and maintaining the historic atmosphere of the island. He cited the restoration of the Jared Coffin House as both preserving a physical symbol of the island's history and a means for assisting Nantucket economically by providing year-round hotel facilities to extend the island season.

Island newspapers arrived at a state of weekly confrontation, as the *Inquirer and Mirror* and the *Town Crier* were often at odds on local issues. Many forces were seeking ways to boost the economy without destroying traditional values. The most visible means of measuring the economy would be found in the value of real estate. The Beinecke purchases were beginning to raise the value of properties in the downtown commercial area. Out of town, ninety-five acres, including 1,500 feet of shore front on Polpis Harbor were advertised for $40,000, and 2,400 feet of waterfront on the south shore were available for $24,000.

At year's end, another Nantucket business went up in smoke

when a spectacular December fire on Orange Street destroyed Ryder's Market, one of the last of the neighborhood markets. The blaze came at 2 A.M. and totally engulfed the old store and its stock of groceries, meats, and liquor, causing a loss of over $60,000. In addition, the fire consumed the business records, including the accounts of many charge customers, most of whom were never heard from again.

The year 1963 opened with an icy blast of subzero weather, gale winds, and snow on New Year's Eve. Ice boating and ice skating on the ponds gave the island the appearance of a Currier and Ives print.

Foremost among changes in Nantucket institutions was the *Inquirer and Mirror*'s move from 1 Orange Street, where it had been for sixty-three years, to the southernmost end of that street at the Rotary, where it resumed business in May. The new owner of the paper, George W. Morgan, promised to expand the business, and in September he purchased the *Town Crier*, thus ending an alternative source of news and a distinctive editorial viewpoint.

The newly restored Jared Coffin House opened for business in May and met with great approval, while the Beinecke acquisition and development activity in the downtown area continued to be of primary interest and some concern. The old building beside the Jared Coffin House was demolished and replaced by a hotel annex in 1964. The most conspicuous of the Beinecke enterprises was the new White Elephant Hotel, sprawling along the new bulkhead with accommodations for 110, a huge dining room and lounge, and Nantucket's first waterfront swimming pool. The hotel opened for business on June 28. The first manager was the well-known Gordon Folger Sr., who announced that the hotel would require ties in the dining room and prohibit bikinis at the pool.

In addition to these major projects, Beinecke seemed to be moving buildings all over town. Many waterfront structures deemed unworthy of preservation were demolished and taken to the dump. Five old waterfront gas stations disappeared. Every contractor in town was busy in the spring of 1963, Mike Lamb's trucks and Russell Pope's landscapers moving in every direction. The old Island Service Company was reorganized into two separate corporations, one doing business and one holding real estate.

Nantucket's traditional institutions saw some changes this year. The Nantucket Atheneum garden got a facelift supervised by summer resident and renowned botanist Dr. Emil F. Guba, and a new Children's Room opened in the basement. Doctor B. F. D. Runk became president of the Maria Mitchell Association, taking charge of that institution for the first of many terms. The Pacific Club was sandblasted down to its original bricks, and the Satler House at 96 Main Street, one of the "Two Greeks," was donated to the Nantucket Historical Association, which operated it as a house museum.

On Labor Day weekend, the island received an unexpected but welcome visitor when the presidential yacht *Honey Fitz,* accompanied by a forty-foot Coast Guard patrol vessel, arrived unannounced and dropped anchor in the harbor. President John F. Kennedy and his wife Jacqueline remained on board with their friends while their children Caroline and John (described as "very well-behaved children") were taken ashore by the Coast Guardsmen to climb the ladder of the Brant Point lookout tower. This presidential visit by yacht duplicated the arrival in 1933 of FDR, when he also remained aboard his yacht *Amberjack.*

Nantucket looked forward to more presidential visits from the Kennedy compound in Hyannis during the coming years, but this was the final visit before the tragedy in Dallas in November. His widow did return to Nantucket many times in later years to visit friends.

The summer season was hot and business was beginning to boom. An estimated 100,000 tourists came and left during the summer, crowding downtown facilities. Nantucket Memorial Airport had its lights and instrument-landing system as well as its control tower and FAA personnel, which ensured the safety of the facility.

On Labor Day 1963, the airport announced that the tower had handled 335 landings and take-offs, its busiest twenty-four-hour period.

In town, social life centered around the hotels and restaurants, many of which featured evening entertainment. The newly renovated White Elephant, the expanded Harbor House and Sidewalk Cafe, and the Boathouse on Commercial Wharf were busy places. The old favorite Opera House, with its popular bar and fine food, was always crowded. Part of the social scene were the popular art gallery openings, usually on Monday evenings. George Vigoroux opened the Lobster Pot Gallery on Easy Street where he introduced guests like Beatrice Lilly, Van Johnson, and Gloria Vanderbilt. In Sconset, the old Chanticleer celebrated its fiftieth birthday, still serving breakfast, lunch, and dinner to its faithful clientele. It was a wonderful season.

On November 22, 1963, a bright Friday afternoon, Nantucket was shattered by the news of the death of President Kennedy in Dallas. Flags were lowered to half staff, business came to a standstill, and the churches held evening memorial services. It was the tragic end of a life full of promise and hope, and an event that would critically influence the future of our country.

In what appeared to have become an annual tradition, January of 1964 opened with a northeast blizzard bringing nineteen inches of snow; then three more snowstorms hit the island in February with another twenty inches.

A colony of gray seals was discovered in the waters off Tuckernuck. One baby seal was captured on the beach at Madaket, and his subsequent death led to a movement to protect the animals, which was finally enacted into law in Massachusetts in 1965.

The first development of a major conservation movement on the island occurred in 1964 with the incorporation of the Nantucket Conservation Foundation, whose mission was to acquire and preserve open land on the island. The foundation was sponsored by the Nantucket Civic League and its president, W. Ripley Nelson; other founders and incorporators were Walter Beinecke Jr., Tell Berna,

Alcon Chadwick, Albert F. Egan Jr., Frederick W. Haffenreffer, Roy E. Larsen, John L. Lyman, Robert F. Mooney, and Charles G. Snow.

The big commercial operation of the year was the organization of Sherburne Associates, a partnership consisting of Walter Beinecke Jr., Lawrence W. Miller, and Lawrence K. Miller. The Millers contributed their ownership of Straight Wharf and Sherburne Oil Company to the Beinecke interests in the White Elephant, the Harbor House, and the Marine Lumber Company. This year, the hotels were leased to Treadway Inns Corporation, while the major effort of the business was the development of the waterfront area. Another major change in ownership took place when Old North Wharf was sold to the Sanford brothers, Hugh W. and Alfred E. The sale included eight cottages, the wharf, and the premises of the Wharf Rat Club

Two famous institutions passed from the Nantucket scene this year. The famous Cross Rip Lightship, long the guardian of the midpoint between Nantucket and the mainland, was removed and replaced by an automatic buoy.

More controversial was the decision of the *Inquirer and Mirror*'s publisher, George W. Morgan, to discontinue use of the famous flatbed press that had given the *Inquirer and Mirror* the distinction of publishing "the largest newspaper in the world" for seventy-five years. The old nine-column blanket sheet measured twenty-seven by twenty-two inches and required a long reach to hold it. Morgan wrote an editorial defending the change, then died suddenly on June 28, and, ironically was eulogized in the last paper printed on the old press, on July 9. Many had protested the change to a modern offset press, but the change was inevitable. The old Cranston Press was offered to the Nantucket Historical Association, which had no room for it, and was then sold for junk.

As the format of the old paper changed, a new paper, the *Nantucket Light*, was published in August by the former *I&M* editor James G. Crowley. It offered a fresh format, many photographs, and a strong editorial position on local issues, often beamed at the *Inquirer and Mirror.*

The long-running battle of the Nantucket school system continued in full spate all year long. Basically a contest between liberal and conservative forces in island politics, it focused on the School Committee, resulting in close and bitter controversy that threatened to split the island community. In the course of this year, the committee was divided by several 3–2 votes, the superintendent of schools was fired, and several teachers either resigned or were not rehired. The Nantucket system was the subject of an investigation by the Massachusetts Teachers Association, which threatened to apply sanctions if improvements were not made within a year. The school fight continued for another two years, before changes in committee members and new administrators appeared to calm the troubled waters. This was not one of Nantucket's proudest times.

In September, two more Nantucket businesses changed their profiles as Harbor Fuel Oil Company took over the supply of Mobil Oil to the island and the new Murray's Toggery Shop expanded into the entire Coffin Block on the corner of Main and Fair Streets, with a large and colorful stock of seasonal wear.

September also witnessed groundbreaking for the new Town and County Building at the corner of Broad and Federal Streets. The building had been surrounded by controversy, as the town fathers annually proclaimed the growing community's need for a modern municipal building only to be frustrated by multiple town meeting votes to delay or postpone the project. A particularly painful decision was made to demolish the Sanford house, the Greek Revival mansion that had been the home of Frederick C. Sanford and once the finest house on the island. Years of town ownership had resulted in a state of decrepitude and hastened its demise, along with the nearby Hosier house, a building so weary it came down in one day. The old Killen house on the corner of South Water Street went soon after, and the town saw construction start on the new red brick building, which was opened for business in 1965.

In November of 1964, Nantucket voted Democratic in a national election for the first time since that of Woodrow Wilson. This year Nantucket went overwhelmingly for Lyndon B. Johnson with 1,197 votes to Barry Goldwater's 586 votes.

January of 1965 was a record-setting month; the month's snowfall of 38.9 inches made it the snowiest since 1904. The winter snows had hardly melted before the construction season got under way in full swing.

A great Nantucket figure, Doctor William E. Gardner, 93, died in April 1965, and was widely celebrated for his long and illustrious life. The beloved Doctor Will had made a career as an Episcopal priest before retirement to his boyhood home in Nantucket, where he became an author, historian, and active writer and speaker on Nantucket history. He is memorialized in a handsome bronze portrait relief by island sculptor Elizabeth Schaeffler; it is mounted on a boulder in the garden of the Nantucket Atheneum.

The Beachside Motel, the island's first such facility, opened for operation in May, and the old Sea Cliff Inn, long a feature on the Nantucket skyline, was purchased by Sherburne Associates. The cost of bringing the old hotel up to modern building codes was prohibitive, so it was demolished and carted off to the town dump. In July, Sherburne Associates announced its plans for development of the waterfront, and a tugboat arrived to commence the work on the boat basin, under contract with Mike Todd. The cornerstone for the new Town and County Building, although plagued by foundation problems, was laid on August 3, and the new Boys Club building on Sparks Avenue was started on August 18.

Changes were taking place in other institutions. At the Atheneum, a new librarian, Miss Barbara Andrews, took over as librarian, a post she would hold for twenty-six years. Her aunt, Miss Clara Parker, had served in that office for fifty years. The Atheneum also began construction on the Kynett memorial wing, containing a research center and book vault; it was financed by a $45,000 gift from H. H. Kynett in memory of his late wife. The demise of the old Island Service Company resulted in two new entities: Bud Egan's Marine Lumber Company, and Charles Fisher's Island Lumber Company. There would be plenty of lumber needed in the New Nantucket. A retail hardware business was opened by Robert Hardy on South Water Street, and barges were arriving from New Bedford, loaded with granite paving blocks for the new waterfront streets.

On November 8, the entire eastern seaboard was hit by an electric power blackout, the result of an electrical grid failure from Canada to Washington. The sole exception was Nantucket, where the diesel generator kept the lights on while the mainland suffered through the unexpected ordeal.

In November, Walter Beinecke Jr. spoke to the Sons and Daughters of Nantucket and described proposed improvements on the waterfront: construction of the boat basin and replacement of the commercial and industrial sites with smaller business and cottages in the Nantucket character. He predicted an increase in summer tourism to as many as 36,000 people daily, and emphasized the need for a zoning bylaw and restrictions on the sizes of vehicles.

Nantucket historian Edouard A. Stackpole responded to the Beinecke message with a personal plea to the Nantucketers to take an interest in preserving the unique heritage of the island. He saw Nantucket as more than a mere summer resort, a place with a year-round attraction for people if the historic island remained alert to protecting itself from the onrush of "our modern scene." Citing the preservation efforts at Salem and Plimoth Plantation in Massachusetts and Strawberry Banke in New Hampshire, he called for the people of the island to play a part in preserving the island for the future.

The bright lights of the Christmas season, the decorations at the new Jared Coffin House, and the pageant of Gibby Wyer's Surfside Road stable of live animals and lighted statues seemed to promise a bright future for Nantucket.

The transformation of the Nantucket harbor front in the mid-sixties was described by Paul Morris in his book *Maritime Nantucket*:

> The entire appearance of the Nantucket waterfront was modified, with much of the Island Service wharf being shortened in length. Its scallop shanties were moved around and a stockade-like structure built from the end of Straight Wharf around to the end of Commercial Wharf, with an entrance for the yachts and the fuel tanker in the middle. Both Straight Wharf and Commercial Wharf were changed with the addition of more commercial shops and cottages. Among other structures, the ice plant, the Island Service office building, and the lumber yard were torn down with a parking lot replacing much of the space formerly taken up by the lumber yard. More slips for visiting yachtsmen were provided inside the stockade. It was the biggest construction project in Nantucket's history and dramatically changed the appearance of the old waterfront, replacing it with a modern marina—styled a "boat basin"— dozens of waterfront shops, and rental cottages surrounding the scene. Such change provoked controversy and complaints about the loss of the traditional harbor scene. But it was generally considered a necessary upgrading of the area, and with the elimination of five gas stations and a sprawling lumber yard, together with the renovation of three old wharves, it marked a symbol of the New Nantucket for the remainder of the century.

In 1966, Nantucket realized the full implication of the U. S. Supreme Court decision in the 1962 case of *Baker* vs. *Carr*, which decreed that state legislative districts must be apportioned on the basis of population. The voters of Nantucket (2,090) were far below the statewide average of 10,460 per legislative district, but the island had maintained its representative in the great and General Court of Massachusetts based upon its status as a county, which entitled it to one vote. Now the court reaffirmed its decision and the legal fiction of the island's independence was about to end, thus depriving

Nantucket of its small but powerful voice in state government.

The long-running School Committee controversy came to an end in March, when a town election seated two new members, Tell Berna and David B. Voorhees, who brought peace and common sense back to the school system. The appointment of a new superintendent of schools and other reforms soon brought the school system back as a successful educational operation.

More good news came in the spring of 1966 when the new Town and County Building was completed and ready for occupation on April 25, the first genuine municipal building ever built on Nantucket. The new Marine Lumber Company was opened on Lower Orange Street, with a new home center and garden shop. Amid heavy spring rainfall, the new waterfront parking lot was completed by Sherburne Associates—a remarkable facility with granite paving stones, reproduction antique lights, and extensive landscaping, making it one of the most attractive sites on any waterfront.

Far from the bright days of Nantucket, the Vietnam War was raging, and the impact of that far-off struggle suddenly hit home as the news arrived of the death of a Nantucket boy, Sgt. Antone Marks, who was killed in action on June 5. He was the only Nantucket man to give his life in that war.

The town responded to public pressure to control development by appointing a committee to investigate a zoning plan. Nothing came of it. The town did vote to extend the airport runways to accommodate the new jet planes, and July traffic, 6,062 operations, was reported as record breaking. The new A&P supermarket opened in July and soon produced enough traffic to fill the new parking lot. The development met with increasing approval, and editorials predicted a record season for the tourist business.

Business activity on the island was increasing in all directions. In rapid order, Sherburne Associates bought Robinson's Five and Ten building on lower Main Street for $42,000 and the Breakers Hotel on Easton Street for $121,000. The Breakers had been a private guest house on the harbor for thirty years and would now be an annex of the White Elephant. In Madaket, the new Hither Creek Boatyard was purchased by a group of local investors, and at the edge of town, the old Fairgrounds site was targeted for the new home of the Nantucket Gas and Electric Company after the stock of the company was acquired by a Nantucket group headed by Robert D. Congdon. "Gas" would soon be dropped from the name of the utility. The Nantucket Historical Association announced a record summer with 67,879 visitors, nearly double the figure five years before.

In November, the Nantucket High School football team, newly revitalized under Coach Vito Capizzo, completed its first eight-game undefeated season, giving Nantucketers the perfect ending to a successful year.

Also in November, the island of Nantucket was designated by the Department of the Interior to be a National Historic Landmark. The new editor of the *Inquirer and Mirror,* Edouard A. Stackpole, called this "An Honor and a Responsibility." He repeated his call for the island's citizens to take part in preservation of this heritage in an editorial titled "Who Owns Nantucket?"

> Who owns Nantucket? For all intents it is the collective grouping of citizen and business—the present owners. But in a larger sense and truer measure, it is to be those who are to become the future—the next generation. We of today must be aware that we have inherited a town and island created by a race of people who were the maritime leaders of their time. They were the true builders of what we have temporarily become the owners, and it is our responsibility to preserve it for those who are to become the next custodians. . . . We cannot escape the obligation; we must not forget the potential within our grasp.

The year 1967 opened to the sound of a thousand-pound hammer driving the pilings and steel sheathing along the bulkhead around the wharves, as Mike Todd and his marine construction crew continued development of the new waterfront. The Beinecke plan for the New Nantucket focused on the potential of the harbor as a singular attraction for private yachts, which was seen as an appropriate and lucrative business. This was to be a new concept, not a marina but a boat basin, with protection from the northeast storms and facilities for tending to the needs of visiting yachts. In the process, the area available to commercial fishermen was reduced or eliminated, which provoked much grumbling in the old town, but the work continued and the results were commercially successful.

Rumbles of discontent were heard from other directions. Town employees at the airport and the department of public works took advantage of a recent state law to organize the first municipal employees union on the island, a movement that raised some eyebrows and many salaries. A strike of Finast supermarket employees took place later in the year, lasting seventeen days. The high cost of living on the island became more and more a general concern of the public. The Wannacomet Water Company raised the cost of water service to a flat rate of $33 a year, provoking a movement for public ownership of that utility.

The Steamship Authority filed a bill in the legislature to permit its service to and from the port of Hyannis. This was a popular move on Nantucket and Martha's Vineyard as it foretold change for the better in the transportation patterns of both islands.

With much publicity and debate, Nantucket tried again in the spring of 1967 to establish a zoning bylaw, a move that was solidly supported by the newspaper, civic groups, and most of the summer community. The outcome was determined in March by a four-hour town meeting debate in which the zoning plan was rejected by over fifty votes. Voters felt the implications of the law would seriously impair their traditional rights to do business and provide for their families. The effort to establish the bylaw would continue for several years.

In April, another air tragedy struck the island when a U.S. Air

Force Constellation radar picket plane, on a practice flight from Otis Air Force Base, caught fire over the island and crashed into the ocean off Madaket, killing fifteen of the sixteen men on board. The lone survivor was thrown from the plane as it exploded and was rescued suffering from burns and shock. Later, it was learned that the pilot, Col. James P. Lyle, a twenty-six-year veteran of the Air Force, had deliberately driven the plane out to sea to avoid crashing into the houses at Madaket—a heroic effort that cost him and most of his crew their lives.

The summer of '67 brought the problems of the sixties to Nantucket, mainland pressures finally surfacing on the island. The young crowd flocked to Cisco, where the open beach was conducive to those who wanted to sun, surf, or smoke. Various night spots catered to the new Nantucket visitors, mostly young working people who found the island compatible with their life styles. But the scene turned ugly in August when an employee at Nobadeer Restaurant was shot in the stomach in what was reputed to be a drug-related assault. Thereafter, state and local police raided the restaurant and night club and arrested seventeen people and seized a quantity of marijuana. Another raid on an Orange Street house bagged a nineteen-year-old female student and more marijuana. Nantucket District Court, which had not seen a drug case in recent memory, suddenly became a tourist attraction as the public crowded in to view the action and stare in amazement at the new breed of criminals. At the time, the individual defendants were all visitors, and there was great public indignation at their appearance and behavior. It would not be long before Nantucket youths were in court, and attitudes would begin to change in the community.

In October, the carcass of a 44-foot right whale washed ashore on the beach at Dionis, and Nantucket found itself back in the whaling business. It was the inspiration of Walter Beinecke Jr. to recover and preserve the skeleton of the whale as an exhibit at the Nantucket Historical Association. The task was formidable, as Mike Lamb and his crew donned oilskins and gas masks to sever the flesh from the huge mammal, then collected the carcass to be contained in screened boxes that were hung overboard for the winter until the bones were cleaned by natural forces. The whale's skeleton was reassembled and put on display in an annex to the Whaling Museum, where it remains a popular exhibit—a tribute to the whale and to the blubber-hunters of Nantucket.

The year ended with a good Christmas season. The island was making rapid progress, but the direction of island life was beginning to trouble many.

The momentous year 1968, which was to contain so many traumatic events, dawned with the usual cold spell that froze the scallop fleet in Madaket Harbor and a February snowstorm that drove a New Bedford scalloper ashore on South Beach. The winter months were so severe that harbormaster Allen Holdgate organized a food shipment to Muskeget Island to save the lives of hundreds of ducks and geese threatened with starvation in the snow.

The first big change of the year happened in the court system, housed in the new Town and County Building. First came the retirement of the District Court clerk Grace Henry Klingelfuss after thirty-six years in office. Then District Court Judge Caroline Leveen announced her retirement after thirty-two years on the bench, having been the second woman appointed in Massachusetts. The clerk's office was soon filled by the appointment of Nantucket police sergeant Wesley E. Simmons, and in April, attorney C. George Anastos was appointed by Governor John A. Volpe to the Nantucket judgeship.

Another familiar figure passed from the Nantucket scene in February with the death of veteran newspaperman Joseph Indio, who had been founder, editor, and publisher of the *Nantucket Town Crier* during its existence, and best known for leading the campaign for independent steamship service for the islands.

Another zoning bylaw was proposed by the Finance Committee

and promptly shot down by town meeting in the spring. It was announced the town budget had risen eight per cent to over $2 million, and the passenger fare on the steamboat had risen to $6.50. The Steamship Authority obtained passage of legislation permitting its operation to "other ports," thus opening the future for Hyannis service, a move greatly supported by Nantucket citizens. This was facilitated by purchase of the property of a competing line and assurance that the Town of Barnstable would not bear any deficit from the operation. Prospects for Hyannis service were shattered when Governor John Volpe vetoed the bill in response to opposition on Cape Cod.

In April, Nantucket experienced its worst forest fire since 1949 when sparks from a front-end loader ignited roadside brush on Old South Road, starting five separate fires. Old South Road was closed down as the flames spread through the pines toward Milestone Road, the smoke and flames billowing so high they could be seen from Cape Cod. Then the flames leaped the Milestone Road and headed toward Polpis Road, swept into the Glowacki Construction Company on Old South Road, and threatened the Holdgate homestead, but no homes were damaged. Volunteer drivers Donald Visco and Albert Coffin led a swarm of bulldozers into the blazing pines and cut a firebreak through the woods that kept the fire from spreading toward town and contained the conflagration, which was declared all out at 5:05 P.M.

One of Nantucket's most beloved professional men, Doctor George A. Folger, died in April, ending a fifty-year career on Nantucket. He was a true family doctor, practicing from his home office on India Street, diagnosing patients in Coffin's Drug Store, and handing out a supply of "little sugar pills" to those with imaginary ailments. He was a passenger in the first automobile brought to the island by his father in May of 1900. He returned to Nantucket in 1915 to recover from tuberculosis contracted through overwork in the Boston emergency wards, and he liked to say he came to

Nantucket to die but it took him fifty years to do it.

The deaths by assassination of Senator Robert F. Kennedy and Doctor Martin Luther King stunned the community. Improbably, two of the nation's most inspiring leaders were cut down in the prime of their lives, creating a void in the national leadership and leading to future national calamities.

A new Nantucket enterprise opened on Main Street in June when Mr. and Mrs. Henry Mitchell Havemeyer opened Mitchell's Book Corner on June 28, offering iced tea and birthday cake to their customers. It became Nantucket's first fully stocked, year-round bookstore and a welcome refuge for Nantucket writers and readers. The store did not yet have the services of the Havemeyers' daughter Mimi, who was abroad in Italy for a year of foreign study.

It was a big summer for the arts in Nantucket. The Siasconset Casino ran a program of first-run movies every other night. The art galleries were in full swing, with featured artists like Bobby Bushong, Reggie Levine, Mary Sarg Murphy, and Andrew Shunney. The Straight Wharf Theatre featured its production of *A Streetcar Named Desire,* by Tennessee Williams, who had spent several summers on Nantucket and had finished the play on the island. The production starred Ward Everitt as Stanley, Ruth Everitt as Stella, and Shirley Yerxa Perkins as Blanche DuBois, under the direction of Joseph "Mac" Dixon.

The turmoil of the sixties and its effect on the youth summering in Nantucket became the subject of a panel discussion at the Establishment, a coffee house in St. Paul's Church parish house. A representative panel of island leaders, local youth, and visiting teenagers discussed their problems for several hours in a constructive atmosphere. Problems arising from the long-hair "hippie" element so visibly present on the public streets, the lack of a place to congregate, and the failure of communication between the various elements of the community, the police, and the youth were emphasized, while fifty elders listened thoughtfully.

Another appeal from the popular summer resident Arthur "Red" Motley called for defining the island's attraction in the "out of season" months and for decreasing the emphasis on the summer season by attracting more people to the island during the quieter time of the year. The peak of the season travel schedule showed departures from the island almost every fifteen minutes, with air service provided by Northeast, Executive, Cape & Islands, and Mass Air. An unfortunate article in *Time* magazine referring to Nantucket's efforts to curtail the day-trippers from Hyannis met with many local complaints and counter-arguments. The trippers were as welcome as anyone else, was the conclusion, and preferable to some of their critics.

"When the history of Nantucket in the second half of the twentieth century is written (and this should be a revealing study), one of the most significant studies will be the accomplishments of the Nantucket Conservation Foundation," wrote Edouard Stackpole in November of 1968. Roy E. Larsen, president of the foundation, then announced the acquisition of over 2,283 acres, including important tracts on the moors, the south shore, Eel Point, and most of Coatue. Preservation and education were the themes of the foundation's mission, and the island was fortunate to have this opportunity to save its natural resources from the tide of the future.

In an airborne spectacle, the First Congregational Church was capped by a thirty-three-foot steeple, delivered by a giant helicopter in still air at six o'clock in the evening. The steeple replaced an old unsafe structure that had been removed in 1849, and its renovation was the fulfillment of a thirty-five-year dream of the Rev. Fred D. Bennett. Finally pushed to completion by an eager congregation, the steeple was built by the firm of Howard Jelleme, then held on the construction site to await the proper wind conditions. While hundreds watched the scene, the steeple was hoisted and carried through the air to a perfect landing atop the church, where five men waited to bolt it into position. Rev. Bennett retired with honor later that month.

November brought another Presidential election, in which Nantucket voters cast 991 votes for Richard Nixon and 744 for Hubert Humphrey. In the same month, the First National Store honored its past three managers—Melvin Ray, Albert Fee, and Charles Ferreira—who together had served over 100 years and were well remembered by all of Nantucket.

The year, and the decade, ended with a full gale on Christmas Day and 4° temperatures, bringing a chilly end to a busy year.

By 1969, Nantucket was advertising several new business enterprises, as the development of the downtown area spawned increased activity. They included Charlie's Market on Main Street, the Country Store and La Crepe Restaurant on the harbor, Claudette's in Sconset, Schell's Steak House on Surfside Road, Smokee's on Steamboat Wharf, and Key West Fabrics on Centre Street. Nantucket was ready for business of all sorts.

The population was growing with the economy. From a population of around 3,600, which had remained stable for decades, the population grew to 4,150, with a reported 857 children in the public schools, the largest figure in history.

Efforts to preserve the island centered on the jurisdiction of the Historic District Commission to cover the entire island and the continued growth of the Conservation Foundation, thanks to a gift of 520 acres from Roy E. Larsen. Big news was the purchase of 200 acres on the south shore by Mr. and Mrs. Paul Mellon for a reputedly enormous sum of $200,000, a figure that set an unheard value on vacant land. Town meeting having approved the transfer, the old Town Building on Washington Street was conveyed to the Nantucket Historical Association to be preserved intact after many years of hard public use. The association immediately launched a campaign to raise $750,000 to preserve its many historic properties.

On the waterfront, the Nantucket Anglers Club was established, giving local mariners and their friends a port of call in informal social surroundings, with Capt. Edward "Pete" Guild as the first president.

In mid-summer the club announced the first Nantucket Billfish Tournament—to pursue the big fish offshore and restore islanders' identity as offshore fishermen.

At the easterly end of the island, Sankaty Lighthouse was renovated and equipped with a new 900,000-candlepower light, sufficient to be seen forty-five miles at sea. The light was automated and required no more faithful keepers. A federal decision to remove the old cap of the lighthouse met with vehement opposition, and the old cap was soon restored.

The Nantucket Weather Bureau, which had existed for several decades, came to an end this year. From its original office in the Pacific Club Building, the bureau had moved to the old town building on Cash's Court off Orange Street and then to Nantucket Airport. It had been like a mother ship in the ocean with its weather reports and warnings. For reasons of economy, the government shut down the station and transferred its services to Cape Cod, thus ending another venerable island institution.

The Steamship Authority made its third try to obtain legislative permission to sail into Hyannis, a move that had been opposed by Cape Cod interests who were partial to the private boat lines. This time, the bill sailed through the General Court and was signed into law by the hand of Governor Francis Sargent, himself a Cape Cod resident, who stated, "The greatest number of people will be best served by expansion of the ferry service." Thus the historic 115-year-old line to Hyannis was finally restored to serve Nantucket.

On Steamboat Wharf, a small restaurant at the corner of Easy Street was taken over by Henry Fee for a full-fledged sandwich shop under the name of Henry's, which began the trend to well-prepared fast food for the busy summer season. Henry's became enormously popular and soon expanded into another outlet just out of town.

On Lower Orange Street, Marine Lumber Company also expanded by adding a garden shop; the housewares, decorating, and patio shops; and several other retail outlets in addition to its traditional lumber and construction business. The company was soon supplying most of the households on the island and employing scores of Nantucketers on a year-round basis.

In Sconset, the owners of the Chanticleer Restaurant were ready to retire, and the village was fortunate in having the right people ready to buy it. Led by Roy E. Larsen, William Matteson, and John Rhodes, a group of Sconset summer residents purchased the restaurant and its surrounding cottages and promised to restore it to provide the village with a first-class restaurant. They set about spending some real money to create the establishment and promote its attractions to the public. Within a year, they found the right man to operate the business in Jean-Charles Berruet, a fantastic Frenchman, and his wife Anne, who brought the establishment into the new decade as the island's premier restaurant.

Beinecke brought the island into the twentieth century.

Walter Beinecke Jr.

THE MAN WHO MADE THE DIFFERENCE

IN WALTER BEINECKE JR. AND HIS DEVELOPMENT PLANS FOR the island, the man and the moment came together to create the New Nantucket. Beinecke came from an establishment family long resident in Sconset, but he was not personally active in island business until the sixties. With his inheritance from his family, he set forth to implement his plans. In doing so, he first relied on established Nantucket individuals like Henry B. Coleman, George W. Jones, and Frank S. Sylvia. The island did not immediately realize the impact his plans would have, but it appreciated the results.

Nantucket emerged from the fifties with many forces vying for its destiny. Fast flights from New York, day trips from Hyannis, low real estate values, and cheap rentals appeared to threaten the old island traditions with a flood of new comers and new money. The island was changing but no one knew how much. One of the biggest questions was the future of the waterfront.

With the renovation of the Ocean House into the Jared Coffin House, Nantucket had its first class year-round hotel. The Nantucket Looms was established to create island employment in the weaving trade. Then the old White Elephant Hotel was completely rebuilt into a modern waterfront hotel, with cottages and swimming pool. These were truly impressive accomplishments of the early sixties.

The climate of the times was conducive to economic development. The town had the manpower to accomplish major projects with island workers, the infusion of money into the island economy was greatly appreciated, and the political climate was almost perfect: there were no zoning or building regulations in force. A man of means could build anything, anywhere, and be appreciated for doing it.

When Walter Beinecke Jr. joined forces with Lawrence W. Miller, owner of Straight Wharf and Sherburne Oil Company, to form Sherburne Associates, the pieces fell into place for major development of the Nantucket waterfront. This was a long-discussed project, but never before had the plans and the means come together. With the new Nantucket Boat Basin, Nantucket could attract luxury yachts and waterborne wealth for long stays on the island. The area was also landscaped to perfection with the Harbor Square parking lot and the new Wharf Cottages, while the old scallop shanties were transformed into waterfront shops and art galleries.

While it was happening, there was grumbling from displaced fishermen and some businesses that refused to pay the escalating rents. Islanders protested with buttons reading "No Man Is an Island," but the results were generally accepted. Beinecke also contributed generously to island preservation and conservation efforts. He talked about his philosophy of "Less Is Better," and urged the island to raise its standards to attract better business.

There is no doubt the Beinecke revival made many people wealthy. There was no end of construction contracts, building moving, and endless landscaping. He paid the bills and the contractors were grateful. Almost any property offered for sale was bought up. The Beinecke purchases started the rise in real estate values on the island.

As real estate development increased, Sherburne Associates made the decision to sell off the operating businesses, resulting in the spin-off of Marine Lumber Company, Island Lumber Company, and Hardy's paint and hardware. Other businesses that lost their locations simply disappeared, to be replaced by trendy gift shops, fashionable clothing stores, and other upscale operations. The old waterfront was changed forever, to the regret of many old Nantucketers.

With the completion of the development phase, Walter Beinecke Jr. became a major investor in both the Nantucket Electric Company and the Pacific National Bank, the major commercial entities on the island. This gave many islanders cause for worry about the concentration of power in one place, and there were many changes of personnel in those businesses during his term.

Amid the rising tide of Nantucket prosperity, Beinecke remained calm and confident, calling for more historic preservation and conservation efforts. He supported the zoning bylaw of 1972 (after his major construction had been completed) and did not complain when the Hyannis boats disgorged more passengers each year, paying his company fifty cents per customer. The island continued to support his efforts. Many believed the valuable Sherburne Associates properties would some day be owned by the town or a charitable trust established by Beinecke.

This was not to be. Events overtook Walter Beinecke and his plans for the future, resulting in the sale of Sherburne Asspociates' holdings in 1987, for a reported price of $55 million. Even this did not go smoothly, as Beinecke intended to make the sale to a consortium of Nantucket residents, who, when their financing failed, assigned the sale to First Winthrop Corporation of Boston.

The long-term judgment of Walter Beinecke Jr. and his development of the New Nantucket is generally favorable: he was the right man for Nantucket at the right time. The changes were beneficial to the island, and island history proves that change is inevitable. Someone was bound to do it.

Never far from the waterfront, Joe Lopes settled just a block away on Washington Street.

Joseph Lopes
DOCKMASTER

JOE LOPES WAS THE DOCKMASTER AT THE NANTUCKET BOAT Basin for twenty years, providing a haven for hundreds of luxury yachts in the summer and scores of Nantucket scallop boats in the winter months. Joe was equally comfortable with the demanding owners of the summer fleet and the salty scallopers, and everyone appreciated his knowledge of the harbor, his attention to his patrons, and his easy-going personality.

He came to Nantucket as a boy with his family, who worked as cranberry pickers and lived in one of the small cottages clustered around the bog. He soon became friendly with the Holdgate boys in Sconset, tinkering with autos and boats and developing a natural talent for mechanics that lasted a lifetime. He made friends easily, and everyone was happy to have Joe around. At one time he and Ken Holdgate owned a boat together, which they cleverly named *Salt and Pepper*.

As a young mechanic, Lopes worked for Al Silva at his garage, where Al considered him the best mechanic he had. His only fault was that he had too many friends, who took their cars to Joe's home for repairs after hours. Al and Joe remained friends for life, but Al remembered, "He did more business after four o'clock than I did all day."

After the Nantucket Boat Basin was constructed in the 1960s, Walter Beinecke Jr. had trouble finding the right man to handle the complex operation, which involved reservations for eighty-eight boat slips, fuel, and supplies for hundreds of transient vessels, familiarity with the waterfront, and endless hours of hospitality and security problems. On the recommendation of John Welch, the job was offered to Joe Lopes. This was an entirely new project for Joe, but he and Beinecke got along famously. They often strolled the wharves together to admire the new Nantucket waterfront, but they also worked together in stormy weather to see that all the vessels were secured. In emergencies, the capacity of the boat basin was expanded to shelter everyone in need.

Joe worked so hard in the summer he was allowed long winter vacations, which he took in Naples, Florida, with his beloved wife Nellie. Their fifty-seven-year romance ended when she passed away in 1998, leaving Joe heartbroken but the same man. After a lifetime of hard work and twenty years of managing Nantucket's biggest waterfront enterprise, Joe could retire and look back: "I had a good life and many friends who were good to me over the years. I treated everyone alike."

After more than a century without a steeple, the Congregational Church received a new one in 1968. A dramatic delivery by heliocopter drew an appreciative crowd.

Top: World news event, the 1976 wreck of the oil tanker *Argo Merchant* on Fishing Rip Shoals.
Bottom: The *Nobska*'s last scheduled trip, September 18, 1973.

The early seventies were marked across the country by civil disobedience, antiwar militance, and turmoil on campuses. The reaction of the Nixon Administration led to the Watergate scandal, impeachment, and the President's resignation. The end of the Vietnam War brought with it a national malaise of drug use and dissent, resulting in a worldwide decline in American prestige. Nantucket was not immune to the national trends as it contended with its own peculiar problems.

Growing
Pains

The decade of the seventies was defined by issues of conservation and confrontation on the island. After the heady rise in the island economy in the sixties, Nantucket seemed to pause and examine its natural and political environment in light of the changes taking place on the island.

On March 7, 1970, Nantucket played a huge part in a celestial drama of national interest as a total eclipse of the sun occurring that day could be seen only on Nantucket Island. The island was host to thousands of serious and amateur astronomers, hundreds of airborne visitors, and innumerable nature lovers who came for the experience. The eclipse lasted from 12:31 to 2:58, treating everyone to the full impact of total darkness for two minutes at midday, when the street lights came on, the birds came to earth, and the town dogs started howling. The island welcomed the people who came to view the spectacular event and loved it. Police and emergency services reported no problems whatsoever.

Problems of another sort were rampant during the summer, however, when state and local police raided several houses searching for drugs and arrested dozens of young people on various drug-related charges. While the defendants were awaiting trial, public protests were mounted against the police action and demonstrations took place outside the court house to raise bail money. Then, one night in August, two deliberate arson attempts were directed against two of Nantucket's historic monuments—the Old Gaol on Vestal Street and the Old Mill on Mill Hill. Both buildings were set on fire, apparently started with kerosene, but were saved by alert police and fire department responses. The town reacted in outrage and expressed widespread resentment of the "long-haired hippies" who were seen to be threatening the island's venerable institutions. Special police patrols were instituted and a special town meeting was called in the fall. The selectmen proposed three "anti-hippie" bylaws: prohibit sleeping in the open, ban hitchhiking in town, and forbid occupation of unlicensed dwellings by more than five unrelated persons. The proposals were quickly voted into law.

A bill seeking to expand the jurisdiction of the Historic District Commission to the entire island was presented in the state legislature and signed into law in June. After its acceptance at town meeting, the law gave the commission authority over the exterior appearance of buildings and structures all over the island and was to prove more complicated than expected.

Early in 1971, the high cost of milk at the local markets set off a boycott by Nantucket housewives, who refused to pay seventy-nine cents for a half-gallon container. The boycott brought Cumberland Farms to the island, and they began to sell the same milk for fifty-nine cents from a truck, eventually opening a convenience store on Orange Street. The supermarkets soon matched the lower price. Meanwhile, the town warrant included the largest budget in town history, over $3.8 million, citing increased costs for the school department, the airport, and union salaries for the newly organized town employees.

A master plan for the island was in the works, the sponsors citing the need to plan for population growth and development. It was argued that town government should work in partnership with private interests on mutual concerns about conservation, recreation, and growth management. Later in the year, it was recommended that the traditional Nantucket dump be replaced by a sanitary landfill, and a survey revealed a great need to provide more reasonably priced housing, a problem that became increasingly acute.

In March of 1971, the selectmen appointed attorney Robert F. Mooney as the first town prosecutor, to handle local police cases in the District Court, which was experiencing a rising tide of criminal cases.

In June, fifty-five members of the Paradis family held a reunion to honor the matriarch of the family, Marie Paradis, on her eightieth birthday. The Opera House also celebrated a birthday, its twenty-fifth, in the friendly red building on South Water Street that had seen so many celebrated guests. Another establishment began with a different clientele when Ginger Rock opened the Compass Rose restaurant and lounge at the airport.

The Nantucket Conservation Foundation, the leader in the field, announced on July 4 that it had acquired the entire unspoiled acreage of Ram Pasture, a 625-acre tract almost entirely surrounding Hummock Pond, saving it from inevitable development. About the same time, the foundation hired James F. Lentowski as its first executive secretary, a position he would successfully occupy for the rest of the century and beyond.

Two portable classrooms had to be added to Cyrus Peirce School because of the increased school population. The October session of Superior Court was extended for two weeks to handle the many pending criminal cases. Even the steamer *Uncatena* had to be lengthened by fifty-two feet to accommodate more freight and cars.

A most significant change in local government took place in 1972. After being shot down for several years in a row, a zoning bylaw was finally passed by a vote of 463 to 221 at March town meeting. The adoption of zoning required the town to establish planning, building, and appeal boards, with related support staffs, and led to huge increases in municipal expense.

In April, Senator Edward M. Kennedy introduced a far-reaching piece of congressional legislation known as the Nantucket Sound and Islands Trust Bill, which proposed broad federal controls over land use on the islands of Nantucket and Martha's Vineyard. The bill, crafted by Washington staffers and selected summer residents, designated large portions of the islands as "forever wild," and severely restricted construction over much of the islands. It came as a complete surprise to islanders, who erupted in a storm of protest and town meeting resolutions. Many pending real estate transactions were postponed as banks hesitated to grant mortgages. The "Committee to Save Nantucket," with Bernard Grossman as chairman, was formed to seek amendments to the Kennedy bill.

As a federal measure, the Kennedy bill gained nationwide publicity. Many who had never heard of Nantucket now focused on the island and its special place on the east coast. Islanders were forced to take positions, and although most residents were opposed to the idea of federal control of the island, a sizable number of retirees and summer residents saw the legislation as the salvation of the island (although they would never vote for its proponent). The result was a polarization of island opinion as never before seen. Nantucketers felt that they no longer controlled their future. Public hearings were held on the island and private meetings in Boston, at which Senator Kennedy explained his legislation and welcomed input from the islands' representatives. Discussion continued until 1976, when in a special town meeting the voters of Nantucket turned down the Kennedy bill and lost forever the possibility of preserving its shore-lines for the public benefit.

The increased interest in Nantucket land soon focused on the manner in which the town had traditionally handled its real estate tax assessments and disposal of tax-delinquent land. Early use of the island for grazing sheep, with hundreds of acres of unfenced and unclaimed land, caused real estate titles to become confused over the years, and the land was of such low value it was often untaxed by the town fathers. In the 1950s and 1960s, with the approval of state authorities, town assessors had adopted the practice of taxing this land of unknown owners to "John Doe, a fictitious person," the true owners being unknown. The town then took a tax lien on the land and sold the lien for the unpaid taxes. The new owner then had to follow a procedure in the Land Court to foreclose the tax lien before he had a clear title. The whole procedure was speculative, but some valuable land was conveyed for minimal amounts. Problems arose, however, because the town failed to advertise the properties for sale at public auction, thus allowing them to be bought by anyone who took the trouble to take the necessary steps.

After receiving several complaints, District Attorney Philip A. Rollins launched an investigation of Nantucket "John Doe" land and advised the town to stop the practice of selling tax liens. He alleged that $2 million worth of land had been sold in the 1960s for about $5,000. The rising value of real estate made such a result possible, but the town fathers claimed they were just following the law and approved practice. A grand jury was convened in September to hear ten witnesses in the "John Doe Case" over a period of two days in which they heard from four town officials. The grand jury was not convinced of any wrongdoing, no indictments were handed down, and the case was closed.

The town entered its objection to cases pending in Land Court, and other titles remained undisturbed. Much of the John Doe tax-title land was dedicated to conservation; the remainder became tax-paying property. New legislation required the town to sell off tax titles in the future at public auction, which seemed to satisfy every-one, and modern comprehensive maps of the island soon identified all remaining property for tax purposes. Thus, the old spectre of John Doe faded into the mists of island history, but the memory of his march through the records of Nantucket real estate remains.

The old hotels of Nantucket were undergoing changes to keep pace with the new era. The grandest old lady of them all, the Sea Cliff Inn, whose 106 rooms had dominated the Cliff Road area since 1857, was purchased by Sherburne Associates but was deemed impossible of renovation under existing building codes. The rambling structure was thereupon torn apart and razed. A proposal to bury the old lady on the grounds was vetoed by the Department of Health, and the remains were hauled away for salvage material. The valuable space atop the hill was soon occupied by private homes. At the foot of Cliff Road, after operating for thirty-seven years, the old Gordon Folger Hotel was sold by its namesake to Mr. and Mrs. Robert Bowman, who renovated it for more contemporary tastes.

Modern communication in the form of the first Nantucket Cablevision operation came to the island in 1973. The company built a 465-foot transmission tower and laid seventy miles of cable to the most populated area before broadcasting its first show on April 2. The old Wannacomet Water Company office on Main Street was taken over by a retail business, and on June 30 the company moved its entire operation to the Wyers Valley location, where electric engines replaced the diesel pumps.

Three highly respected public servants passed from the scene. In 1972, the venerable Herbert P. Smith, ninety-four, Nantucket's last surviving Spanish-American War veteran and a longtime selectman, passed away. In 1973, after serving over fifty years as Register of Probate and Town Assessor, John J. Gardner II, went to his reward after a lifetime of public service that will probably never be equaled. (His successor was his secretary, Irene M. Smith, daughter-in-law of Herbert P.) Later that year, the remarkable jurist, George M. Poland, ninety-six, judge of Probate for thirty-three years, died on November 3. The old order was passing.

Nantucket's steamship line was also undergoing change. The old *Nobska*, after forty-nine years on the line, made her last run on September 18. She was to remain afloat to become a museum piece by the end of the century. A modern steam vessel was launched in Florida and became the M.V. *Nantucket,* the older steamship Nantucket being renamed the *Naushon.* For the first summer, the Steamship Authority ran regular service to Hyannis, which met with wide approval.

On August 13, an open jeep carrying several young people on an island outing turned over on a bend of Polpis Road, causing several minor injuries and permanent paralysis to one passenger, Pamela Kelly. The driver of the jeep was twenty-year-old Joseph P. Kennedy III, son of the late Senator Robert F. Kennedy. The driver was tried and convicted in Nantucket District Court a week later, fined and admonished. Judge C. George Anastos told young Kennedy, "You carry an illustrious name, and I hope you will use that name for doing good and set an example for other young people, rather than appearing in a courtroom such as this."

During the summer of 1973, continuing debate over the Kennedy Bill continued on both islands and in the newspapers. In July, a subcommittee of the Senate's Interior Committee held a public hearing on Nantucket and toured the island. Island opinion on the bill was divided, with Selectman Robert G. Haley and Representative Arthur S. Desrocher speaking in opposition to the bill as an excessive intrusion of federal authority into a matter that called for home rule. Selectman Charles J. Gardner and Conservation Commission chairman Bernard D. Grossman spoke in favor of the bill as a necessary measure to protect the island from the pressures of modern growth and development. From Martha's Vineyard, where he had a summer home, came a statement from the other Massachusetts senator, Edward W. Brooke, voicing his opposition to the sweeping provisions of the Kennedy Bill, which made it unlikely that the bill would ever get through the Senate. The bill pended for a few more months, then died a quiet death. The divisions in the Nantucket community, however, remained for years thereafter.

At the end of the year, Miss Grace Brown Gardner, ninety-three, died after a long stay in the hospital. She was the daughter of Arthur H. Gardner, newspaper editor, tax collector, state representative, and historian. Miss Gardner became a teacher and earned a master's degree from Brown University, teaching in Nantucket, New Bedford, and Framingham. She was a trustee of the Nantucket Atheneum and an active force in the Maria Mitchell Association and the Nantucket Historical Association, where she is best remembered for her voluminous collection of scrapbooks on every aspect of Nantucket history. Her contributions to the life and history of the island were exceptional and her memory of people and places was legendary.

With the onset of the energy crisis brought on by the oil shortage of 1973, the state ordered a curtailment of energy usage across the Commonwealth, limiting the use of fuel by homes and businesses. The most apparent result on Nantucket was the discontinuance of the traditional outdoor Christmas displays, which had been one of the joys of the season. The church steeples lost their lights and the familiar display of trees on Main Street was canceled. Many homes simply remained dark for the season, costing the island another of its winter attractions. Daylight Saving Time was imposed in January to save fuel expenditure, and long lines at the gas stations resulted from the state-imposed gasoline limitations, which caused drivers to gas up at all hours of the day, probably wasting more fuel than was saved. It was a strange season, but a temporary one.

As the school committee had been the center of public attention in the sixties, the focus now turned to the agencies in control of the island's environment and development, especially the Planning Board, the Board of Appeals, and the Conservation Commission. Week after week, the news centered around the various hearings, proposals, and heated issues generated by the new zoning bylaw and the rising tide of residential and commercial development. A new hotel at the airport, housing developments on the Milestone Road, new health regulations in Madaket, and major residential subdivisions in Surfside and Tom Nevers were the center of attention. Islanders became aware of the pressures for development, which were seen as threats to the environment and traditional life style of the island. The town responded by increasing regulatory pressure on developers, which provoked more lawsuits and appeals by disgruntled petitioners. The Planning Board hired its first professional director, William R. Klein, at a salary of $15,000, and he became a valuable adviser on planning issues.

Many legal issues were under discussion, dozens of court cases were pending, and the legal fraternity was thriving. Zoning and land-use issues were the cause of ever-lengthening court sessions. The town attempted to settle the old issue of ownership and control of the great ponds (over ten acres in area) and the proprietors' roads (ancient abutters' ways), by taking advantage of its role as the Proprietors of the Common and Undivided Lands of Nantucket, and for the token sum of one dollar the proprietorship deeded all its interest in the ponds and roads to the town. That action probably ended the proprietorship, which had existed since 1659, but in this litigious world, one never knows. Another long-running legal contest in the Nantucket courts, *Sanguinetti* vs. *Rounsville*, revealed some interesting legal manipulations of real estate during past years and was finally put to rest in 1975 with the deeding of 625 acres of land to the town.

A hot topic in 1974 was lifelong Sconset summer resident Peter Benchley's novel *Jaws*, which became a best-seller and popular movie. With Nantucket's pride in the local author came a sense of relief when the actual movie was filmed on Martha's Vineyard, styled as a fictional Long Island resort. Nantucket publicists hastened to assure vacationers that the local sharks were harmless to tourists.

The town meeting of 1974 adopted Nantucket's first official flag, a blue-and-white burgee with a sperm whale superimposed on a compass rose.

In June 1974, legislation was finally enacted giving the Steamship Authority the right to maintain year-round service from the port of Hyannis, and in anticipation of the service the authority began running the new modern motor vessel *Nantucket* on the line. The old *Nobska* was laid up in Nantucket for three months before being sent south, where she was intended to become a floating restaurant in Baltimore, but was rescued toward the end of the century and became an operating maritime museum ship.

Two Nantucketers would be remembered with permanent memorials for their contributions to the island. John Hussey Bartlett Jr., called "June," died suddenly at age seventy-four, after working his farm and selling his vegetables on Main Street up to the last day of his life. One of Nantucket's most popular and respected citizens, he was memorialized in a bronze plaque mounted on a granite slab on the sidewalk where he parked his farm stand on Main Street. On the Polpis Road, another memorial was unveiled to the memory of Harold H. Kynett, a founder and benefactor of the Nantucket Life Saving Museum. "Doc" Kynett, who died in 1973, was a longtime summer resident of Nantucket with a particular interest in its maritime history and its library facilities, which resulted in generous donations to the Life Saving Museum and the Nantucket Atheneum.

In midsummer, the island was shocked by the details of a bizarre hit-and-run incident on the Sconset bicycle path, which resulted in the death of a twenty-year-old blond visitor from Sweden, Anne Christine Anderson. Her body was found on the bicycle path early on July 21, near the remains of her mangled bicycle. Following up on the available evidence, the Nantucket police arrested a U. S. Navy man at the nearby Tom Nevers Naval Facility. Arthur Roy was tried in Nantucket Superior Court in November and convicted of driving under the influence and manslaughter, which resulted in a sentences to Barnstable for two and a half years.

The highly respected Wall Street lawyer and summer resident Arthur H. Dean delivered to the U. S. Senate his opinion that Kennedy's Nantucket Sound and Islands Trust Bill had serious constitutional flaws—principally its broad extension of federal regulation of land within one state. This was a serious legal challenge to the bill, which was quietly put to sleep in the Senate.

In the November election of 1974, the islanders voted Yes on all ballot questions, including Question 2, which called for the reducing the size of the Massachusetts House of Representatives from 240 to 160 members, thus deliberately removing Nantucket's one seat in the House. The vote was carried by forty votes, with 290 blanks—certainly one of the strangest votes in Nantucket history. Many island voters later claimed they did not understand the question.

On December 13, 1974, Nantucket celebrated the season with its first Christmas Shoppers Stroll, with music by the high school band, lighted trees on Main Street, and free refreshments in every store. The event was promoted by the Chamber of Commerce and other island business organizations as a means of keeping the Nantucketers at home to do their shopping, instead of flocking to the newly built Cape Cod Mall and other mainland outlets. What started as a warm, small-town celebration in a cozy Christmas atmosphere soon developed into something quite different. News of the Nantucket Stroll reached the mainland, causing summer residents and tourists to flock to the island for the weekend, and Nantucket found itself overwhelmed with winter visitors intent on seeing the spectacle. Hotels and restaurants reported in future years that profits from the Stroll weekend exceeded anything seen in the summer. Nantucket had been discovered again, in December.

Also in December, District Court handled more criminal cases than ever when a drug raid netted thirty-five defendants and several island businesses were broken into, including the Atheneum where the thief managed to find ten dollars. In response to the increased business of the court, District Attorney Philip A. Rollins appointed Nantucket attorney Robert F. Mooney as an Assistant District Attorney, the first such island appointment.

Preservation of the island's vital resources continued apace this year, with the gift of 310 acres of land at Coskata by the Backus and Sziklas families, a gift of 625 acres on the moors from the Sanguinetti family, and a vital parcel on Nantucket Harbor by the Lovelace family. All these gifts went to the town or to conservation agencies and helped offset the threat of several new developments. The developers' plans were continuously displayed and publicized in the newspaper, while public hearings and correspondence indicated almost total opposition, with many local decisions subject to reversal by the courts.

The pressure on the climate and the population resulted in a 1975 proposal for construction of a new $5 million high school, which proved so controversial that 1,200 voters turned out to defeat it at a town meeting in April. The wisdom of this decision was questioned at the time, but in December, the U. S. Navy announced its plans to close the Naval Facility at Tom Nevers in June. The Navy personnel, a fertile source of school-age children, would thus be leaving the island, taking away a large number of prospective students, and leaving Nantucket schools in a state of confusion for years.

The future of Nantucket's outstanding Straight Wharf Theatre, the home of the Theatre Workshop for decades, was guaranteed when a five-year lease on the property was signed in February. Then, on a windy April evening, the old building went up in smoke and flames, totally destroying it and damaging the nearby Cap'n Tobey's Restaurant. The theater's props and costumes had been removed just that day in preparation for renovations of the building, and it was surmised that some departing act of carelessness was the cause of the blaze. The building was a total loss and was soon replaced by a court-yard of retail enterprises.

It was announced in May that the famous old Nantucket light-ship was to be removed from its historic post on South Shoals and replaced by an electronic signal. The town fathers seized the oppor-tunity to acquire the lightship as a permanent historic display in the harbor, and, in cooperation with the Nantucket Historical Association, the proposal soon became a reality. The plan was for the big red lightship to be maintained at a wharf in Nantucket where it would become a tourist attraction, as well as a colorful postcard sub-ject. In December, the lightship was sailed into Nantucket Harbor by a volunteer crew of Nantucket men with maritime talents, who named themselves the "Dirty Dozen," and cheerfully autographed photographs of the occasion. She was a colorful sight at the dock, the object of many photographs and a good museum piece for the island's maritime history. However, she proved to be an expensive exhibit, one which required constant maintenance and painting, as well as a permanent curator. After several years of effort, the Historical Association ended its lease and the town let the ship go, with regret, to a mainland port.

During the summer, the very first cases of babesiosis were diag-nosed on the island, most of the known cases spread by the deer tick, which later became the carrier of the dreaded Lyme disease, with Nantucket a primary site of infestation.

Madaket's own unofficial Coast Guard commander, Mildred Jewett, was honored by the Coast Guard in July for her many years of service to the establishment, dating back to 1925. "Madaket Millie," as she was affectionately known, did more than any person on the island to assist the Coast Guard while it still maintained the Madaket Station, and she became the guardian of the western end of the island after the station closed in 1947. A truly extraordinary per-son in many ways, she was honored with an appointment as the ser-vice's first honorary warrant officer.

Two more veteran office holders retired from the public scene. In June of 1975, Chief of Police Wendell Howes announced his retirement after thirty-nine years on the police force. In January 1976, the much respected Charles Clark Coffin, one of the last of the old-timers in the town building, retired after thirty-five years as Town Clerk. The old order of town government was changing.

Traffic figures from the Steamship Authority again showed a substantial gain for the year 1975, with Nantucket passenger traffic up over twelve percent at 323,710 and motor vehicles up over ten percent to 42,763. The authority also released the interesting results of a poll taken of 325 Nantucket and 370 Vineyard residents, dealing with authority operations, service, policy, and traffic. In the poll, sixty-five percent of Nantucketers felt the authority should deliver the traffic and let others deal with the growth problems, and sixty-seven percent opposed the idea of controlling the volume of passengers. However, sixty-four percent thought some limits should be imposed on the cars brought to the island by summer residents and visitors. Nantucketers took much more interest in the comfort and facilities of the boats, calling for better seating, more cleanliness, dog control, and a better choice of food. Nantucketers registered more satisfaction with the line than complaints.

A severe gale from the southwest struck Nantucket a damaging blow in February, with winds of hurricane force smashing into the Madaket area and raising havoc with the scallop fleet in Madaket and Nantucket Harbors. Nantucket was hit harder than any part of the coast. In town, the great elms were toppled on Main, Pleasant, and Centre Streets. At the height of the storm, the 325-foot Consolan Tower of the FAA navigation system snapped like a toothpick and crumpled to the ground, a loss estimated at $80,000.

Morris Ernst, famous New York civil liberties lawyer and long-time summer resident of Monomoy, died on May 21, leaving his two favorite islands, Nantucket and Manhattan. On June 30, retired District Court Judge Caroline Leveen, died after thirty-three years on the bench, during which she never took one day of vacation or one day of sick leave, a remarkable record for a state employee.

Town meeting voted down the Kennedy Bill in a nonbinding vote, after which the U. S. House of Representatives sent it off for an eighteen-month study. The same meeting voted to build a $3.5-million elementary school, but narrowly rejected a $4.3-million high school, which lost by nine votes.

The big event of 1976 was the national bicentennial celebration on July 4, which fell on a Sunday, forcing the town to reschedule its public events until noon or later. At noon, every bell and whistle on the island was sounded, and a parade started through the downtown streets. A human chain was formed to stretch across the island and sing "God Bless America." Parade floats, sailboat races, beard contests, and athletic events made up the public schedule in Nantucket, while in Boston the spectacle of the Boston Pops and its red, white, and blue theme was watched by thousands. Even Queen Elizabeth II visited Boston to celebrate Independence Day. In the evening, Nantucket fog overtook the festivities and the $4,000 worth of fireworks disappeared into the gloom.

Art flourished during the summer, with Old South Wharf gradually becoming the favorite spot for Nantucket artists to work and show their wares for the eager inhabitants of the boat basin. Another type of artist plagued the town that year, as art thefts were reported from the Whaling Museum and the Atheneum, the work of a team of professionals who were never apprehended. This was followed by a string of thefts and vandalism that created a heavy load for the police department, with crimes reported all over the island, culminating with the theft of a police cruiser on a night call.

The arrival of the first mopeds in the summer of 1976 was another threat to the already burgeoning traffic problem. Billed as a cheap solution to the energy problem, claiming 150 miles to the gallon, the new motorized bicycles had a top speed of twenty-five miles an hour. The laws of Massachusetts recognized the moped as a motorized bicycle, not a motor vehicle, and thus capable of operation without registration or insurance, provided the operator was a licensed driver. All the bicycle shops were swept up in the new craze for mopeds. But the moped was subject to abuse by thrill-seeking tourists on Nantucket's narrow and sandy roads, and many accidents resulted in serious injuries. This resulted in an attempt by the town to license the moped dealers and bring the operation under the zoning bylaw, which produced more litigation and conflicts for a few years. The resulting court cases were finally brought to a head in the summer of 1978, when, for the first time since the days of Daniel Webster, a federal district court judge came to Nantucket and held a trial in the county court house. The judge declined to overrule the town regulations. Moped dealers were licensed, helmets were required, and instructions were given the operators. Mopeds were now free to join the increasing variety of traffic in the streets and byways of Nantucket.

Continuing litigation over the subdivision and development of Nantucket real estate became standard fare for the courts and the newspapers. Big developments in Surfside and Tom Nevers were pending in the Planning Board and contested in the courts. Dozens of cases were pending in Superior Court and Land Court, as hastily organized citizen groups tried to stop the development plans, usually meeting with limited success.

The November 1976 election showed a trend in Nantucket, away from its traditional Republican loyalty toward a more Independent, if not Democratic, state of mind. The Republican ticket of Ford and Dole won 1,399 votes, but the Carter-Mondale ticket scored 1,115 votes; the ever popular Senator Edward M. Kennedy carried Nantucket with 1,623 votes and Congressman Gerry Studds topped them all with 2,213. The total vote was a record 2,633 voters, attributed to an influx of politically active young people and the large numbers of retired people who were registered and active in public affairs.

Three Nantucket institutions celebrated events this year. The Wauwinet House celebrated its centenary in July with a village clambake; the site of the first Macy's store at 2 Fair Street was memorialized with a plaque in October on the site where Rowland Hussey Macy worked in his father's store before departing for bigger things in New York; and the old Ocean House, now the restored Jared Coffin House, celebrated its new island owners, Philip and Margaret Read, who bought the historic inn from the Nantucket Historical Trust in October.

The most dramatic event of the year came right before Christmas. On December 15, the Liberian-registered tanker *Argo Merchant* went aground on Fishing Rip Shoals. Settling in fifty feet of water, the hull split apart, releasing 27,000 tons of heavy oil into the Atlantic Ocean and precipitating a major marine disaster. Nantucket became the center of an international news story, and reporters and photographers rushed to the island where the survivors of the wreck were comfortably settled in local hotels. Under the leadership of Jim Lentowski of the Conservation Foundation, many Nantucketers organized to help out in the emergency. The immediate problem was the hundreds of oil-soaked birds that were floundering on the shore and could not be collected or buried without federal permits: "Do not touch the birds." The problem of handling a major oil spill in the rough open ocean was more difficult, as was the threat of having the entire mass wash ashore. The Coast Guard had a major burden on its hands, and for weeks the public worried about the unthinkable: a total blackout of the island beaches, contaminated water all around, and dead fish and birds everywhere. However, the powerful tides that pulled the *Argo Merchant* onto the shoals soon reversed and swept the problem out into the Atlantic from which it came.

A study commission opened the year 1977 with a recommendation that the old wooden police station be abandoned and the department moved to occupy the brick fire station on South Water Street (which was even older but capable of rehabilitation for modern police purposes). The new fire station was to be located on town property at the intersection of Pleasant Street and Sparks Avenue while the police department would maintain its in-town presence. This was one proposal that met with almost universal acceptance, and soon came to fruition. (Nantucket may be the only town in the world with its fire station on a Sparks Avenue.)

More developments and more controversy were the order of the day, with large subdivisions pending in the Fishers Landing area at the west end, the Milestone Road development of Pierce and Gumley, and the controversial proposal to build a motel on airport land. The first two proposals eventually were approved and became highly desirable residential areas, while the airport motel, shot down by the town meeting, was eventually built by private parties on adjacent land and continues to operate as the Nantucket Inn.

The biggest story of the year was one that drew national attention as the islands of Nantucket and Martha's Vineyard took up the cause of secession. Each island, since its inclusion in the Massachusetts Bay Colony, had been entitled to one representative in the state legislature, known as the Great and General Court of Massachusetts. This anomaly was allowed to continue due to the islands' status as counties of Massachusetts, with each county entitled to at least one vote, although Nantucket's population was far below the statewide average for a representative district.

Following the U. S. Supreme Court decision in *Baker* vs. *Carr,* which declared that each state must create legislative districts roughly equal in population, the handwriting was on the wall and the island representatives would soon become relics of political history. However, it seemed to come as a surprise when the legislature proposed to the two islands that they become part of a new legislative district that included Falmouth on Cape Cod. To the cry of "Disenfranchisement! Unfair! Taxation without Representation!" was added the ultimate threat of secession—a proposal to leave

Massachusetts for another state. The islands drew up a "Declaration of Independence," which Representative J. Sydney Conway delivered in the State House. At the time of the secession movement, Nantucket had a population of about 5,700, while the average legislative district was about 36,000. The islands did, however, have legitimate grievances, which they considered unique and compelling reasons to honor their political integrity. They were isolated from the mainland by water, with no free highway to the capital city; they had special needs for transportation by sea and air, which the state did not pay for; they were first-class tourist attractions for the state; and they contributed in taxes far more than they got back from the state treasury. None of those factors, however, influenced the court mandate for population-based representation.

The fun started when the publicity hit mainland news media. Hundreds of Nantucketers were interviewed for their thoughts on the subject, while proposals for a new Nantucket flag with a defiant seagull replacing the eagle were spread abroad. The islands' bid for adoption struck a responsive chord in several states, with New Hampshire, Rhode Island, Vermont, and Connecticut expressing an interest in the island colonies. The most publicized proposal came from New Hampshire, where the flamboyant governor, Meldrim Thompson, quick to seize the publicity value of the cause, flew to Nantucket and delivered a speech to the Chamber of Commerce, along with four bottles of maple syrup. He promised unlimited state aid and freedom from taxation (New Hampshire being one of the few remaining states without an income tax) in return for Nantucket's offer of a mild climate and eighty-eight miles of beaches. Massachusetts Governor Michael Dukakis, who admired Nantucket as a vacation retreat, was skeptical of the proposal. Averse to losing any part of his state, he cordially received a Nantucket delegation and suggested that Governor Thompson might want the island for another nuclear power plant.

Although the two islands went so far as to file a secession bill in the legislature, and voted overwhelmingly in straw polls for the idea, the practical politics of the matter soon caught up with the daydream of secession. Such a move of one populated community from one state to another would require the affirmative vote of both state legislatures and an act of Congress, neither of which was likely to happen. Faced with public scrutiny and the assurance of a gubernatorial veto, secession died a happy death, fortunately without a civil war, but with the possibility of rising again when the islands are sufficiently provoked.

During February 1977, Nantucket lost one of its finest public figures—W. Ripley "Rip" Nelson, a tireless civic leader of many good causes, including the Conservation Foundation, the Historical Association, and the Civic League. He was remembered by a motion of the town meeting as "one whose unpaid public service to this town and its people can never be rewarded, but should never be forgotten."

The summer was marked by more youth and fewer jobs, as the island's popularity spread through the college world. Idle hands and immediate needs, the spread of the drug culture, and the easy availability of summer trouble resulted in many cases of vandalism and theft. Increasing trouble with mopeds caused the Nantucket Cottage Hospital to demand action from the town to control their operation, with Dr. David Voorhees telling the board about six skull fractures due to inexperienced and unhelmeted operators.

Excavation of an early native American dwelling site at Quidnet revealed for the first time the antiquity of the Nantucket Indian culture. Archaeologists sponsored by the Nantucket Historical Association found a number of artifacts including spear points and pottery in the area and indications that the native diet consisted of game and shellfish. For the first time on Nantucket, the technique of carbon dating was used to analyze a deer bone, which was dated to A.D. 375, the first reliable dating of the native culture.

By the end of the year, the town was concerned about the possibility of offshore oil becoming a factor in the marine environment.

The federal government proposed to lease a huge area near Georges Bank for oil and gas exploration. Of more immediate concern was a Steamship Authority plan to remove the large-capacity motor vessel *Nantucket* from the Hyannis run and force more Nantucket traffic through the longer route to Woods Hole. Nantucket was to be serviced by the unpopular *Uncatena,* a vessel that always had trouble keeping to its schedule.

The summer of 1977 witnessed a novel stage production of *Dracula* by the Nantucket Stage Company, a new enterprise that got its start by renting the Cyrus Peirce School during the summer season. The production and stage effects went over with the public, and the fall saw the show performed at the Wilbur Theatre in Boston, under the direction of Dennis Rosa with designs by Edward Gorey. After Boston, it moved to New York and became an off-Broadway hit for several seasons.

The banking scene lost another prominent figure when Robert D. Congdon retired as president of the Pacific National Bank on September 1, but Mr. Congdon continued to be associated with the insurance company that bears his name. He was active in many business and civic organizations and was a sportsman and collector of note. His place at the bank was assumed by Henry "Hank the Bank" Kehlenbeck. The old order at the bank was changing forever. The new president was a genial, casual type who worked in shirtsleeves, puffed a cigar, and treated all bank customers alike, no matter what their station or bank balance.

On the last day of 1977, one of the most shocking crimes in island history took place, when an intruder broke into the home of a sixty-three-year old widow near Fairgrounds Road and brutally attacked and stabbed her in her bedroom. The Nantucket police launched a most thorough investigation, collecting evidence to send to the FBI crime laboratory in Washington and combing the island for suspects. After recovering from the attack, the victim was able to give the police an accurate description of her assailant, and as a result the police held a lineup of several men, from which the woman selected and identified the attacker. On February 16, Captain George Rezendes arrested a twenty-two-year-old man named Ronald Leftwich, a summer worker who had stayed over on the island for the winter. He was quickly indicted by the grand jury but protested his innocence. Because he was young and friendless, Leftwich attracted the sympathy of several people on the island who raised money for his legal defense. Due to the publicity and the tension created by the crime, the trial was moved to New Bedford Superior Court. When he was called for trial before Justice Augustus Taveira in July, the defendant changed his plea to guilty and admitted all the elements of the charge. He then offered a public apology to his victim and to the people of Nantucket for all the harm he had done, an expression of sincerity never before heard by the court. The judge then sentenced Leftwich as a sexually dangerous person to an indeterminate sentence at Bridgewater House of Correction, a potential life sentence. The island breathed easier. Ronald Leftwich served almost twenty years in Bridgewater, after which another judge held a hearing and determined he was no longer a threat to society. He was released from confinement to live in western Massachusetts, where, in 1998, he attacked and stabbed to death a Catholic priest who had befriended him.

The Leftwich case had an impact on the Nantucket community, which was forced to realize that it was not immune to the social evils of the times—crime, drugs, and violence. In a town where people once boasted of unlocked front doors and keys left in cars, many habits of a lifetime were changed. The hardware stores did a brisk business in padlocks and house keys, and the police chief was deluged by requests for firearm permits. The police department itself was soon upgraded in personnel and training, and the town took a serious interest in public safety.

The winter of 1978 would be remembered for two of the worst storms in recent New England history, which struck on January 20 and February 6. The latter storm was the Blizzard of 1978, when Boston received thirty inches of snow and Nantucket had seventy-eight-mile-an-hour winds but only four inches of snow. The mainland situation was so bad that Governor Dukakis closed all the highways, airports, and transit services for several days. Nantucket escaped the full fury of the blizzard, but could validly claim the storm had "cut off the mainland."

With spring came Daffodil Weekend at the end of April, featuring the Nantucket Garden Club show and the parade of antique cars. Since 1973, with Garden Club sponsorship, thousands of daffodils had been planted all over the island and the event became the "end of winter" signal, though the official opening of the season would wait for Memorial Day.

That summer, island voters authorized the expenditure of $1.2 million for a new Our Island Home, a modern nursing home for the elderly. Housing of another sort was in short supply, as the pressure of the summer population created a serious housing shortage for working people and families. The soaring price of Nantucket real estate resulted in a taxpayer protest against the traditional Nantucket tax-assessment practices, the result being low assessments of older properties and high assessment for newer construction, which often resulted in startling disparities. One house assessed at $3,900 sold for $74,000. Despite the fact the state had ordered communities to make true hundred percent evaluation of all real estate, Nantucket was still awaiting the completion of new tax maps and professional revaluation. In the meantime, the old way continued.

Recent criminal cases and the rise in concern over public safety prompted the selectmen to appoint a select committee to survey the police department. The committee reported the need for more and better trained officers, which would definitely involve a higher standard of pay. The starting salary for patrolmen was $10,700.

Summer social life centered on the art galleries, various charity events, and gala events at the Yacht Club and the Siasconset Casino.

205

The town band concerts, given on Main Street and at the gazebo in Harbor Square, were now in their eighteenth year, constituting one of the most popular of summer events and one of the few free benefits of Nantucket's summer season.

The year 1978 saw many changes in town government, with new candidates winning election to the board of selectmen and school committee. The rising cost of living, taxpayers' complaints about assessments, and the prospect of unionized public employees prompted a study by professional consultants of the salary schedule for all town employees. A new plan was adopted by town meeting and was to lead to more and more expensive public services. This was also the year Nantucket merged into a new legislative district with Martha's Vineyard and part of Cape Cod and elected its first nonresident legislator, Howard "Rick" Cahoon, of Chatham.

In September, a strong gale with high winds and seas struck the island without warning one afternoon, forcing the town to provide emergency accommodations for 250 passengers of the HyLine vessel *Brant Point,* which was unable to return to Hyannis. The Nantucket Police Department took charge and found room for everyone in the new high school auditorium and in Gardner Hall at St. Paul's Church. The tourists' unexpected evening on the island proved a great success, and the next morning they were sent home on the vessel *Point Gammon,* full of good will and DownyFlake doughnuts.

Nantucket High School launched two popular programs: the Academic Achievement award ceremony for gifted students, featuring U. S. Senator Edward Brooke as the speaker, and the annual Homecoming football game, featuring Nantucket's first Junior Miss contest winner, Susan Boyd. Public spirit was running high.

With enthusiasm for preservation of the island's open spaces, the public was cheered by the Nantucket Conservation Foundation's announcement that it had purchased 242 acres of land on the south shore from William J. Braun, a Boston real estate investor who had bought the land in 1954 for $14,000 and sold it for $925,000. This was considered a good investment to protect the south beach land. That purchase may have inspired town meeting's vote to purchase the forty-six-acre site of the Tom Nevers Naval Facility for $525,000. The same meeting appropriated $550,000 to build a new fire station on Sparks Avenue, which coincided with the expansion of commercial and public facilities to the edge of town. Talk of moving the police department out of town was just talk, as the public felt the need for a downtown police presence.

The last year of the seventies witnessed the passing of several citizens who had made important contributions to the Nantucket of their era. They included Parker W. Gray, pioneer aviator; Margaret Harwood, first director of the Maria Mitchell Observatory; Gus Bentley, Nantucket's favorite musician; Henry B. Coleman, popular realtor and public official; Gardner Russell, former District Court justice; George Parmenter, founder of Cape & Islands Airline; Harriet Backus, owner of the Wauwinet House; Marjorie Mills, popular newspaper and radio pioneer; and Roy E. Larsen, one of the founders of the Nantucket Conservation Foundation.

On a clear afternoon in April, in a spectacular blaze visible from Cape Cod, Preston Manchester's Airport Lounge at Nobadeer burned to the ground. Two bartenders valiantly held their posts until the flames forced them and twenty-five patrons to give up hope for their favorite establishment and leave ahead of the flames. The loss of this location led to the later construction of the Nantucket Inn on the site.

Another establishment was opened for business in May when the Harbor House opened to the public after major renovations, offering 111 rooms at $55 to $85 per night. Placing several buildings in traditional Nantucket style along a replicated Nantucket street with lavish landscaping made this the premier downtown hostelry, and it soon became popular for business and social gatherings.

During the summer, a mounting concern was the erosion of the shorefront at Great Point. One of the historic lighthouses of the east coast, the original Great Point Light was erected in 1784. The light-house was once 420 feet from the shoreline, but was now only twelve feet from the water, with the shore eroding at the rate of ten feet every year. An appeal to the federal government, with some heavy help from Senator Edward Kennedy, eventually saved the site, not from the surf, but from the Coast Guard administration, which had refused to move the light.

During the summer of 1979, a street musician named Robert Goldstein began to play his dulcimer on Main Street without a permit. The town fathers claimed he owed a $50 vendor's license fee because he was soliciting money. Goldstein, who called himself the Nantucket Troubadour, refused to pay and claimed his music was an exercise of his right to free speech. His cause was championed by the American Civil Liberties Union and the case went to the U. S. District Court in Boston. On September 25, Judge Rya Zobel ruled the street musician was protected by the Constitution; thereafter, any musician could play on the sidewalks of Nantucket. After proving his point, the Nantucket Troubadour mysteriously disappeared perhaps to play in another jurisdiction.

Other complaints were heard that summer: the Civic League and the Chamber of Commerce appeared before the selectmen to protest the "deterioration" of the downtown area. The complaints centered on the unchecked display of offensive merchandise, sidewalk sales, handmade signs, and fast-food outlets. Police and health inspectors were sent into action against the offenders.

Expansion of commercial outlets to the edge of town increased when the Pacific National Bank opened a branch office on Sparks Avenue and the new fire station was under construction in the same area. A new hotel with 100 rooms was approved to replace Preston's Airport Lounge. One commentator attributed the decline of the downtown area to a "fast-buck mentality" and the indifference of owners and tenants to the importance and charm of the town's commercial center. There was a noticeable trend to abandon the downtown to the tourist trade and day-shoppers, while the substantial and necessary businesses sought more room and parking space at the south end of the town—a trend that was to continue for some years.

At the end of the year, a midnight fire swept the large commercial building at Zero Main Street, destroying a liquor store, a retail shop, the headquarters of Walter Beinecke's Sherburne Associates, and the Frank Sylvia antiques store. Fifty paintings by Nantucket artists that were being stored for the Nantucket Historical Trust by Sherburne Associates were lost in the blaze. Arson was suspected but never proved.

At the end of the seventies, the Nantucket Civic League heard planning director William Klein describe Nantucket as the fastest-growing community in New England, with 116 new homes built in the past year and a five percent growth in population. At that rate, Klein predicted a population of 12,000 year-round residents and 60,000 summer residents by 1990. These startling figures were accompanied by a demand for more controls on growth in the future.

All of Madaket came under the watch of Millie's "West End Command."

Mildred Jewett
THE SPIRIT OF MADAKET

MILLIE JEWETT WAS THE SPIRIT OF MADAKET FOR SO MANY years that the place has never been the same without her. Born on Nantucket in 1910, she was raised on a farm near Madaket, which was then a small settlement of the summer cottages and fishing shacks of Nantucketers. Her parents broke up early in her life, and she worked the farm, milked the cows, and spent a lonely life by the sea. Her one try at marriage—supposedly to a mail-order husband—ended when he slipped away on the morning boat. Millie developed into a rugged and salty character, suspicious of strangers ("What you looking at? Get the hell outta here!"), but was always helpful to lost fishermen and stray animals.

She settled down in a cottage near Hither Creek, and ran a small roadside store, selling the bare necessities. ("Two kinds of ice cream—black and white!") She also befriended the men of the Madaket Coast Guard Station, which stood near the beach, on a site now long eroded by the sea. The lonely young sailors took a liking to her, and she ran errands to town for them. They soon began calling her Madaket Millie.

During World War II, Nantucket was subject to a total blackout as part of the east coast defense against Nazi submarines. Millie was the civil defense officer and air raid warden for Madaket, which she patrolled on a big horse. Woe to the careless customer who violated the blackout on Millie's watch. The Coast Guardsmen also patrolled the beaches with German shepherd watchdogs. Millie found her love of animals gave her a special talent for training the dogs; she could even train them to climb ladders. She won a citation for her wartime work. After the war, much against Millie's advice, the Coast Guard closed the Madaket Station. On the day it closed in 1947, Millie took up the beach patrol, and located the Panamanian freighter *Kotor*, hard aground on the Madaket shore in a dense fog. Millie called the Coast Guard cutters to rescue the ship. The Coast Guard rewarded her with a sign reading "USCG West End Command," which she proudly displayed on her little cottage. She was later honored with an official appointment as Chief Warrant Officer for her many patriotic and humanitarian services.

Millie never changed. She lived out her rugged and lonely life, surrounded by her dogs, ducks, and geese, talking to her animals and welcoming a few friends. These included such diverse types as Game Warden Ed Metcalf, Boston *Globe* photographer Stan Grossfeld, and TV personality Fred Rogers, who found a tender spirit under her gruff exterior. When she passed away in 1990, all Nantucket knew it had lost one of its original characters, a tough woman with a soft heart.

Jim Lentowski's drive to preserve Ram Pasture was a watershed for Nantucket conservation.

James M. Lentowski

MR. CONSERVATION

JIM LENTOWSKI ARRIVED IN NANTUCKET ON A HOT JULY 4 weekend in 1971 to become the first executive secretary of the Nantucket Conservation Foundation and the man destined to lead the cause of conservation on the island for the next thirty years.

Jim came from Chicopee, the western Massachusetts city best known as the Kielbasa Capital of the nation. He first came to Nantucket on Boy Scout trips on rainy weekends, became a Life Scout, and began the study of natural landscape, graduating from the University of Massachusetts with bachelor's and master's degrees in landscape architecture. The department head at UMass recommended him for a new position opening in Nantucket, and he was hired by Roy E. Larsen, legendary president of the Nantucket Conservation Foundation.

The foundation was incorporated in 1963 by a small

group of Nantucket citizens and summer residents who had the foresight to recognize what was then only a dimly seen threat of over development. The organization at first lacked the funds to purchase large tracts of land, so most of its early acquisitions were gifts from conscientious landowners.

The moving force behind the foundation's growth was the influence of its early leaders: Roy E. Larsen, John L. Lyman, W. Ripley "Rip" Nelson, and Alfred F. "Teeny" Sanford, all skilled promoters and fund-raisers for the cause of conservation.

The movement really took off when Jim Lentowski arrived to spearhead the drive to acquire Ram Pasture, an unspoiled 625-acre parcel of land almost surrounding Hummock Pond. Aided by two generous contributions and individual gifts from many local people, the foundation managed to raise the funds to acquire this unique property. The foundation's acquisition of Ram Pasture set the pace for what would become an island-wide wave of conservation.

For thirty years, Jim Lentowski has led the island's land-conservation movement with a steady hand and knowledgeable performance. He consistently refuses to embark on the political ventures and strident assaults that have degraded other well-intentioned movements. He and his wife Jill and daughters Mary and Molly are very much a part of the island's year-round community.

By the end of the century, with the Nantucket Conservation Foundation controlling some 8,500 acres— more than forty percent of the island preserved forever— Nantucket would be grateful to this former Boy Scout who found his lifetime career on the island.

Henry Fee's sandwich business became a family affair: Andy, Sandy, and Henry.

Henry Fee

SANDWICH MAN

HENRY FEE WAS FORTY WHEN HE GOT THE IDEA:
Nantucket really needed a sandwich shop. After hearing a
radio program encouraging personal enterprise, Henry and
his wife Sandra decided to try it. The decision was not easy,
for they had four young children and no experience in the
business. Henry had to give up his fourteen-year career with
the telephone company, the most secure employment in town,
whose employees seldom left.

Henry's got started in 1969 on Steamboat Wharf, in a
small restaurant owned by Beulah Scully. They quickly came
up with Henry's name and one more important decision:
since they did not like the smell of hamburgers and french
fries, they would serve only sandwiches. The food had to be
good, so Henry insisted on baking the bread, which was
always fresh and tasty. The public was looking for good, clean,
fast and friendly food; the sandwich shop met the need and

became enormously popular. The first two years were a struggle, as they made sandwiches in the Tap Room and rented a store on Main Street during the winters, moving back to the wharf each summer.

Henry attributed their success to his wife, Sandy, who was always there to work and train the help. ("We worked the 7-24 shift; 7 days a week, 24 hours a day.") As the children grew up, they moved into the kitchen, baking or making sandwiches. Hundreds of summer workers—college students, many of them Irish, local youths, well fed and housed by Henry—made for a cheerful crew and friendly atmosphere.

In a few years, Henry bought the Easy Street property from Beulah Scully, reserving her a life interest in her home. When she passed away, they rebuilt the property into the present restaurant. Moving down the wharf, the Fees purchased the Skipper Restaurant in 1974, and used the old waterfront boat deck for dinner and entertainment. After operating for a few years, they were overtaken by the expansion plans of the Steamship Authority, and forced to sell that property for $1.3 million, retiring from the restaurant while providing the authority with a new and expensive parking lot.

With four children obtaining college educations and working on the island, Henry and Sandra could retire from active business. Matt was running Something Natural; Sydney and Andrew were running Henry's Jr. on Lower Orange Street; Barrie was married and settled down; and son Andrew and niece Terry Hastings were managing Henry's on Steamboat Wharf. After thirty years of hard work and thousands of sandwiches, Henry could look back with satisfaction: "At least I saved Nantucket from McDonald's!"

The fall of Great Point lighthouse during a storm in 1984 brought sadness to the entire island.

The turbulent early years of the new decade brought images of American hostages and international terrorists threatening the world with a dangerous future. A new American administration brought about a rising tide of capitalism and confidence, which by the end of the decade brought down the Berlin Wall and the "Evil Empire" of European communism. Nantucket was its own microcosm of the national mood during those years, as it struggled with the issues of the eighties.

More People, More Problems

Early in 1980, Nantucket became aware of its true value. Prior to that year, islanders had enjoyed their favorite form of taxation—low assessments and reasonable tax bills, issued by local assessors who were elected to keep things that way. The rising tide of Nantucket property sales and the decisions of several courts mandated that cities and towns assess their property at fair market value. The town hired a professional firm of real estate appraisers who issued a report in the spring. It found that the average home on Nantucket was worth $125,000 and the total valuation of island property, which the local assessors had estimated at $32 million, was currently valued at $660 million. These staggering values would soon soar even higher, and the island spent much of the ensuing decade dealing with Nantucket's escalating value and the consequences of all that new wealth.

The big story of the year, which became Nantucket's most baffling mystery, began to unfold on a cold windy night in January on a hillside in the new Tom Nevers development. After spending an evening at dinner in her home with her brother and friends, Doctor Margaret Kilcoyne, fifty, a research physician from New York, mysteriously disappeared. When her brother, Leo Kilcoyne, could not find her next morning, he called the Nantucket police. With no signs of violence or forced entry, the case was deemed a missing-person incident. A check of the airport and steamship reported no such person leaving the island.

Fifty volunteers was mustered to sweep the countryside, without success. Her brother told the police Margaret was highly agitated, talked about lavish parties, and stocked the house with hundreds of dollars worth of food and liquor for a party that never happened. In her house, police found a long tape of a phone conversation that was described as "a verbal suicide note," although none of her friends thought her suicidal, only manic.

The mystery deepened two weeks later when people walking a dog near Tom Nevers Pond, about a mile from her home, found Margaret's wallet, passport, and some articles of clothing. Then came reports of her appearance on the mainland, which were investigated and proven erroneous. A psychic divined that she had been murdered in a lovers quarrel. The Nantucket police followed every lead, traveled to Boston and New York, but never found any evidence.

The search for Margaret Kilcoyne continued into the spring and summer without success. New police chief Paul Hunter delivered an opinion that she had been secretly removed from the island, possibly for confinement in a mental hospital. Police captain George Rezendes believed she had committed suicide by walking into the ocean. Everyone who dealt with the case had a different opinion, including the possibility of an alien abduction. Seven years after her disappearance, the Nantucket Probate Court decreed that she was presumed dead, based on the common-law presumption of death after seven years' unexplained absence. That ended the police case, but not the controversy, and the Kilcoyne case will remain Nantucket's greatest mystery.

A minor mystery developed on the neighboring island of Muskeget, which was declared a National Natural Landmark by the U. S. Department of the Interior in April, based in part upon the island being the sole habitat of the famous "Muskeget vole," which is found nowhere else in the world. It is not recorded how the vole reacted to the publicity.

During the summer, the Nantucket Planning and Economic Development Commission issued a report on the island's population, showing an increase to 7,306, due almost entirely to settlement on the island of about 250 persons per year. This was accompanied by increased consumption of gasoline and electricity, and a rise in truck traffic of 347 percent in the past decade. The passenger traffic on the steamship line was increasing by ten percent a year.

In a midsummer speech to the general public, Governor Michael Dukakis called Nantucket a "national treasure," and called for a balance between natural resources and economic growth. He warned the island against over-development and stated, "It is important that Nantucket's unique character be preserved for generations to come."

Public projects were making progress throughout the year. The new Our Island Home was begun in April; town meeting voted to convert the former Academy Hill School to apartments for the elderly and the town entered into an agreement with a private developer to renovate the property for that purpose. The Fire Department moved into its modern station at the corner of Sparks Avenue and Pleasant Street, and after renovations were made the Police Department moved into the old fire station on South Water Street in October.

Private projects continued apace. The old Glowacki sand pit on Old South Road was acquired by a consortium called the Nantucket

Collaborative, which announced plans for a major development that would include a 250-room hotel, a restaurant, a convention center, and twenty-five single-family homes. It was met with almost unanimous opposition and more legal action. The Nantucket Electric Company changed management as the former stockholders sold the controlling shares to a group headed by Walter Beinecke Jr. and new officers were installed. The Nantucket Conservation Foundation acquired the 250-acre Windswept Cranberry Bog on Polpis Road. In October, the Town of Nantucket took over ownership of the old Navy Base at Tom Nevers, acquiring the valuable acreage and dilapidated buildings for some unspecified uses in the future.

September 13 was a date for celebrity visits. On that day, former President Richard M. Nixon arrived on a yacht together with his friend Bebe Rebozo. They toured the island and dined at the Chanticleer. On the same day, a World Business Council conference was held on the island, featuring appearances by former Attorney General Elliot Richardson and future Secretary of State General Alexander Haig.

A longstanding controversy between the town fathers and island contractor Augusto Ramos went to court in the fall, and a local jury awarded the contractor a judgment of $100,000 after finding that town officials had conspired to deprive him of public works contracts. The finding also involved seven town officials, and there was a threat of mass resignations by selectmen and members of the town finance committee if the decision was not overturned on appeal. It was.

The year 1980 ended on a high note on December 6, when the undefeated Nantucket High School football team went to its first Super Bowl to play a heavily favored team from Boston, Christopher Columbus High School. Nantucket won by a score of 44 to 20, to end an eleven-game season undefeated. The star of the day was flashy halfback Beau Almodobar, one of three brothers on the team, who scored four touchdowns. As luck would have it, the team returned by steamboat in the middle of the Christmas Stroll and rode aboard the fire trucks in a spontaneous parade that had the street crowds going wild with welcome to the local heroes.

Nineteen eighty-one got off to an old-fashioned start with a January freeze that brought the island bitter temperatures, frozen water pipes, and six inches of ice in the harbor. Steamship service came to a halt, as both Nantucket and Hyannis harbors were frozen out of service. The Coast Guard icebreaker *Bittersweet* forced a channel to Nantucket, permitting one boat per day, but it was no pleasure trip: on January 19 the vessel *Uncatena* made the trip from Woods Hole to Nantucket in fifteen hours. The scallop season came to an early end, costing the town a half-million dollars in winter income.

The forces of nature seemed dominant on the island. The eroding shoreline at Great Point came within forty feet of historic Great Point Light, whereupon the Coast Guard announced that the government had released no money to save the structure and nature could take its course. (It eventually did just that.) Other authorities were seeking ways to harness the elements: The school department received a grant to establish solar-heating panels on the roof of the high school. The brightest idea of the year was use of the winds continuously sweeping across the island for the potential generation of electric power. One proposal sought to build 100 windmills to solve the power problem, followed by a more modest proposal from the Nantucket Electric Company to set up a small experimental wind farm, which was eventually approved and installed at Bartlett Farm. The first private windmill, owned by Ernest Whelden on Mill Hill, proved to be a noisy apparatus that had to be turned off at night to satisfy the neighbors. The Historic District Commission stepped forth with regulations limiting the height of wind towers to sixty feet and with only white vanes. Windmills began whirling at Bartlett Farm with the completion of the first three in August and the approval of seven more by the Planning Board. The wind overpowered the mills, and they did not last long. Nantucket had too much wind and the terrific power the mills generated could not be stored. Wind power was not the answer.

In the spring, the Nantucket Historical Association announced its plans to expand, creating a "navigation room" and a Museum Shop. The new exhibition hall was named for longtime public servant and former NHA president Leroy H. True, and the Museum Shop became an important source of revenue for the NHA.

March 25 saw the passing of one of the great Nantucket school teachers, Julia F. Williams, who taught commercial subjects for forty-five years, a record career at the time. Hundreds of Nantucket students learned their basic skills in her classrooms—and went on to successful business careers.

The 1981 town meeting was a lively affair, with several important growth-related proposals on the warrant, which included 111 articles. The most important proposal was a building cap, limiting construction to eighty residential building permits per year and allowing building on only ten percent of new subdivision lots. This proposal sparked a flurry of new subdivision plans to be filed before the effective date of the new bylaw. Among these was the first of several Surfside Realty Trust plans for new subdivisions of 600 acres of land in Surfside. This was soon followed by the subdivision of 230 acres of land near Miacoment golf course by the trustees of 3M Realty Trust. Other builders rushed to get plans on record ahead of the building cap, effective in November.

The same town meeting considered a "head tax" of twenty-five cents on all passengers landing on Nantucket. Although it was supported by some of the selectmen and civic groups, it was criticized for being both elitist and unconstitutional, and went down to defeat. The meeting did approve the first of Nantucket's parking limits (for one- and two-hour locations) in downtown areas and the first parking charges at Nantucket Airport. Starting on April 7, the meeting did not adjourn until May 12.

New enterprises and entities appearing this year were the VFW headquarters at the old navy base; the Iron Man Relay Race, sponsored by The Muse restaurant; the new Nantucket Conservation

Foundation headquarters on Cliff Road; and the new Our Island Home, containing forty-five beds for elder care at a cost of $2.4 million, dedicated on August 1. That summer, Nantucket Police Department appointed its first female police officer, Donna M. Mayo.

Another institution was honored in September, when Walter Beinecke Jr. was given a testimonial at the Nantucket Yacht Club in recognition of his efforts in combining the planning of the new Nantucket with the preservation of its historic heritage.

In one week of November, the founders of three notable Nantucket dynasties passed from the scene, leaving hundreds of mourners on the island. Marie Paradis, ninety, died leaving eight living children, twenty-seven grandchildren, and twenty-six great-grandchildren. Antone Oliver, seventy-nine, died leaving ten children, twenty-nine grandchildren, and fourteen great-grandchildren. Gertrude Holdgate, ninety-five, left seven living children, forty-four grandchildren, eighty great-grandchildren, and fifty-three great-great-grandchildren. That is a lot of Nantucketers!

A man who was known as Nantucket's favorite author of his day, Nathaniel Benchley, died in December. He was remembered for his humorous works with Nantucket backgrounds: *The Off-Islanders* (which became the popular movie "The Russians Are Coming, The Russians Are Coming!"), and the tale of Nantucket's flirtation with secession, *Sweet Anarchy*. His family were long-time residents of Sconset and included his father, the well-known humorist Robert Benchley; his wife Marjorie; and his son Peter, author of the enormously successful novel *Jaws*, which was also made into a movie, parts of it filmed on Martha's Vineyard.

The year that started with a deep freeze, ended with a howling gale that brought high winds and seas and dropped thirty inches of snow in the middle of the Christmas Stroll weekend. Thousands of visitors who arrived on the island for the day had to spend the night. The town opened its doors and found shelter and food for 2,000 stranded people in fur coats and Christmas finery. The weather cleared by morning so everyone went home with another tale of Nantucket hospitality. However, another group of visitors was not so fortunate; seventeen pilot whales stranded themselves on the South Shore during the tempest and could not be rescued, although dozens of whale-lovers and marine-mammal rescuers turned out to help. Unable or unwilling to return to sea, the whales ended their days on Nantucket, like many of their ancestors.

Plans for a 250-room motel and commercial development on Old South Road, presented to the Planning Board by the Nantucket Collaborative, were heard in early 1982 and produced a storm of protest. After several noisy hearings, the plan was denied in May, which provoked a $20-million suit against the town. Without coming to any decision, the issue was finally resolved by the sale of the property to another developer, who replaced the big motel plan with a large residential complex of more than 200 residences on 5,000-square-foot lots. This was eventually approved and became Naushop Village.

Another controversy developed in town when the Sanfords, who owned Old North Wharf, disclosed plans to lengthen and expand the wharf with the addition of more waterfront cottage units. After more protests, the plan was withdrawn. Then the Steamship Authority began construction of immense cement caissons whose bulk seemed to overwhelm the catboat basin. The SSA claimed the new pilings were needed for alternative docking space, and they were erected despite vehement protests from townspeople concerned with aesthetic values on the waterfront. Finally, the Steamship Authority announced plans to reconstruct the entire Steamboat Wharf, aided by a $2.8 million federal transportation grant. The plan was immediately approved and construction went forward.

The Unitarian Church on Orange Street commenced a four-year preservation program in May, calling upon the Nantucket community to help restore the historic structure, which houses the Town Clock. For the first year of the construction phase, the Unitarians held their services in the Nantucket Arts Council's auditorium on the second floor of the Methodist Church.

In October of 1982, the Planning and Economic Development Commission sponsored a public seminar—"Nantucket 2000"—at the Coffin School to discuss the island's future. Planning director William Klein described the growth of the island in the past twenty years, with a 500 percent increase in the number of building lots, a 300 percent increase in passenger traffic, and a 600 percent increase in electricity usage. The best suggestion to come from the session was for a land-transfer tax to fund the acquisition of land for preservation.

In November, Governor Michael Dukakis proved his popularity with Nantucket voters by winning over his Republican opponent by 1,274 to 970. Senator Kennedy also won 1,274 votes to his opponent's 966. Democratic Congressman Gerry Studds won with 1,579 votes. Nantucket had turned Democratic and liberal. In the same election, Nantucket's veteran Register of Deeds, Josiah S. Barrett, after forty-eight years in office, was defeated by his former assistant, Margaret Chase Pignato. After his long career as Nantucket's favorite accountant, surveyor, and civil servant, Si reflected upon his surprising defeat: "That's politics. It wasn't an election, it was a beauty contest." He continued to visit the office on a daily basis.

It was a year for turnover in the office of the police chief. After the long tenures of Chief Mooney and Chief Howes, Nantucket could not seem to settle upon their successor. Over a short period of time the office was filled by Anthony Hopfinger, Paul Hunter, Peter Caputo, and David McCormick—before the selectmen finally promoted Randolph Norris to the office in January of 1984. He was to serve the remainder of the century (but he never found Margaret Kilcoyne!).

August 1982 saw the publication of Robert diCurcio's important and handsome work *Art on Nantucket*. Published by the Nantucket Historical Association in cooperation with the Nantucket Historical Trust and financed by Albert F. Egan Jr., the book displays and discusses Nantucket art and artists from the beginning to modern times and is now a standard reference work.

Major changes in Nantucket government and personnel occurred in 1983. Selectman Bernard Grossman was appointed the Nantucket member of the Steamship Authority, giving him a powerful position in both town and transportation issues. Norman Beach became the Nantucket member of the authority's Finance Advisory Board. The Steamship Authority signed a $5-million contract for the reconstruction of the Steamboat Wharf terminal and broke ground on June 1. The Nantucket Historical Association opened its Museum Shop beside the Whaling Museum with Grace Grossman as manager and founding mother. Robert F. Mooney resigned after twelve years as Town Prosecutor and Assistant District Attorney to devote more time to private enterprises. The principal of Nantucket High School, the much respected Robert H. Diamond, died of cancer at the age of fifty-nine, receiving tributes from his colleagues and students. Nantucket's representative in the state legislature, Arthur S. Desrocher, resigned to take a management position at Massachusetts Maritime Academy in Buzzards Bay—and later returned to serve several terms on the Board of Selectmen.

The Nantucket Jewish community held its first services on the island on July 8, 1983, after which Congregation Shirat Ha Yam (Song of the Sea) was formed, with Morgan Levine as president. Services were held in the newly renovated ground-level meeting hall of the Unitarian Church.

A survey commissioned by the town recommended that the current form of government be retained with an executive secretary appointed to manage the day-to-day work of the office. Over the objection of the incumbents, it was also recommended that the three financial positions of town treasurer, town accountant, and tax collector be appointed rather than elected. These changes were later adopted by town meeting vote.

In the meantime, the building inspector announced that the cap of eighty building permits per year was a flat failure, 461 permits having been issued during the two preceding years. This was alleged because the new law did not apply to existing subdivisions approved within the past five years, as provided by state law. Furthermore, an exemption to the local bylaw was provided for those owners who claimed to be building their principal residence. New owners from Texas and Europe were signing Nantucket residency covenants. Even the proposal to impose the building cap did nothing but accelerate growth, and buildings had increased, not decreased. The number of permits for 1983 was estimated at 216, compared to 221 in the year the building cap was introduced.

Real estate matters were in the forefront of business activity. A survey of local real estate brokers indicated a change in the quality and purpose of the new Nantucket buyers: more young and aggressive people, many from the financial worlds of New York, Texas, and California, looking for quality investments, not homes. Nantucket was definitely becoming a rich man's island, and the first of the million-dollar properties were appearing in the real estate advertisements. There were, however, houses still selling for under $100,000. The real estate boom would continue to 1987, then pause for a few years.

The April 1983 town meeting took up two matters of importance. Near unanimous approval was given to ask the state legislature to permit the town to purchase and preserve land by establishing the Nantucket Islands Land Bank, which would be funded by a transfer tax. This was a major breakthrough, because for years it had been settled doctrine that a town could not go into the real estate business. Now Nantucket was to become the first community in the state to break into the real estate market to preserve its open space. The same meeting rejected a far-reaching plan to rezone the Somerset Road area to permit construction of a 100-room motel and recreational area adjacent to the Miacomet golf course. This plan, by the trustees of 3M Realty Trust, met the same fate as other motels proposed at the airport and on Old South Road, where similar commercial ventures had been turned down. The news was not all bad, for the proposed motel site was later divided into forty-five house lots for island residents who were allowed to purchase homesites at bargain rates, and the golf course itself was sold to the new Nantucket Land Bank for $4.5 million, guaranteeing the island a public golf course forever.

The summer scene in town was one of road renewal, as the selectmen started a project to replace perfectly good paving with cobblestones. The slow and steady work of laying cobblestones left many Nantucketers frustrated while the dust and fill made the downtown area look like a minefield. Opinions differed on the final result, which left Nantucket with more artificially quaint streets and uncertain footpaths. To replace the victims of Dutch elm disease, Nantucket Historical Trust volunteered to plant fifty new hardy specimens along the town streets, while the Garden Club planted 5,000 more daffodils.

The year ended with a loss in the Super Bowl, the appointment of Elizabeth "Libby" Oldham as executive director of the Chamber of Commerce, the most successful Christmas Stroll in terms of weather and revenues, and a White Christmas for the first time in twenty years. None of these events was related.

Great Point lighthouse, a 166-year-old rubblestone structure guarding the northern point of Nantucket, fell silently into the surf one night in March of 1984, a victim of years of erosion on the open shoreline. The U. S. Coast Guard, which had been reluctant to move the old structure, announced it would be willing to build a new one if the money were available. In October, Senator Edward M. Kennedy pushed through Congress a bill to finance the new lighthouse for a cost of $2 million.

A tragic altercation at Madaket Landing in the summer of 1983 produced the first murder trial on Nantucket in a hundred years, in May of 1984. Thirty-year-old Robert Aguiar of Nantucket was charged with fatally shooting twenty-eight-year-old David King of Sconset after a long period of hostility between the two young men. Superior Court Justice John J. Sheehan and a Nantucket jury heard the case over a period of two weeks. The defendant claimed he had fired one shot in self-defense after the victim had threatened him several times. The jury found Aguiar guilty of first degree murder and he was sentenced to life imprisonment. The judge then took under consideration a defense motion and ordered a new trial, at which Aguiar was convicted of a lesser offense and sentenced to a shorter term in prison, which he served. The case left Nantucket with a bitter taste of modern crime and its consequences in the community.

The continuing expansion of town government was marked by the appointment of multiple committees to study varying subjects, from the Dog Pound Committee to the Street Light Inventory Committee. When the newspaper mentioned this "government by committee," of which thirty-two were cited, chairman Bernard Grossman defended the practice as necessary to obtain public input into multiple fields and defended the committee system as valuable to town government.

This was also the year the Nantucket Land Bank would begin its program of purchasing properties to preserving open space on the island. Purchase of the 143-acre Miacomet Golf Course was a popular move, and other acquisitions also helped retain open space threatened by development. The effectiveness of the Land Bank served to quiet some of the previously strident conservation efforts of several private groups.

Expansion of real estate activity in 1985 was still uppermost on the Nantucket scene, with the announcement that the previous year had seen the approval of 508 lots for potential development. The new building inspector, Carl Borchert, started work with 150 applications for building permits on his desk. Among pending developments was the highly controversial plan for twenty-five lots at Woodbury Lane, off North Liberty Street. Such development of this in-town site provoked great opposition and required forty-five public hearings before it won approval. By that time the original developer was in bankruptcy and the banks took over; the lots were sold and houses sprung up quickly in this desirable in-town residential area. Meanwhile, a far more visible development of twenty-five lots on North Pasture Lane went forward, with all approvals for the first large houses overlooking Polpis Road and the moors. Among many descriptions of the local phenomenon, the real estate scene was referred to as "a feeding frenzy."

Meanwhile, the Steamship Authority added to the competition for real estate by purchasing the old Skipper Restaurant property on the edge of Steamboat Wharf for a reported $1.3 million. The old restaurant was immediately condemned as unsafe and torn down, leaving the authority with a convenient but expensive parking lot. The actions of the Steamship Authority were later criticized as wasteful and chaotic by the state inspector general, especially when it turned out that the new Steamboat Wharf reconstruction for $6.8 million was about $3.3 million over budget. Although the state recommended tighter controls over spending for capital projects, the community was happy to see the new project completed and the selectmen backed up the authority and its members for their performance.

In 1985, town meeting went into a spending mode and approved a major project for spending $4.3 million for roads and sewers, $135,000 for construction of a bicycle path to Madaket, and $275,000 for a new fire truck. The Nantucket Housing Authority finally acquired some land at the Navy Base and an additional twenty acres on Surfside Road to construct low-cost housing. The Land Bank purchased sixty-four acres of vacant land on Long Pond for $2.5 million. The Nantucket Conservation Foundation then purchased the 300-acre Sanford Farm adjacent to its Ram Pasture property for a cool $4.4 million, in a joint venture with the Land Bank. The town itself was not immune to the feeding frenzy of 1985.

One highly regarded old friend of Nantucket passed away in June of 1985. Probably the most famous citizen of Martha's Vineyard, Henry Beetle Hough was the legendary editor of the *Vineyard Gazette* for sixty-five years, an author of twenty books, and an outspoken advocate for both islands on political and steamship issues.

In the fall, Nantucket was alarmed by the threat of Hurricane Gloria, which promised high winds at high tide, forcing the evacuation of many waterfront homes and the boarding up of several store-fronts. The big blow was a total bust, passing harmlessly west of the island and dissipating on the mainland. One final natural onset could not be avoided, as the bluff at Sankaty continued to erode into the eastern shoreline, leaving several homes in danger and threatening Sankaty Light with the fate of her sister beacon on Great Point. By the end of the century, Sankaty Light was still there, but there was no doubt that nature would some day take another of Nantucket's favorite landmarks, unless somebody did something.

Private real estate was not faring so well. The newly renovated restaurant at 21 Federal Street, ready for operation, was struck by a devastating fire on March 21, just before its opening. The fire was determined to be arson, but the culprit was never named. The damage cost the owners an additional $250,000, but the restaurant was restored and opened for business on July 4. The flourishing Pacific National Bank, at the height of its real estate success, purchased the solid brick Folger Block at Orange and Main Streets from Sherburne Associates, for $750,000. The building was to house the booming mortgage-loan office, which would soon disappear in a reversal of fortunes.

One of Nantucket's more colorful public employees left the scene in the spring when Henry E. Garnett retired after fourteen years as janitor of the town building—"senior custodian" by job description. After presiding over his boiler-room operation, where he served coffee and popcorn to all the town employees, he encapsuled the town expansion by its most visible result: "It used to take two weeks to get a bag of rubbish; now you get 'em in a day or two." The growth of the town had taken place under his shrewd observation: "This place went from a nothing operation . . . there was no such thing as an HDC . . . Planning Board . . . Probation Office . . . Executive Secretary . . . the Land Bank . . . and all those secretaries—there's just no room. And now we've got a computer!" He was glad to retire with the observation: "These are all the brains we are working under."

In August, ground was broken for the new lighthouse at Great

Point by ninety-four-year-old Elsie Grieder, who had lived there with her husband the lighthouse keeper in the 1930s.

Marianne Giffin, became editor of the *Inquirer and Mirror.*

At the end of the summer, the famous brick mansion built by Jared Coffin on Pleasant Street, long known as Moors End, was sold for a reputed price of $3.5 million, the highest price paid for a home in Nantucket history. The Nantucket Police Department was expanded from eighteen to twenty-five officers at a special town meeting, and the selectmen were informed by town counsel that there were now thirty-five lawsuits pending against the town, mostly related to real estate. Among other problems, the town had to contract for a car-crushing service to dispose of the reported 1,200 derelicts abandoned on the moors. There were also 103 moped accidents this summer. Problems everywhere.

Nantucket's building boom of the eighties peaked in an unprecedented volume of commercial and public construction in 1986. This was due in part to the five-year building cap, which had limited the number of building permits for housing while leaving commercial buildings untouched by the ban. As a consequence, with air travel increasing by nine percent each year and full employment in the contracting industry, real estate prices were soaring,

The first large commercial development to attract attention was Robert Sarvis's ambitious Nantucket Commons on Lower Orange Street, which proposed several large multi-use structures arranged in what was described as a village concept. This was followed by the proposal to subdivide 360 lots on Old South Road for Cedar Crest Realty, the largest subdivision yet. Both these proposals met with opposition, and the town meeting of 1986 confronted a warrant of over 100 articles, many designed to deter further growth.

The town itself was expanding its real estate ventures. The old Our Island Home on Orange Street was renovated and converted into eighteen apartments for the elderly under the name of Landmark House. Renovation of the old Academy Hill School, built in 1929 and once housing all twelve grades of school, was completed with twenty-seven apartments available for people over fifty-five years of age. Originally planned as co-ops, the apartments were subsequently offered as rental units. Under the stipulations of a ground lease with the town, several of them were reserved for residents of moderate income.

The biggest venture of them all was the proposed new Nantucket High School building, to be constructed on the school property at the corner of Atlantic Avenue and Sparks Avenue at a cost of $28.8 million, a figure substantially above previous proposals but far below the final cost of construction. With a well-organized building committee headed by attorney Wayne Holmes, and the persuasive arguments of the superintendent of schools John O'Neill, the school won the backing of most of the community. It was an ambitious plan, fully developed for many varieties of public use, including a modern auditorium, meeting rooms, and swimming pool. The school was approved with almost unanimous support of the town meeting, which included most of the parents on the island. The vote came at a time when many young parents were employed in the booming construction trades. Once the school was approved, half the town meeting voters went home. It then took six months for the Historic District Commission to approve the exterior design of the school, but eventually construction began.

One more big building finished this year was the 100-room Nantucket Inn at the airport, a resort and conference center on the site of the old Nobadeer Restaurant that was finally built after many failed attempts.

Even as the commercial building boom went on apace, the Planning Board and the Historic District Commission went forward to issue a set of guidelines for large commercial developments on the island. Emphasis was on avoiding mainland-style strip development and large shopping areas and the retention of small-scale business operations, well landscaped and planted to buffer the areas from adjacent neighborhoods, with limited-access roads and limitations on obtrusive signs and advertising.

During the winter of 1986, Nantucketers wintering in Florida got together to have the first Florida Reunion in Port Charlotte, with a good turnout of natives and ex-residents who gathered for lunch and memories. This was a revival of the old reunions of the Sons and Daughters of Nantucket, which started in Boston in 1894 and was to continue for several years in the sunny South. It is unlikely any other town as small as Nantucket could command such a loyal following so far from home.

Two more Nantucket men retired from prominent positions on the waterfront this year: Joseph Lopes, dockmaster at the Nantucket Boat Basin for twenty years, who made hundreds of friends among sports fishermen and yachtsmen, retired, leaving many who missed his smiling personality. He was succeeded by George Bassett Jr., a retired Coast Guardsman, who ran the operation for the rest of the century. On Steamboat Wharf, Malcolm Soverino retired as manager of the Nantucket operation after thirty-three years and was succeeded by Paul Harrington, who also lasted through the nineties. Among the last of the old-timers, retired police chief Wendell Howes, perhaps the most familiar face on Main Street for twenty-three years, died in July at the age of seventy-one.

Life was booming on the beach. In August, a spontaneous beach party on the south shore erupted into the Madequecham Jam, with 3,000 college-age students flocking to the beach for an afternoon of music, surf, and suds. The unorganized party received many complaints from the neighbors and was later banned by the town fathers when it was learned that teenagers were coming from the mainland to share the Nantucket hospitality. However, a month later, Nantucket held its own beach party at Great Point, when the new lighthouse was dedicated by a party of local officials and baptized with a bottle of champagne swung by Senator Edward M. Kennedy.

One aquatic feat noted in September was the accomplishment of a twenty-nine-year-old swimmer named Paul Asmuth, who became the first person known to swim from Nantucket to Cape Cod. He did this thirty-one-mile swim from Nantucket Harbor to Craigville Beach in Hyannis in twelve hours and five minutes.

The Nantucket air scene witnessed two new phenomena this year. Nantucket Cottage Hospital instituted MedFlight, emergency helicopter service from the island to mainland hospitals. The cost of a flight to Boston was quoted at $4,000, and was considered essential to the hospital's emergency operations.

Heavy construction programs on the island, in both the public and private sectors, were making more demands than available manpower could meet. The cost of housing workers becoming prohibitive, many contractors opted to bring workers over daily from the mainland to work on Nantucket. This produced the phenomenon of the "flying carpenters," who arrived from Hyannis or New Bedford each morning, complete with tools and equipment, and flew home each evening after putting in eight hours on Nantucket. Despite the cost of air travel, the contractors found daily travel cheaper than Nantucket rentals, and the practice continued to grow in future years.

In August, the demise of the famous Napoleon willow on Centre Street was ordered by the Nantucket tree wardens, not without controversy. The tree was grown from a cutting of a willow that had reportedly shaded the grave of Napoleon on St. Helena island and had been brought home by a Nantucket mariner. Perched on a curb on Centre Street, the tree had begun to lean perilously into the street and was rotten enough to fall, but it was protected by history and sentiment. Finally, the town fathers authorized its removal, and the willow met its Waterloo, but only after several cuttings had been saved for posterity.

This year, the thirty-nine-year career of the Opera House, the distinctive red building on South Water Street, came to an end—sold to a developer of retail space. Pioneering the Nantucket night scene since 1946, the Opera House was host to celebrities, saints, and sinners during the golden years after the war. Hosted by Harold and Gwen Gaillard, its tiny bar and crowded dining room were the place to be seen in Nantucket. Its early years met with some controversy and public disapproval of its lively appearance and tinkling piano, but it soon became part of Nantucket's brightest nightlife, and its departure was deeply felt by many.

The most important story of 1986 came at the end of the year. After announcing in May that he was ready to step down from the management of the full-time operations of Sherburne Associates, Walter Beinecke Jr., at the age of sixty-seven, sold the 160 individual properties of the commercial development company for a reported $55 million. The sale included the Nantucket Boat Basin, the White Elephant Hotel, the Harbor House, and thirty-six retail properties in the downtown area of Nantucket. The buyer was First Winthrop Corporation of Boston, owner and manager of over $5 billion in real estate, mostly in urban areas. The Winthrop organization proudly announced its acquisition of these "signature properties," financed by 2,500 new investors, and credited summer resident K. Dun Gifford with "facilitating the transaction." Walter Beinecke, remembering his simple philosophy of "less is better," repeated his hope that the new owners would carry on with his plans for Nantucket. Thus ended the dramatic venture of Sherburne Associates, which turned the island into the New Nantucket and abruptly disappeared from view on the last day of 1986, leaving the island's future in other hands.

Another familiar Nantucket business landmark passed out of the picture on the final day of 1986. Buttner's, at the corner of Main and Union Streets, had provided Nantucketers with their clothing and household goods for several decades, but fell victim to the rising prices and changing patterns of downtown business establishments. The store was one of a small chain owned by the Buttner family of Plymouth, who were unable to pay the $78,000 annual rent and bear the cost of renovations needed by the old building. After a month of closing sales, Buttner's closed its doors, to be replaced by the

SportsLocker, selling athletic shoes and sportswear in a brighter, trendy environment to a year-round clientele of residents and visitors.

The new year of 1987 was ushered in by three major storms. Heavy snow and ice caused damage that was particularly severe in the Madaket and Dionis areas, where 2,000 people were deprived of electric power for days. One commentator measured twelve inches of snow and called it the worst Nantucket storm since the blizzard of 1952.

As realtors advertised the first of the million-dollar homes, real estate values soared and several developments were going forward. First Winthrop Corporation announced plans to raise $62.8 million, which would include $6.5 million for improvements to its Nantucket properties, by selling $80,000 units to private investors. The plans of Nantucket Commons for a major commercial development on Lower Orange Street were closely watched by public boards and private activist groups. The most obvious changes took place on Sparks Avenue, where the Finast shopping center expanded, adding a drugstore and a liquor store. A new restaurant building would become the SeaGrille, and Sherburne Hall, formerly Odd Fellows Hall on Centre Street, was renovated to become the home of the Preservation Institute: Nantucket. On Beach Street, the family-owned Beachside Motel was sold for $7.7 million to a group that proposed to convert it into a 100-room condominium hotel. Progress seemed unlimited.

Early in the year, the town was surprised to learn that the venerable Wannacomet Water Company, founded by Moses Joy in 1879 and now one of the few remaining private water companies in the country, was up for sale. News that the company had already contracted to sell fifty-three acres of prime land around the water supply area to private developers, without notice to the town, provoked loud public protest and threats of lawsuits. When the town fathers remembered they had the right to take the utility by eminent domain, cooler heads and negotiations resulted in a settlement by which the town purchased the water company and most of its land around Washing Pond.

Another utility undergoing changes was the Nantucket Electric Company, which went through three presidents this year. The final one was Walter Beinecke Jr., recently retired from Sherburne Associates, who promised to move the generating plant from the downtown area and increase its power capacity.

Nantucket's new high school, approved for $28.5 million but stalled by the Historic District Commission and permit problems, was re-voted by the 1987 town meeting to be built for $31.3 million dollars, and ground was broken in the spring. The size of this project, the largest construction project in the history of the island, greatly increased the demand for off-island contractors and workmen, and the daily traffic of workmen flying to and from the island became part of the new Nantucket way of life.

The newspaper reported on the decline of the Nantucket farm scene, once a staple of the Nantucket economy but now reduced to three working farms. The farms of the Bartlett, Gardner, and Slosek families were all that remained. Their owners reported constant proposals from developers.

In July, the new Madaket bicycle path was opened for traffic, adding to the Sconset and Surfside routes. The Nantucket Conservation Foundation bought the Sanford Farm property alongside the Madaket path, thus acquiring very popular and accessible entry to the Smooth Hummocks and Ram Pasture nature preserves and a favorite walking area.

Problems with the summer scene occupied much of the news. In the spring, the annual Figawi Race participants and their followers got out of hand, with drunks and revelers filling the town jail by 6 P.M. This was a town-authorized event, but the Madequecham Jam, a monster beach party, was not. When 3,000 teenagers arrived at the beach with their coolers and surfboards, they were met by state troopers who confiscated the beer and sent them away, while angry neighbors threatened to barricade the roads to defend their neighborhoods. Young and old, rich and poor, all headed to Nantucket.

Perhaps the best news of the year was the disclosure of the enormous charitable gifts made by the will of Oswald Tupancy, who died in May. Mr. Tupancy, known to all as "Tup," first came to Nantucket as a golf pro at Sankaty Golf Club. He left his former golf course property of seventy-three acres along Cliff Road and the north shore to the Nantucket Conservation Foundation and his home at 99 Main Street to the Nantucket Historical Association. His estate combined with his late wife's fortune to establish the Tupancy-Harris Foundation, which would benefit Nantucket nonprofits, including the Cottage Hospital and the Atheneum, for many years to come.

Three admirable senior citizens passed away this year: Ethel Mooney, eighty-two, former nurse and active public figure, died in September; Arthur H. Dean, eighty-nine, distinguished lawyer, diplomat, and conservationist, died in November; and a grand old Nantucketer, Charles Clark Coffin, eighty-seven, town clerk for thirty-five years, died in February.

In October, the Women's Bar Association inaugurated the much-needed service of Safe Place, Inc., to provide shelter and assistance for victims of domestic abuse. In the same month the Oldest House, on Sunset Hill, was struck by a bolt of lightning that almost destroyed the interior while leaving the walls standing; it required a major restoration effort by the Nantucket Historical Association. Almost unnoticed on Nantucket, the New York stock market was struck by another shock wave on October 16 that set off a wave of selling and dropped the market averages by over 500 points in one day. Like the crash of 1929, this "Black Monday" was to have a major effect across the country, and would impact the boom times on the island.

Rising costs and the business slowdown took their toll on Nantucket in 1988. Early in the year, the town announced that it must raise an additional $2.3 million dollars to fund the new school and other town operations. The voters' response was to defeat the necessary override and to cut the town budget by $1.2 million. Then it was announced that the annual budget for the new school department operations would come to $5 million. A heavy voter turnout at town meeting gave the town its operating funds but turned down any new projects. In a nonbinding referendum, a majority of the voters approved a proposal to limit further growth.

While some business projects were going forward, others were in trouble. The elegant new Wauwinet hotel opened in July after extensive renovations and upscaling of the operation. Steamship traffic was reported to be up by forty-five percent. The Sanford brothers announced plans to enlarge and improve Old North Wharf by restoring it to its 1838 configuration, a proposal that immediately drew complaints from neighbors.

By the end of the summer, several Nantucket business operations were in the news and none of it was good. The new Beachside Motel, bought and renovated for millions, closed its doors in November. The Westender restaurant in Madaket was under fire from the neighbors while trying to expand its business against public and legal opposition. The new 100-room Nantucket Inn planned to close for the winter. The real estate bubble was beginning to burst.

Among several reasons for the business downturn was the stock market decline of October 1987, which caused many potential Nantucket visitors to curtail their expenditures, particularly in real estate. This led to a slump in local real estate prices and sales. A major tax reform bill in 1986 had taken effect, drastically limiting the deductions available for speculative real estate ventures, depreciation guidelines, and other features that had made real estate investment popular. A general real estate slump across the country was not only felt but accelerated in Nantucket. During the building boom of the early eighties, Nantucket experienced an excess of commercial construction, resulting in many establishments with "For Rent" signs in their windows. Amid this scene, Nantucket welcomed the new Democratic candidate for the Presidency, Massachusetts Governor Michael S. Dukakis, who came to the island for several days in June. Dukakis and his wife had honeymooned on Nantucket and were very popular on the island. Dukakis was then at the peak of his national popularity and was considered several points ahead of his rival, Republican candidate George Bush. The prospects of a Summer White House in Nantucket were promising until November, when Nantucket's favorite candidate went down to defeat in the Republican sweep of forty states.

At the end of the summer, another Nantucket favorite was honored when the Chamber of Commerce awarded its Business Person of the Year accolade to Pacific National Bank president Henry Kehlenbeck, jovially known as "Hank the Bank." This was a tribute to his successful management of the bank during the best years in local history and his dedicated work on many civic and charitable projects.

Faced with state and federal mandates, the town finally made a move to manage its growing rubbish problem. The old Madaket dump, where all island trash was dropped and burned for many years under the casual management of Andy Lewis, who only needed an iron rake and a book of matches to do the job, was now an environmental disaster. Only after much discussion, town meeting in November voted to approve a trash compacting operation at the newly named Nantucket Landfill Facility.

After a trying year, Nantucket celebrated in December with a hugely successful Christmas Stroll, said to be have brought $3 million to the island.

The difficult times of the previous year led to increasing tensions and public controversy in 1989. Constant conflicts with development plans and attempts to regulate building on the island had by this year embroiled the town in 141 lawsuits, mostly involving the Planning Board, building inspector, and the Conservation Commission. The expansion of town activities saw an agenda listing forty-one committee meetings in February. A sewer-connection moratorium was ordered to hold the waste problem under control until the sewage-treatment plant could be built, but this only inspired more legal action from desperate home builders.

It was announced that tourism to the island was off by twenty-five percent, and steamship revenues were down for the first time in years. With real estate sales lagging, the realtors proclaimed this was a buyer's market, but there were few takers. Instead, the banks became cautious on mortgage lending, and the island saw the first foreclosures on real estate in many years. Most of the foreclosures were levied on speculative properties, but some overextended home-owners were badly hurt.

In the fall, the national auction firm of Larry Latham announced the production of a Nantucket Showplace Auction to advertise and sell island real estate over a Nantucket-only television network beamed at a national audience. This was described as a means to "jump-start sales" on the island, but it failed as only one property was sold. If anything, the publicity and dismal results only served to lower the prospects for Nantucket property.

Under such circumstances, the voters of the town went to town meeting with only one thing in mind. They quickly defeated thirty-four ballot items designed to restrict or increase the cost of building on the island. They denied a move to pledge the town credit behind a $10-million Land Bank bond issue and refused to purchase or take more land at Dionis Beach. They did approve a $9.8-million composting plant at the landfill, a major project required by environmental laws.

A familiar figure returned to the Board of Selectmen when Bernard Grossman was re-elected in a special election, after he had resigned in 1987. He won by a large majority and promised to work to straighten out some of the town's problems.

A new newspaper, the Nantucket *Beacon*, began publishing in March and provided a lively and colorful forum for public and his-torical affairs. Started by Bruce Poor, it was later sold to publisher Ted Leach from New Hampshire.

One noticeable change in the Nantucket employment scene was the increasing number of immigrant workers in the summer industry. Hundreds of young Irish men and women were working all over the island—in the building trades, the tourism businesses, and the banks. They were joined by numbers of workers from the Caribbean islands who found the island jobs appealing. First Winthrop began to employ many Jamaicans in its hotel operations and the two supermarkets soon followed suit. It became clear that the heavy summer business of Nantucket could not be sustained without imported help.

In May it was announced that the old African Baptist Church at the corner of York and Pleasant Streets would finally have a benefactor. The decaying building had long been studied for its historic potential, but this year it was acquired by the Museum of Afro American History in Boston, which promised an ambitious program to restore it as the African Meeting House on Nantucket, a memorial to the rich tradition of the Nantucket black community.

Other institutions were not doing so well. The Nantucket Cottage Hospital announced it was facing an $800,000 deficit, which threatened its existence unless financial support could be found. The Nantucket Historical Association announced the retirement of its executive director, John Newell Welch. Finally, the islanders' favorite restaurant, the comfortable old Mad Hatter on Easton Street, announced it was closing its doors. It had been a rooming house, a bed-and-breakfast, and a cocktail lounge, where Nantucketers remembered Happy Hour drinks for forty-nine cents each, but it had developed into a friendly and popular restaurant for the Nantucket crowd, open every day but Christmas. Purchased by Sherburne Associates and First Winthrop, it was ordered closed by the new owners so it might become part of the Harbor House conference center. It never happened. With its closing, Nantucket lost one of its best.

Thus ended a year and a decade, on a solemn note, made even more so by a blast of freezing weather in December that put a chill on everyone.

The later years of the eighties had proven that Nantucket was not immune to national forces, that prosperity was not endless and good times did not last forvever. It was time to pause and plan for the future.

243

Bill Macomber wrote the book on diplomacy: *The Angels' Game.*

William B. Macomber
MR. AMBASSADOR

BILL MACOMBER REPRESENTED THE BEST OF AMERICAN life and culture before he retired to continue an active and valuable retirement in Nantucket, becoming widely admired for his contributions to the life of the island.

Born in Rochester, New York, he graduated from Yale during World War II, going from the Yale football team into the U. S. Marine Corps. After earning graduate degrees, he moved to Washington, working in the State Department and on Capitol Hill. The State Department was headed by Secretary John Foster Dulles, and while working for him Macomber met his future wife, Phyllis, who was Dulles's private secretary. He also impressed the future president from Massachusetts, who in 1961 gave him his first diplomatic appointment as ambassador to Jordan. Macomber eventually served under five U. S. presidents, finishing his career as Richard M. Nixon's ambassador to Turkey.

Bill and Phyllis Macomber investigated the possibility of retirement on Cape Cod, but found it "too crowded," so they followed their Rochester friends to Nantucket where they settled on Monomoy Road, in an expanded cottage full of books and memorabilia. There, in his study surrounded by photographs of presidents, foreign dignitaries and secretaries of state, Bill wrote his book on diplomacy, entitled *The Angels' Game*, which soon became a handbook for American diplomats. Then he was persuaded to accept the position of president of the Metropolitan Museum of Art, where he skillfully managed the nation's most prestigious museum for another eight years.

Finally retiring to Nantucket in 1984, Bill could not be idle. He offered to teach history at Nantucket High School, where he also coached the junior varsity and helped develop one of Nantucket's best teams, saying, "The kids made the coach look good." Although he enjoyed working with young people, the career change to teaching cost him membership in the *Social Register*. He taught from 1986 to 1991, when he retired for health reasons.

Bill Macomber looked upon island life as an opportunity for retirees to contribute to the needs of Nantucket. He was elected to the School Committee, served on the boards of the Artists' Association, the Historical Association, Theatre Workshop, and the Nantucket Atheneum, always giving active service and sound advice. He saw the greatest need of the island to be planning and constructive improvement of an outmoded system of government, a recognition that Nantucket's future was in the balance, to be carefully safeguarded. With few exceptions, the island's retirees had the time and talent to help out, and should learn that to enjoy the island fully, one should contribute to its life. Certainly Bill Macomber showed the way.

By the season of 1966, Vito had become a builder of winning teams, and of young men.

Vito Capizzo
A COACH WITH CHARACTER

WHEN VITO CAPIZZO BECAME COACH AT NANTUCKET High School in 1963, he arrived to find a discouraged squad of fourteen boys wearing leather helmets and playing a four-game schedule. The School Committee was considering dropping football as a useless and expensive program. Within three years, Capizzo produced an eight-game undefeated season that set Nantucket on the way to football fame. By the end of the century, Capizzo was recognized as one of the outstanding coaches in Massachusetts, with over 250 victories, and Nantucket High, the smallest football-playing school in the state, was a perennial powerhouse.

Capizzo was born in Sicily in 1940, and immigrated with his family to Natick, where he excelled in football and hockey, which led him to a scholarship at Alabama and the start of a teaching career. He soon developed his own philosophy and methods of coaching: "These kids want some discipline in their lives . . . they want to be winners." Using the colorful language of his native land, he provided the discipline and demands to learn his system: "You don't want to do it my way, you sit down and watch the game!" As athletic director, he also recruited boys for his team, gave everyone a chance, and never cut a player from his squad. He mandated their grades and behavior, and managed the complex problems of travel to and from the mainland: "No more time outs—we have to catch the boat!"

Football demands long hours of practice. Fortunately, the Nantucket Boys Club started an early program to begin training boys from the age of seven, matched for size and talent, learning the basics of the game. From the midget to the junior league, they moved up to weekly games, using the high school system. From this incubator of talent, players moved into Capizzo's varsity high school teams, ready for action.

The entire Nantucket community responded to the fall programs with enthusiasm. Home games were crowded, lights were installed-for night games, and hundreds of fans followed to attend the mainland games, Nantucketers often outnumbering the home-team fans. Despite Nantucket's many appearances in their division Superbowl games, the climax of the season is always the inter-island rivalry with Martha's Vineyard—the Harvard–Yale of high school football. The island game was described by Charles McGrath, sports editor of *The New Yorker:* "The game is a celebration of small-town high school football, played there in a simpler and purer form."

Like the game itself, Vito Capizzo became a tradition on Nantucket. He gave the island winning teams and showed the local boys how to become winners. Even more important, he gave the island a sense of pride, purpose, and school spirit.

The Grossmans were active in many sectors of Nantucket life.

Bernard and Grace Grossman

A COUPLE OF GOOD CITIZENS

WHEN THE GROSSMANS MOVED TO NANTUCKET IN 1965 after a successful career in the financial and social world of Boston, they could have retired to a life of ease on their Polpis farm. Instead they elected to become active in the public and cultural sectors, contributing their talents and means toward improving the island's quality of life.

Bernard Grossman was the man to see for any public or charitable project, and he actively promoted many good causes, including the founding of Landmark House, development of the Academy Hill School housing, and the Small Friends child-care center. His private office on Federal Street was practically an annex of town government as he served on the Conservation Commission, the Civic League, the Steamship Authority, and three terms as selectman. Proudest of his many humanitarian achievements was his term as president of the Nantucket Cottage Hospital, where he started the visiting physicians program. His assertive and determined style accomplished more than anyone else in his day.

Grace Grossman, a power in her own right, is respected as a charming hostess and unstoppable fund-raiser for good causes. She willingly took on the financial problems of the Nantucket Historical Association and founded the Museum Shop to increase its revenues, then became a major force in raising over $3 million for the Atheneum building campaign. She was appointed by the governor as a trustee of Cape Cod Community College, and was chairman of the fund-raising campaign that produced $3.5 million and averted its financial crisis. Upon the death of her husband in 1996, she succeeded to his position on the Steamship Authority, dealing with its many problems with energy and determination. Working endless hours in the public interest, without compensation, her energy and dedication deserve the only possible accolade: Amazing Grace.

In a quiet town, Ted's ability to instruct reached as far as his booming laugh.

Rev. Edward B. Anderson

THE PEOPLE'S PREACHER

AFTER SERVING A QUARTER CENTURY IN THE PULPIT OF THE Unitarian Church, the Rev. Ted Anderson's reputation stood as high as the church tower, which houses the town clock. For islanders and visitors alike, he reached out beyond the usual confines of the parish ministry to make people welcome and play a part in the community. His booming voice and hearty laugh were only part of the style of this intellectual with the common touch.

Ted Anderson came to Nantucket with degrees in divinity and education from Yale and Harvard, with additional training in history and archaeology. Once in Nantucket, he became part of the island life, working at his ministry but finding time to take part in building and scalloping. He also became active in community life, teaching, preaching, and serving on the School Committee for six years. His sermons often reflected his varied commitments to local issues of education, conservation, and town government, and he did not hesitate to take stands on controversial issues.

But it was the outgoing personality and humanity of this man that marked his tenure in Nantucket. With his patriarchal beard and his checkered shirts, he reached out to everyone, whether in church, in the hospital, or on the street. The young and the old, the rich and poor, were welcomed as friends and remembered his warmth. He not only performed hundreds of happy wedding ceremonies but managed several happy funeral services.

With a variety of interests in his retirement years, Ted Anderson hoped to return to teaching, qualifying his plans for the future with his experience of the past. With a burst of sound and spirit, he marked his retirement from the church and the arrival of the new century by ringing out the last hour of 1999 on the old Portuguese bell in the Old South Tower, a fitting salute shared with the entire community.

Top: An important restoration of the African Meeting House was completed by the century's end.
Bottom: This scene from a 1992 storm video shows the sea destroying a cottage in Codfish Park.

The decade of the nineties had everything: a short and successful war in the Persian Gulf, the breakup of the Soviet Union, a decline in foreign terrorism and a rise in domestic terrorism, guns, and violence. The Cold War ended and global warming began. The wonders of the Internet brought the worldwide web into millions of homes. The peace process brought hope to Northern Ireland and the Middle East. Through all of this economic progress and financial boom times, Nantucket sailed along to the end of an extraordinary era.

Here Comes Everybody

At the beginning of the new decade, statistics that showed the results of the past revealed an uncertain future for the island to contemplate. The population figure for 1990 was 6,600 year-round residents having a median income of $41,600 per household and owning a home with a median value of $290,000. Despite the fact the building boom of the eighties having slowed to the point where only seven new permits were issued in the month of January, the cost of houses continued to increase, resulting in an "affordability gap" for Nantucket residents. The shrinking real estate market resulted in more affordable homes, but unemployment existed in the building trades and jobs were scarce. The slow summer of 1990 was followed by worse news for Nantucket fishermen when the price of scallops dropped to $4.50 a pound.

By 1990, the entire east coast was feeling the effect of the banking crisis that had started in the southwest when several federal banks and savings and loan companies failed after a heady period of speculative investments and under-performing loans. Federal regulators demanded that banks begin to collect their debts and tighten their credit policies. On Nantucket, the newspapers began to carry foreclosure notices, new businesses were closing shop, and automobile sales, a good indicator of local prosperity, were off. In the fall, it was recommended that the town begin to cut services and eliminate nonessential personnel.

In this atmosphere, the response was to increase regulation of the town's growth by utilizing matters of public health to restrict development, which took the form of increased restrictions on septic systems that required larger lots, smaller houses, and a moratorium on sewer hookups. The fee for a sewer connection was raised to $2,000. Forewarned of the new restrictions, three major landowners filed subdivision plans to avoid the regulations. and noisy hearings were held to protest the actions of the selectmen as the Board of Health. It was announced that the zoning bylaw had been a failure so far as growth was concerned, the law itself was a confused mess, and that all attempts to regulate the island's growth had only resulted in a flood of lawsuits—results that were accentuated by the disclosure that the town's legal bill for 1989 was $589,000.

In March, the venerable *Inquirer and Mirror* was sold to Ottaway to become part of the thirty-four mainland newspaper chain, thus ending island ownership of the 169-year-old newspaper. The sale price was never disclosed, but was rumored to be around $2 million. The sale brought the *Inquirer and Mirror* into a newspaper empire that included the Cape Cod *Times* and the New Bedford *Standard Times*, both former competitors for Nantucket news.

April brought the first showing of "Wings," a new television comedy with a Nantucket connection. Opening shots featured the Nantucket airport and other familiar island scenes, but the sitcom, centered around the owners of a commuter airline and other denizens of the airport, was filmed in a Hollywoood studio. It soon spread the Nantucket name across the country and sent summer visitors seeking to find the location of the fictional "Tom Nevers Field."

This summer another famous name was launched from Nantucket when the first Nantucket Nectars went on sale. This juicy enterprise was the product of the "long winter of 1990," when Tom First and Tom Scott spent the dreary months concocting a variety of fruit juices into a vendable product, with the first bottling done on the island. They eventually expanded into a major bottling enterprise and a nationally distributed product, carrying the Nantucket name across the country. Not bad for a couple of Juice Guys.

On March 1, the island was saddened by the death of Mildred Jewett, 82, the legendary "Madaket Millie," honorary Chief Warrant Officer, guardian of the Coast Guard's West End Command. The selectmen named a bridge in her honor after her ashes were scattered in Madaket Harbor.

Constant erosion on the south shore brought three cottages at Cisco to the water's edge. Unable to be moved, two were claimed by the sea and one of them was torched by the Fire Department as a drill for the firefighters. In an interesting test of historic preservation, a grand old mansion at 17 Lincoln Avenue was demolished rather than restored. The property had been acquired in 1987 for $2.2 million by the Pittsburgh philanthropist Richard Mellon Scaife, who planned to restore it and add a cupola. When the Historic District Commission denied the cupola, Scaife scrapped this project and purchased Walter Beinecke Jr.'s nearby property for $4.4 million. The old house remained as an eyesore to the neighbors for two years until the owner had it demolished—this time with the permission of the HDC.

By the end of the summer, it was reported that real estate sales had slumped by thirty-eight percent in Nantucket, the average home price had dropped to $412,000, and the median-priced home was down to $315,000. Many houses were selling for less than assessed value and Land Bank revenues were off considerably.

Town facilities continued to expand. The selectmen agreed to purchase a laundromat property on Washington Street for the marine and building departments at a cost of $450,000, which was considered to be a bargain price. The cost of the proposed composting plant at the landfill was raised to $13 million, and the Airport Commission announced plans to undertake a $2.2-million renovation of the terminal building. By the end of the year, it was predicted that town expenses would exceed revenues by $2 million, requiring more budget cuts to make ends meet.

In January of 1991, Nantucket responded to President George Bush's call for action in the Persian Gulf against the Iraqi invasion of Kuwait. While several local men and at least one woman were called into service to bolster the military forces, a sizable group paraded through the streets in January in a silent Walk for Peace. Fortunately, the Gulf War ended in February with a victory for the allied forces and there were no more effects on Nantucket other than a steep rise in prices for gasoline and heating oil.

An explosion of a liquid propane tank at the DownyFlake Restaurant on a February morning caused heavy damage to the popular restaurant and also seriously injured the owner, Karsten Reinemo, who was pulled out of the building by local police officers. He was flown to a Boston hospital for treatment and recovered, but the DownyFlake never recovered its location; it went on to quarters at Children's Beach and eventually settled on Sparks Avenue, where its popularity is undiminished

The cost of town government having soared from $14 million to $26 million in the past six years, the voters, beset by rising prices and a slow economy, went to town meeting in the spring and promptly defeated five spending referendums. The town continued to search for more laws to preserve its environment, resulting in eighteen Nantucket bills filed in the legislature. Despite the island's declining fortunes, its legal bill was up to $666,597 for the previous year.

In May, the Nantucket Atheneum reported its accreditation as a certified public library by the Massachusetts Board of Library Commissioners, bringing the town into the mainstream of public libraries. This made the Atheneum eligible for state and federal grants, building construction funds, and access to interlibrary loans from libraries across the state and nation.

The weather blew in on 1991 with two big storms of hurricane force that gave little or no warning of their severity. In August, a tropical storm named Hurricane Bob struck the island with winds up to 102 miles an hour, but no rain. Coming while the trees were in full leaf, the winds toppled dozens of mighty trees, including a stately elm in the Atheneum garden. The wind carried salt spray that scoured the treetops, leaving them dry and brown, some of them permanently damaged. At the end of October, an unusual combination of ocean storms and extremely high tides united to create the "No-Name Storm," which had eluded the hurricane forecasters and which meteorologists labeled a "perfect storm," later to be dramatically recounted in the book by Sebastian Junger that was later made into a hit movie. Hitting the island on October 30, the storm brought unusually high tides surging ashore all along the waterfront, smashing against the cottages on the wharves and creating havoc in the boat basin. Waist-deep waters flooded the waterfront streets and at Brant Point; boats were driven ashore on Washington Street and cottages were demolished on Old North Wharf. It was reckoned the storm damage amounted to $30 million in the worst storm to hit the island since 1908. Small consolation that the disaster was a boon to the construction industry, as every man and piece of equipment was soon fully employed in cleaning up and repairing the damage, which took a year.

Despite the storms and the depressed summer season, there were some signs of a real estate revival. Buyers took advantage of lower prices for Nantucket property—down about twenty percent—and came back into the market. Real estate agents were advertising houses for $2 and $3 million, but most were selling well under $300,000. Reported sales increased by forty-four percent, the average house selling for $281,000 and the average lot going for $70,000.

In August, the Atheneum helped to celebrate the 150th anniversary of Frederick Douglass's appearance in the library's Great Hall at an anti-slavery convention in August of 1841. It was the occasion of the first speech to a white audience made by the great black American orator and statesman. The Unitarian Church joined in the celebration by sponsoring a performance by Fred Morsell, an accomplished actor who vividly portrayed Douglass through his own writings and speeches. The performance was a benefit for the newly recognized African Meeting House on Nantucket, which would begin a restoration project that year.

The Atheneum sponsored a live and lively speaker in September, when it inqugurated its fund-raising campaign with an event at the Harbor House, hosted by the Friends of the Atheneum. The nationally famous NBC television host and longtime summer resident John Chancellor delivered a stirring address on world events, launching the Atheneum's series of public speakers with popular appeal.

Among local celebs, Elizabeth "Libby" Oldham announced in September that she would retire in March as executive director of the Chamber of Commerce after twelve years; Joseph "Mac" Dixon retired after thirty-five years of directing and playing in hundreds of productions for the Theatre Workshop; and former Ambassador William "Bill" Macomber, previously retired from a career in the state department, now retired from teaching history at Nantucket High School.

For the first time, the newspapers acknowledged the wedding phenomenon in Nantucket, hundreds of brides and grooms finding the island just the right place for gala nuptials. Every weekend in the fall saw dozens of well-dressed young people rushing to local churches, shrines, and natural sites for elegant nuptials, which became an important part of the off-season economy. (In 1999, it was reported there were thirty weddings on the Columbus Day weekend.)

Nineteen ninety-one was the year the long-discussed issue of pond openings was finally resolved after much waste of time and money. The large freshwater ponds of the island—Hummock, Miacomet, Long, and Sesachacha—were all separated from the ocean by narrow barrier beaches. In a centuries-long practice dating back to the island's Native Americans, Nantucketers were accustomed to opening the ponds each spring to freshen the water quality and relieve flooding on the lowlands. The practice involved digging a channel through the barrier beach, which state environmental laws had prohibited since 1981. On Nantucket, a solitary activist, Steve Scannell, took it upon himself to open the ponds. One by one, he began to dig channels across the beaches, eventually opening several ponds until he was stopped by police officials. Scannell went to court several times, was warned to stop, but continued to dig. After every arrest, he lost his shovel and his case to save the ponds. He was sent to jail in Barnstable but never gave up. In 1991, after a Pond Opening Committee had spent $200,000 on environmental surveys, the state abandoned its position, permitting Nantucket ponds to be opened to the sea, thus restoring the ponds and vindicating Steve Scannell.

By the end of 1991, the Christmas Stroll was working in reverse, as hundreds of Nantucketers began flocking to Hyannis to do their Christmas shopping. The phenomenon of the island families, who could not afford to shop in their own town, was greatly appreciated on Cape Cod. "They really mean business . . . they know what they want and come to get it," was the Cape merchants' refrain. Loaded with shopping bags and hamburgers, Nantucketers proved to be great customers for the mainland stores, their shopping sprees ending only in fear of missing the last boat or plane home.

Three more prominent citizens passed away this year. In April, a plane crash took the life of U. S. Senator from Pennsylvania John Heinz, fifty-two, a highly regarded summer resident of Hulbert Avenue. His neighbor, Alexander "Sandy" Craig, seventy-three, former president of Nantucket Cottage Hospital and the Nantucket Chamber of Commerce and veteran member of the Airport Commission and Steamship Authority, passed away in July. The last of Nantucket's "old time" doctors, Wylie L. Collins, ninety-two, died in October. Three good men who made their mark on Nantucket and were sorely missed by many.

Business began to pick up early in 1992 and there was a general feeling the worst of the economic woes were over. Five restaurants changed hands, houses were more affordable, and the prices for commercial property was much lower than in the peak times four years earlier. At the airport, a new $2.2-million renovation project was completed, giving Nantucket a bright new terminal building. Two commuter lines, Nantucket Airlines and Island Airlines, competed for the lucrative Hyannis route, flying airplanes every fifteen minutes to handle the steady traffic. Many of the passengers were tradesmen, off-island workers flown over to work on public and private projects as it was more economical for contractors to do that than to provide housing for them on the island. Local workers in the building trades found that there were plenty of jobs to go around.

The Pacific National Bank, beset by the troubles of past years, announced a public sale of 1.6-million shares of stock, which was quickly absorbed. The proposed $3.3-million Polpis Bicycle Path was announced. Real estate sales climbed by thirty percent, the average house going for $304,000. Dependent on almost nothing but the weather, the Nantucket Boat Basin announced it had ninety-eight percent occupancy that summer.

The summer of 1992 saw thirty-four art galleries operating in town; fourteen religious services; theater companies flourishing at several locations; movies at the Dreamland, the White Dog, and the Siasconset Casino; the scenic presence of the Figawi Race, the Opera

House Cup, the Swan Regatta, and the Iron Man Race. Nantucket's most popular spectator sport, the Demolition Derby, also served to remove dozens of junk cars from the scene forever. There was something for everyone.

Nantucket went to the polls in November and elected President Bill Clinton by a vote of 2,030 over incumbent George Bush, who tallied 1,153 votes. An unusually large (for Nantucket) number of voters—4,227—were counted in the Democratic column, giving the popular Congressman Gerry Studds 3,184 winning votes.

Spending by the town on capital projects in the eighties had now tapered off, with the town debt standing at $48 million. The papers commented on the "binge" of the eighties and the expansion of town payrolls, which were defended by the town fathers as necessary to comply with state laws to bring town government under more professional management. Amid the turnover in executive secretaries and finance managers, the selectmen did dissolve eight outdated and unnecessary boards.

After a well-financed campaign by beachfront owners, town meeting went along with a program to restrict access that called for an annual fee of $20 for personal cars and $200 for rental vehicles—a controversial measure that aroused the ire of many Nantucketers who claimed vehicle access as a right.

One Nantucket institution made progress when the Atheneum announced the appointment of a new library director: Charlotte Maison was selected to succeed Barbara Andrews, who was retiring as only the sixth librarian in the history of the Atheneum. Maison announced plans for a $3-million restoration and renovation of the historic 1847 library building. A complete renovation would provide for structural and public safety, access for the disabled, restoration of the historic Great Hall, and a bright new children's library. The project to give Nantucket a modern public library and restore the heart of downtown Nantucket met with universal approval.

In the summer, the prolific Coffin family held a reunion on the island attended by over 300 family members. Plans for restoration of the African Meeting House at Five Corners were announced at a ceremony attended by local officials and followed by a rousing gospel concert in the high school auditorium. The historic structure was purchased in 1989 by the Museum of Afro American History in Boston. Local support for the project would be promoted by the newly formed Friends of the African Meeting House.

One tide that could not be stopped was the big storm that came as a powerful northeaster on December 11–13, which flooded the downtown streets again. Heavy surf pounded the eastern shore, where four cottages were swept out to sea from the bank at Codfish Park, a scene captured on video by photographer Rob Benchley. Nantucket was again reminded of its fragile perch on the edge of a powerful sea.

The Nantucket building boom resumed in 1993; 1,080 building permits had been issued in 1992 and 797 in 1991. Single-family houses under construction were larger and more expensive than ever before, a fact attributed to higher land costs and more affluent home-builders. This year several major residential developments were under construction and finding ready buyers. Among them were the Old South Road spread at Naushop, building "A town out of town," with 198 lots affordable at $50–70,000; Fishers Landing on Madaket Road, with eighty-seven "very attractive lots" at $95,000; and Woodbury Lane in town, with twenty-four lots and several impressive new homes. Not many more subdivisions could be developed, as the Planning Board had approved only forty-three new lots the previous year. The real news was the size and expense of the new houses.

Other building sights were to be seen: After a ten-month battle with the Historic District Commission, the Wannacomet Water Company obtained approval for a 2.9-million-gallon water tower atop its hill on the north shore; thirst and gravity won the battle. Plans for a new animal hospital on Crooked Lane were revealed, with a 7,800-square-foot building and a fifty percent increase in boarding capacity. The town finally agreed to go forward with its plans for a $9.5-million trash-composting plant. The Nantucket Electric Company announced that it would remove the existing generating plant and replace it with an underground cable from Harwich to Nantucket at an estimated cost of $28 million. Big projects were sprouting everywhere.

Other real estate was not doing so well. At Codfish Park several homes were still endangered by the erosion from last winter's storm. At Cisco, houses were toppling over the bluff, undermined and impossible to move. Steady erosion at Sankaty Head was a growing concern for all the homeowners along the bluff and resulted in several ambitious proposals to save the shoreline.

Nantucket lost two popular citizens in March as two brothers died within a week. Walter Barrett, seventy-five, a genial operator of the boat to Tuckernuck, veteran fireman, and member of the Planning Board died on March 20. His elder brother, Josiah Barrett, eighty-six, longtime town accountant, register of deeds, and surveyor, died on March 26.

Amid much controversy, the town meeting of 1993 defeated a proposed Domestic Partnership article to permit the registration of unmarried couples of either gender and allow them to share employment benefits. The vote against the proposal was 455 to 186 but the issue was to come back in later years. One indication of the change in island sentiment was the arrival in July of the cruise vessel *SeaSpirit* with ninety allegedly gay travel agents on board who came to survey the island's attitude toward alternate life styles. Nantucket was available to everyone. In August, the newspaper advertised the existence of fourteen self-help organizations, providing meeting places and services for everyone from alcoholics to potential suicides.

Environmental concerns led to the closing of Great Point to automobile traffic from June through August, which brought howls of protest from fishermen and drivers of sports vehicles. The issue focused on a small bird, the piping plover, which had once been a popular target for small-game hunters but was now an endangered species that nested in tire tracks. The issue continued to dominate the press as bird lovers now pitted themselves against beach lovers and surfcasters, while the perky little plovers were caught in the middle all summer.

On July 15, the Nantucket Atheneum launched its summer season with an outstanding lecture by author and historian David McCullough on the subject of his Pulitzer Prize-winning book *Truman*. Speaking to a capacity audience at the Unitarian Church, McCullough delivered an eloquent and inspiring speech that thrilled the crowd and gave a great boost to the Atheneum's building campaign. Later that summer, famous author and Nantucket resident David Halberstam gave the Atheneum another star performance with a talk on his new book *The Fifties*.

A new Board of Selectmen and a new series of changes in the governance of the town was the order of the day in 1993. The position of executive secretary gradually evolved into an administrative/management position, while the problem of control over the position of finance director—a combination of the old town treasurer, tax collector, and auditor—was more complex. During the year, the town went through three finance directors, bought out one contract for $20,000, and hired a one-month replacement for $10,000. The town was growing, and its problems were growing even faster than the population.

In the fall, the Steamship Authority announced the end of the line for the workhorse vessel *Uncatena* after twenty-eight years of service. Built in 1965 and enlarged by fifty-two feet in 1977, the *Uncatena* was a sturdy but unlovable craft, carrying 650 passengers and tons of freight but sporting blue plastic seats and few conveniences, which earned it the nickname "Junkatena." She was to be sold at auction and replaced by the sleek 1,166-passenger *Nantucket*.

With November, Nantucket's thoughts turned toward its football season, capped by a 7–6 win over traditional rival Martha's Vineyard. The victory marked the 200th career win for Nantucket coach Vito Capizzo, named Coach of the Year in Massachusetts and the Rotary Club's Man of the Year in Nantucket. Faith Oldham was named Woman of the Year in recognition of her contributions to the Council on Aging and on the Finance Committee.

At the end of a busy year, Nantucket paused to remember the well-known island residents who had passed away: the Rev. Frank Pattison, eighty-nine, former Methodist minister; Harold Anderson, seventy-five, island sportsman and conservationist; Captain Jack MacDonald, eighty-seven, one of the last fishing captains; Gilbert Burchell and Gibby Nickerson, popular fishermen; Esther Gibbs, eighty-two, only the second woman to be elected selectman; Clarence Wilson, ninety-one, friendly face from Sconset; Edouard Stackpole, eighty-nine, highly esteemed Nantucket historian; and Judge C. George Anastos, seventy-six, former presiding justice of the Nantucket District Court. All were highly regarded citizens of the town, and their passing was a loss to the community they served so well.

The opening month of 1994 was marked by intense cold and ice, and it was claimed to be the coldest January in memory. The port of Hyannis was frozen in for weeks, requiring service from Woods Hole to the two islands. Electric heating bills soared while morale slumped on the island. The economic upswing of 1994 was marked by increasing values in the Nantucket real estate and construction businesses. Local banks were experiencing a rising tide of business, as the Building Department reported 399 permits for the year, compared with 192 the previous year. The boom was marked by fewer subdivisions but larger and more expensive homes being built in all parts of the island. Even the remote island of Tuckernuck, with no utilities, was being built up with more houses added to the thirty-two already there. One real estate salesman optimistically advertised that there were still homes available on Nantucket for under $300,000. When

265

Daffodil Weekend brought 8,600 visitors to the island to kick off the season, everyone knew things were definitely on the upswing.

Some island entities were not doing well. The venerable Pacific Club, a social organization of more than 100 members, had maintained its traditional ground-floor observation post on Main Street—home of endless games of cribbage and conversation—for over a century. It was now faced with $22,000 in unpaid taxes owed the town, which threatened their ownership of the stately brick counting house built by William Rotch in 1772. The club tried to keep its historic building intact, at a time when every other location on Main Street was turning into a gift shop or T-shirt store. The Egan Foundation sought to lease the building to preserve its historic tradition, but no agreement could be reached.

Meanwhile, the operations of First Winthrop Corporation, the new owner of the waterfront and resort hotels, came under criticism for making changes in the Harbor House operation, closing the Mad Hatter restaurant, and laying off employees. One correspondent called for the island to "Bring Back Beinecke," while another writer lamented that the man who knew Nantucket best had sold out his interests to those who did not. Some of the real estate developers of the eighties found that their ambitious projects were too far ahead of their time and finances. The developer of Nantucket Commons, which was heavily financed in several banks, was accused of bank fraud and convicted in federal court. It was revealed that the Nantucket Land Bank, after leasing 100 acres of land off Milestone Road for five years at $100,000 a year, could not afford to buy the land, now slated for development as Tetawkimmo Commons. The Nantucket Land Council, once an opponent of the project, came to endorse it because it favored fewer, but larger, houses on the moors.

Following the turmoil in town government, which had seen three tax collectors come and go within a year and a long dispute within the planning department, the town seemed to be making improvements. Andrew Vorce replaced the retiring Alan Gordon as Planning

Director, William Macomber was overwhelmingly elected to the School Committee, and Bernard Grossman took over as chairman of the Steamship Authority. Veteran teachers who retired this year were Charles P. Flanagan, after forty-one years of teaching high school, and Nanette Small, with twenty-nine years' service in the elementary schools.

In June, Nantucket Memorial Airport dedicated its Hall of Fame, with a wall display honoring the accomplishments of the six aviators who were Nantucket's pioneers in aviation. They included Jean Adams Shaw, Vice Admiral Marcel Gouin, Captain Parker Gray, Captain David Raub, Lieutenant Alexander "Sandy" Craig, and Lieutenant Allen Holdgate. Holdgate was present for the occasion, the only survivor of the honorees.

The Nantucket business community was changing rapidly: Philip Murray was elected president of the Pacific National Bank, David Worth retired after running the Wannacomet Water Company for thirty years, and the Nantucket Electric Company applied for a twenty-five-mile cable connection to the mainland, running from Harwich to Jetties Beach. The company supplying the power line, New England Electric Systems, also made an offer to buy the Nantucket utility for $3.5 million, offering $125 per share for the company's $50 stock. The results of the offer were predictable.

This was a good year for the Nantucket Atheneum and its plans for restoration of the historic structure. A scale model approved by the Historic District Commission displayed the new children's library, made possible by the Weezie Foundation, a gift of Lucile W. Hays as a memorial to her sister. The Pittsburgh philanthropist Richard Mellon Scaife and his wife announced a gift of $600,000 from the Allegheny Foundation. With this assurance of success, the Atheneum moved into temporary quarters in the Coffin School, under a lease from the Egan Foundation

It was a summer for celebrities: Pierre Salinger lectured on the Gulf War and political issues in August; renowned author, compos-

267

er, and Nantucket home owner Ned Rorem published his new biography; and the popular musician Jimmy Buffett literally dropped into Madaket Harbor in August when his Widget seaplane crashed in four feet of water, leaving the singer bruised but smiling.

Continuing attempts to turn the tide at Sconset were frustrated by the weather. The antierosion measures under way at Sankaty Bluff were frustrated by a northeast storm in August that swept away much of the work in progress. One survivor of all seasons, however, was the plucky little piping plover, soon to become the most controversial bird in island history. During the summer, it was discovered that ten pairs had nested in the tire tracks on Great Point and Eel Point, thus requiring the authorities to close those popular fishing areas to the public at the height of the season. The howls of the jeep owners went unheeded and the island's favorite beach retreats were turned over to the birds for the season.

The ongoing saga of the sixty-nine-year-old steamship *Nobska* continued. The legendary old ship, now owned by the Friends of the Nobska and berthed in Providence, was offered as a passenger-carrying vessel once again, proposing to sail between New Bedford and the islands. Although inspiring much nostalgia, the last of the coastal steamers did not attract the amount of money needed to cover the rising cost of restoration. By the end of the century, she was still awaiting restoration in drydock in Boston.

Perhaps the most illustrative picture of the New Nantucket economy was shown by the many advertisements for services published in the local paper. Island residents were offered accommodations, banquet rooms, caterers, wedding cakes, and tent rentals. All these services were in demand and plenty of entrepreneurs were available to fill the needs of the growing populace.

Nineteen ninety-four marked the tenth anniversary of the Nantucket Islands Land Bank, one of the most successful conservation efforts ever launched. The Land Bank was now a major force, along with the private conservation efforts of the Nantucket

Conservation Foundation, the Land Council, the Sconset Trust, and other such organizations.

The Nantucket Fire Department released interesting figures that showed the growth of that municipal service, which used to be a part-time voluntary outfit. The department now had a budget of $1,034,442 and listed twenty-two full-time men, sixty-five part-time volunteers, and one Dalmatian. The department also handled emergency medical services: 1,088 EMT calls and fifty-three emergency flights off-island.

Every year took its toll, and 1994 saw the passing of several highly respected citizens: In January, Charles F. Sayle Sr., eighty-five, Nantucket's maritime expert, fine craftsman, and Commodore of the Wharf Rat Club; in February, George W. Jones, ninety-two, noted civic leader and twenty-seven-year assessor; and in November, Harry Gordon, ninety, former Ford dealer, craftsman, and beloved citizen died, leaving much of his estate in scholarship funds for Nantucket High School graduates. One of the legendary characters of Sconset, Clement Penrose, eighty-seven, died at his home, proud of his career as founder of the ultrasecret BOF Society and his reputation as "the oldest living continuous summer resident of Sconset."

The year ended on a high note, with a Christmas Stroll described as "just like August," with 450 flights delivering 4,000 airline passengers, and a seaborne invasion of 8,700 visitors on the Steamship Authority vessels. Nantucket had finally extended its season into December.

Expansion and expense were the overwhelming issues in Nantucket in 1995. The population was announced to be 6,794, a thirteen percent increase in the past five years. Everything was headed upward, from the population to the cost of government. The School Department announced an increase of $982,590 in its budget due to increased enrollment. The town budget, stated to be $41.5 million, had quadrupled in the past ten years from $11.6 million in 1985. Capital projects alone resulted in a per-capita debt of $5,371, the highest such debt in the state. Taxes and fees were going up, with the price of a beach-driving permit raised to cover the expense of the Beach Management Plan. Beach driving had been curtailed on Great Point and Smith's Point, frustrating many local sportsmen but stimulating the return of the piping plover, which now returned in force with twenty-seven pairs of happy birds.

Town meeting faced dozens of amendments to the zoning bylaw, which attempted to regulate everything from building sizes to family matters. In general, the forces of conservation were successful, while domestic partnerships were rejected for the third time. Town meetings, once perfunctory affairs, were now stretching into several evenings as voters became involved with more issues on the public scene.

The bigger the business, the bigger the numbers this year. The Nantucket Electric Company, one of the island's long-standing locallyowned enterprises, agreed to a merger with its mainland connection, New England Electric Systems (NEES) in March, for a reported $3.5 million. The old Wannacomet Water Company, now a public-service corporation, dismantled its old black water tower, which had been a landmark on the north shore for eighty-seven years, and replaced it with a sleek gray 415,000-gallon tower, soon to be surrounded by trophy houses on the hills. First Winthrop Corporation, which had bought the Sherburne Associates properties in 1987, sought a solution to its financial problems by borrowing $41 million, then underwent a change in management as it was taken over by a New York real estate partnership, Apollo Real Estate Advisers, which purchased ninety-two percent of its shares.

Winthrop also made news when it attempted to demolish the Mad Hatter restaurant building, a 100-year-old landmark on Easton Street had once been the islanders' favorite restaurant. The Historic District Commission granted the request, but public disapproval halted any action, and the building lasted out the century. Walter Beinecke Jr., who had sold the Sherburne properties to Winthrop, lamented the actions of the Winthrop "absentee owners," and delivered his opinion that the island needed more local control.

One hopeful sign for the island was the purchase of the 250-acre portion of the Henry Coffin farm on the Milestone Road by a group of summer residents with plans to design and operate the Nantucket Golf Club, an eighteen-hole course with the modern facilities demanded by new island residents. The vast project received speedy approval and was soon under way. Entry into cyberspace was announced when the Internet Cafe connected island computers with the latest in modern technology. And the good news from the hospital was its acquisition of a CT-scan to add to its medical arsenal.

On May 26, Nantucket's Hulbert Avenue was the location for a happy event when U. S. Senator John F. Kerry married Teresa Heinz, widow of the senator from Pennsylvania John Heinz. Mrs. Heinz became a benefactor of many Nantucket institutions, and her husband gave Nantucket another powerful voice in Washington.

The news in public transportation was the inauguration of the Nantucket Regional Transportation Authority (NRTA), Nantucket's first municipal shuttle-bus service, with free transportation around the town area for the first year in an attempt to limit automobile use. The buses proved popular, although the traffic did not decline, and were planned for expansion to Sconset and Madaket another year. Complaints from the taxi drivers were heard but not heeded.

Announced in the spring and started in December, the first of the high-speed ferries, the *Gray Lady,* was put in service by the HyLine Corporation. This was a sleek white catamaran that could make the Hyannis run in about an hour, and was to prove quite popular with the traveling public.

Other vessels did not fare so well. In June, the Bermuda-bound luxury cruise ship *Royal Majesty* ran aground on Rose and Crown Shoal, a sandbar east of Nantucket that local mariners had successfully avoided for centuries. This time, a faulty radar fix and a Global Positioning System landed the liner on the shoal, where 1,400 passengers were stranded for twenty-three hours until six tugboats towed her back on course.

The bad news of the season was the spread of Lyme disease on the island, which brought warnings to use extreme care in tick-infested areas. The sea continued to take its toll, with erosion on the south shore taking houses in the Madaket area while officials studied various proposals to save the shoreline. Heavy surf at Surfside resulted in eighteen rescues by the lifeguards in five days of July. Then the island lifeguards, claiming they were overworked and underpaid, went on strike. They were fired and sent home, while the town mustered a skeleton crew of guards to serve through Labor Day, which they did without further casualties on the beach. These problems were not the worst news, however, for Wesley Tiffney, director of the University of Massachusetts Field Station on Nantucket, announced that because of rising sea levels and global warming Nantucket would be entirely under water in 600 years. Time would tell.

The island lost a powerful friend in Congress when U. S. Representative Gerry Studds announced he would retire after twenty-two years in Washington. The island's second newspaper, the *Nantucket Beacon,* announced in October that it had been bought out by Ottaway, the parent company of the *Inquirer and Mirror* and said, curiously, that it would continue to compete with the old paper. In the Super Bowl, Coach Capizzo's Whalers defeated East Boston 40 to 6, the islanders led by their outstanding quarterback and captain John Aloisi. With this victory, the island counted 1995 a very good year.

Nantucket had lost three more respected citizens in 1995: Robert Caldwell, seventy-five, founder of the Nantucket Life Saving Museum and former president of Harbor Fuel Oil Corporation, died in April; Roger J. Roche, sixty, native business executive, died in October. In November, the island mourned the passing of Merle Turner Orleans, eighty-four, daughter of longtime publisher and editor of the *Inquirer and Mirror* Harry B. Turner and herself a writer/editor of the paper from girlhood. She wrote the paper's obituary notices for most of her career, served as president of the Nantucket Atheneum, and loved the island and its wildlife.

The Blizzard of 1996 opened the new year with howling winds and a foot of snow in mid-January. Winds of sixty miles an hour and driving snow virtually closed the town for two days; the schools and public buildings shut down while snow plows worked around the clock, wiping out the town's annual budget for snow removal with $80,000 spent in January. The worst of the storm battered the fragile shoreline at Codfish Park in Sconset, where four seasonal homes were swept away, making a total of six houses lost to the sea since 1991. Along the south shore, Sheep Pond residents were threatened by more erosion as the soft sand washed away the foundations of their homes while the town pondered the problem. One bright light shone through the blizzard as the maternity room of the Nantucket Cottage Hospital delivered three snow babies during the height of the storm, a phenomenon that one commentator blamed on the low barometric pressure that accompanied the blizzard.

Even more wind and energy were expended in connection with the proposed Nantucket Market, a plan to build a 48,000-square-foot shopping center and supermarket on Old South Road. This huge commercial scheme aroused the energy of every antidevelopment and conservation group on the island in reaction to the perfect target: off-island commercial development on a huge scale. The issue occupied much of the year with news stories, public hearings, inflammatory rhetoric, letter-writing campaigns, and "Bag the Market" bumper stickers. The plan never really got off the ground, and the planning board voted unanimously against it. Despite the growing population and crowded summer shopping sites, the defeat of the Market was seen as a victory for the forces of preservation and controlled growth on the island. More and larger houses continued to be built, but the island would not tolerate more business expansion, at least for now.

The April town meeting showed a distinct liberal turn, as the newspaper commented, with big money spent for purchasing the Loring property on Washington Street for $2.75 million and a vote to increase the Land Bank tax to four percent of a property's selling price. The biggest change came in the acceptance of the domestic partnership bylaw, providing benefits for unmarried couples in alternative life-styles, which after three defeats was passed by a margin of two votes.

Changing life-styles resulted in many new problems that were now commonplace on the island, situations that would have been astounding a few years earlier. One survey indicated that alcoholism and drug abuse ranked highest in the public concern, followed by lack of affordable housing and rising crime problems. The police department reported an increase in property crimes and a dramatic rise in heroin use on the island. In April, a drug raid brought fourteen suspects into court, several of them well-known local youths. Two Nantucketers were arrested at the Hyannis airport with $4,500 worth of heroin headed for the island. Another serious statistic was the increase of the suicide rate on the island: with five suicides within the past six years, Nantucket was far ahead of the state average. The new era was not the good old days.

One happy note was the opening of the restored Nantucket Atheneum in April, followed by a dedication of the Weezie Library for Children in May. The success of the $3.3-million renovation of the historic library was celebrated with a formal dedication in the Atheneum Garden on July 6. In an all-American scene, with the Nantucket Community Band playing and the Coast Guard presenting the colors, the library was formally dedicated by a stirring speech delivered by the great American historian David McCullough. It was a day to remember.

With speeches and events in the Atheneum, July brought the anniversary of the Great Fire of 1846, which had devastated the town 150 years before. This was followed by the threat of Hurricane

Bertha in July, which caused pounding surf but little real damage as it swept past the island. Nothing could stop the air travelers, however, as Nantucket Airport set a record on Sunday, July 7, with 1,211 air operations, surpassing Logan Airport with 1,165 operations on the same day. The season was best remembered for its terrible weather, with fog shrouding the island for seventy percent of the summer days.

Nothing, however, could stop the soaring Nantucket real estate market. Fueled by a sizzling stock market surge, Nantucket real estate prices seemed to have no limit. Downtown stores like the traditional Hardy's hardware store, which had served the island's homeowners and builders for seventy-six years, passed out of existence to become the site of six trendy boutiques. A population of about 40,000 summer residents now brought 10,000 automobiles to the island, and needed the services of sixty-seven restaurants. Two members of the Kennedy family bought homes in Quidnet for $1.4 million, and fashion designer Tommy Hilfiger bought a mansion on the Cliff for $4.6 million. The new members of the Nantucket Golf Club were paying $250,000 each for their memberships, and the October sales of real estate reached $58 million. The average price of a house was $538,000. The rising demand for Nantucket real estate was attributed to the galloping stock market and the numbers of successful young corporate executives and professionals buying family homes in a highly desired location. Thirty percent of home sales exceeded $1 million.

Nantucket women were in the news this year. Upon the death of her husband, Bernard Grossman, Grace Grossman was appointed to his place on the Steamship Authority. Following a turnover in the Chamber of Commerce, Maia Gaillard was appointed as executive director, a position once held by her mother, Libby Oldham. In November, following the retirement of Phyllis Visco as Register of Probate, Sylvia Howard was elected to that office in a spirited election.

The November election also produced a new Congressman when former District Attorney William Delahunt was elected to succeed Gerry Studds. The island was consistently electing Democrats to Congress.

Major public projects under way included the long-awaited Polpis bicycle path, in the planning stage for nineteen years and scheduled to be completed in two more; the new animal hospital and shelter, spread over 8,656 square feet on Crooked Lane; and the new $4.2-million recycling plant at the Nantucket landfill, the first in a large complex of environmental improvements in that area. Ground was broken for the restoration of the African Meeting House on York Street, a fine memorial to Nantucket's community of black Americans. The biggest project of them all, the electric cable connecting Nantucket to the mainland, got under way. New England Electric Systems would be the beneficiary of the $33-million extension cord from Harwich, which promised the removal of the old diesel generating plant and two smokestacks that had long been eyesores on the waterfront. The proposed use of this property was under intense study.

Nantucket Nectars, the popular fruit juice bottling business, announced a number of island benefits in the summer of 1996. Founded by two college boys on the Nantucket waterfront, the business had now grown to a $35-million enterprise in 1996. Tom First and Tom Scott, now twenty-nine and thirty, expressed their gratitude to their home base by supporting the Nantucket Film Festival and other island benefits.

Two storms added to the news of Nantucket '96 by timing their arrival for critical weekends. In September, Hurricane Edouard moved slowly up the east coast headed for Nantucket, causing residents to rush for food and supplies, barricade the storefronts, and evacuate the waterfront on the usually profitable Labor Day weekend. The storm hit with eighty-five MPH winds and four inches of rain, driving summer yachts up on the beach and sending thousands of summer visitors home early. Then, on the first weekend of December, the Christmas Stroll was belted with gale-force winds of seventy-five MPH, canceling the Friday boat service and the plans of many strollers. December continued to be rainy and foggy, until the last day of 1996 brought a light snowfall and a white New Year's Eve for the island.

The saddest news of 1996 was the passing of so many good friends and friendly faces from the Nantucket scene. Among the departed this year were Frederick W. Haffenreffer, seventy-five, long-term conservationist and island benefactor, who died in January; Bernard Grossman, seventy-five, who died in March after a lifetime of public service in Boston and Nantucket; Joseph "Mac" Dixon, beloved actor and former director of the Theatre Workshop, who died in March; Manny Souza, fifty-nine, local lobsterman who died at sea in June; John Chancellor, sixty-eight, greatly respected journalist and television commentator, who loved his autumns in Nantucket, died in July; and Paul J. Burns, former Boston attorney and Nantucket resident, passed away in December. It was a year of great losses.

Growing pains were the theme of 1997, as Nantucket faced more and larger problems with its unprecedented prosperity. In January, the National Conservation League listed the island as one of the most endangered communities in the nation, threatened with over-development and environmental dangers. The town launched a master plan to curb uncontrolled development, including attempts to curb the building rights of pre-existing homeowners and restriction of the previously protected right to build second homes on house sites.

Evidence of the town's growth was told in statistics. The town budget was now $45.8 million, mostly composed of $17 million in salaries for 450 full-time and 250 part-time employees, a figure described as "eating up the town." School enrollment rose as many new young families moved to the island, drawn by opportunities in construction and other businesses. Capital requirements included a new $27-million sewage plant on the south shore and $15 million for the Sconset treatment plant. The bicycle path was creeping slowly along the Polpis Road, costing far above its estimates. Bicycle traffic was up, along with road rage, which was the result of increased traffic congestion. During a dedication ceremony for the Polpis path with Acting Governor Paul Celucci officiating, noise from airplanes almost drowned out his remarks. As congestion went up, the trees came down: Nantucket's stately elms were falling victim to Dutch elm disease and were felled by chain saws on downtown streets. Almost everyone had a complaint that summer. Road traffic, air traffic, and finally bird traffic: in the spring a flock of a thousand starlings crashed into the Milestone Rotary, and twenty-five of them met their doom when they were run over by a Nantucket police cruiser. Good thing they were not piping plovers!

There was some good news on Easton Street, where the old Gordon Folger Hotel, built in 1891 as one of the grand dames of Nantucket's big-hotel era, was bought and renovated at a cost of $3.2 million. The previous owners had paid $250,000 for it in 1972. The hotel, which had been named for a longtime owner, was originally called the Point Breeze, suffered through fire and depression, and was now reborn with its original name—a grand revival for a grand old lady.

The new HyLine ferry *Gray Lady II* came into service this year, destined to carry more passengers to the island more quickly, while the Steamship Authority also announced a new $15-million vessel to replace the *Islander*. The city of New Bedford began to take interest in the Steamship Authority, suggesting that the line needed a new port and the city was available. The suggestion of a longer and more expensive route to and from the mainland reminded many islanders of the old days before 1961 when the islands fought to be rid of the New Bedford port. Although the city interest was mainly directed at improving its own lagging economy, the Nantucket *Inquirer and*

Mirror, which had once opposed the idea, on July 3 editorialized in favor of adding the city as a mainland port to increase freight traffic to the islands.

Town meeting opened with a new moderator: Sarah Alger, island attorney, was elected as the first female moderator in history. The meeting also voted to favor a $25-million bond issue for the Land Bank to purchase more property with the backing of the town's credit, thus adding to the public's bonded indebtedness. A proposal to increase the Land Bank tax from two to four percent, however, was defeated in the legislature by strong opposition from the real estate industry and the governor's office.

In June, the Pacific National Bank, which had dominated the financial scene on Main Street since 1818, was sold to the Bank of Boston, now known as BankBoston, in a multimillion-dollar sale of its bank stock. The Pacific Bank, which in 1992 had been listed among 350 of the nation's troubled banks, had sold a private offering of its stock for $9.50 a share in that year; those fortunate stockholders now sold out to Boston for $50 a share, creating several instant millionaires on the island. For the rest of the community, it was seen as another loss of a Nantucket-owned, locally controlled institution. Now the Big Three of the island economy—the electric company, the commercial bank, and the vast real estate holdings of Sherburne Associates—were all controlled by off-island interests.

At the lower end of the street, the Pacific Club gave up its famous view of Main Street when it leased its club rooms for a commercial art gallery on a seasonal basis, to provide revenue to pay its taxes. The Nantucket Historical Association also leased out the 1847 Thomas Macy Warehouse, the old whaling warehouse on Straight Wharf that had been its Museum of Nantucket History; it was turned into a commercial art gallery and helped to solve the association's financial problems.

Big and bigger, the island now had its biggest summer spectacle when the Boston Pops played for the first time on Nantucket. This outdoor concert at Jetties Beach was a big fund-raiser for the Nantucket Cottage Hospital. It attracted more than 4,000 people for an evening under the stars and featured Senator John F. Kerry delivering the Gettysburg Address. The evening was a huge social and financial success.

Smaller but equally festive was the party for the American Ireland Fund at the home of Bob Matthews on Cliff Road; it featured Irish musicians and celebrities including Frank McCourt, author of the best-selling *Angela's Ashes*. McCourt came to the island to lecture for the Atheneum's summer author series, and proved a popular figure wherever he appeared. This summer the island also had its first Island Jazz and Folk Festival, which, added to the Film Festival, the Art Festival, the Wine Festival, the Daffodil Festival, and the Cranberry Festival, gave a new description of the Nantucket summer scene: Infested.

The end of August brought the sad news of the death of Princess Diana, whose passing was felt deeply by persons of all walks of life in every country. The newspaper recalled the passing of the old Bosun's Locker on Main Street by resurrecting a photograph of those celebrities of the sixties gathered on the sidewalk. The airport reported thousands of workers flying in and out of the island every day to work on the many construction projects, while the Historic District Commission complained about the sheer weight of its workload.

The fall was a time for honoring those Nantucketers who had done much for the island. Named Man and Woman of the Year by the Rotary were Alan Newhouse and Grace Grossman. Honored for service to the Maria Mitchell Association were Edith Andrews, Eileen McGrath, Dorrit Hoffleit, and Henry Albertson. More good news was the $350,000 gift of the Gifford family to ensure the new skating rink projected by Nantucket Ice. News that the property assessments of the island had reached $4.3 billion prompted the selectmen to set the tax rate at $5.18, one of the lowest rates in the state. Growth had its benefits.

Not so lucky was the deer population. From the single pair set loose in the twenties, Nantucket deer were now so numerous, and their habitat so encroached upon, the herd had grown beyond reasonable limits. Furthermore, they were carriers of the dreaded deer tick, source of Lyme disease and babesiosis. A remedy was the extension of the deer season to two weeks with the hunters allowed a greater take of does to limit the herd.

Nantucket opened the new year of 1998 with a scene from its past: shore whaling, complete with fresh blubber and sperm oil. The occasion was the stranding of a forty-six-foot sperm whale on the eastern shore of the island, where it died on Low Beach on New Year's Day. Instead of participating in a riotous scene out of the eighteenth century, the Nantucketers of 1998 treated the whale as a respected and endangered species, protected by federal law and supervised even after its demise by state and federal officials. The body of the whale, which could not be handled intact, was carefully dissected and examined for the cause of death, probably the first whale autopsy ever held on the island. Under veterinary supervision, the blubber was removed and the carcass examined, with samples taken for laboratory purposes. Nantucketers were especially happy to collect seventy-five gallons of sperm oil, gathered in buckets from the head case. Workers from the Nantucket Historical Association gathered the bones and teeth of the great mammal, which one day will be a valuable exhibit in the Whaling Museum.

Early in the year, realtors tallied the results of the island's real estate activity for 1997 and announced that sales had amounted to $311 million in the past year, up from $119 million in 1990, the lowest recent year, with twenty houses selling for over $2 million. The average cost of a house on Nantucket was now $475,000.

Professional planners, who came to the island at a cost of $135,000, held a four-day seminar, afterwards announcing that the island could benefit from avoiding uncontrolled growth, which was obvious, in favor of planning around the "village concept" of closely constructed, self-contained areas, where nobody wanted to live. Starting with little knowledge of the Nantucket community, they suggested the island divide itself into small units, preserving the open spaces in between and limiting auto traffic. They also suggested construction of employee dormitories for working people who would live cheaply and harmoniously without any automobiles whatsoever. The island took their recommendations under advisement and sent them back to the mainland.

In February, Codfish Park was blasted by more shore erosion, adding to the damage of the big storms of 1991 and 1992. Half a dozen homes were gone along with 200 feet of beachfront in the area.

The best news of the winter came from Japan, where the U. S. Women's Olympic Hockey Team swept to victory and the gold medal in the Olympics of 1998 by defeating all opponents in Nagano. The star defense player on the team was twenty-two-year-old A. J. Mleczko, a Harvard student with a family home in Nantucket. The whole town turned out to honor her upon her return to the island in March, with a fire truck parade up Main Streetto the Pacific Bank, where she graciously signed autographs and chatted with admiring youngsters.

Building continued apace. There seemed to be no stopping construction on the island, although building costs and wages had tripled in recent years, so that the cost of building now reached as high as $350 per square foot. That did not seem to affect the plans of Roger Penske, the automobile magnate, who planned to construct an estate at Pocomo with a 9,300-square-foot house, a 2,200-square-foot guest cottage, and a 2,500-square-foot garage for some of his vehicles. Plans for a lighthouse-type tower were not approved, however. It was announced the building cap of 225 houses had been reached in July, after which it was theoretically impossible to obtain a building permit for the year. On the site of the electric company plant on Candle Street, the company was demolishing the old diesel-generator building, the storage tanks, and two brick chimneys. With the new cable connection, the structures were excess property, and Nantucket Electric had its new neat brick building on the corner of Commercial Wharf and Washington Street.

The biggest real estate transaction, however, happened in March, when First Winthrop Corporation announced the sale of its waterfront boat basin and cottages, the White Elephant Hotel, and the Harbor House to Boston-based developer Steven Karp, the owner of the renovated Wauwinet resort. The sale price was said to be $40 million dollars, which, if true, was a lot below the 1987 purchase price of $55 million. However, Karp was a Nantucket homeowner and had the blessing of Walter Beinecke Jr., who hailed the change in ownership as a benefit to the island. Karp soon announced plans to upgrade the properties.

The Steamship Authority followed the HyLine into the fast-ferry business by introducing its own vessel, the *Finest,* which would deliver 360 passengers to the island in one hour for $40 each. Next, the HyLine requested the authority's approval of a larger passenger capacity on its own vessel, now limited to seventy persons, which set up a confrontation between the public and private carriers that was to continue for some time.

The Steamship Authority also had another problem looming on the horizon in New Bedford. In another attempt to revive its lagging economy, the city was in the process of building a $3.2-million freight terminal, aided by $2 million in state and federal funding. The city announced plans to attract the islands' business by making the Steamship Authority divert its freight traffic through the city. This problem continued and became a source of controversy in the future.

The island economy was still booming, with the Nantucket Bank proving that islanders preferred their home-owned bank to the new Pacific/BankBoston combination. The former savings bank, with its modern and convenient building on Pleasant Street, was rapidly surpassing the older island institution, which also had parking problems on Main Street.

Traffic problems continued to mount. Several accidents on Old South Road called attention to the heavy traffic all day on that main thoroughfare connecting the airport and many outlying businesses to town. Meanwhile, the long-expected Polpis bicycle path was stalled in midstream; a pesky willow tree stood in the way of its progress and a stretch of wetland seemed to defy the intentions of the builders. Two selectmen voted to move the Polpis Road rather than touch the wet spot, but the public reaction was vociferous. Two years in the building, the Polpis Path was becoming the Big Dig of Nantucket.

The summer season was a good one—long and dry with many visitors. The Boston Pops returned to the Jetties and thrilled a crowd of 11,000 people. In July, the Nantucket NectarFest was added to the FilmFest and the other festive occasions that filled the island calendar. At the east end of the island, the new Nantucket Golf Club was going strong with a full membership and eighty caddies adding to the thirty-five other employees. Warm weather also brought the marine scene to life, as several right whales were sighted close to the south shore. The sad story of the summer was the demise of Willie the Town Cat, victim of a careless driver on Lower Main Street. He was a fixture on Main Street for many years, ate at the best restaurants, and maintained a cool attitude that brought him hundreds of admirers. He was memorialized on Main Street—a cat of nine years but only one life.

This was not a good year for President William Jefferson Clinton, who was forced to admit his improper relationship with a twenty-one-year old White House intern. The ensuing scandal would dominate the news for the rest of the year and prove to be a severe test of national emotions.

The year 1998 marked the passing of four Nantucket men who had been prominent on the island scene: J. Sydney Conway, seventy, Nantucket's liaison to the state legislature, former postmaster, and representative (when Nantucket had a representative), died in January; Roger Young, seventy-three, Nantucket bicycle man, tour guide, and popular public figure, died in March; Carl Borchert, sixty-one, public official and conservation leader, died in April; and the highly regarded Bruce Killen, forty-nine, skilled craftsman and builder, died in April, mourned by a crowd that filled the Unitarian Church and overflowed into Orange Street.

At the end of the season, Nantucket builder Del Wynn reflected upon the changes he had witnessed in the past thirty years since he arrived on the island as a "bearded hippie" and settled into the cheap housing at Flossie's on India Street and the rich conversation at the Bosun's Locker. From the "vibrant, unpretentious" Main Street scene, he heard the lively debate over the value, or threat, of the Beinecke enterprise in changing the dilapidated waterfront and its ancient shanties into a thriving marina and modern marketplace. While many saw the changes as ruining the old atmosphere of Nantucket, others were cheering the coming economic boom. No one, however, saw the extent of the change. The downtown stores were modest operations, providing a living for a few owners in the marginal economy. Construction was, at best, a seasonal occupation, providing wages for the workers and a certain amount of stability for the owners of businesses, most of whom supplemented their income by caretaking empty houses in the off-season. Scalloping kept a few people in cash during the winter.

The change, according to Wynn, came with the Kennedy Bill in 1972, which was fervently opposed by the Nantucket community as unwarranted federal interference in home-rule matters. It ran against the Nantucket grain to take advice or orders from off-island, especially from Washington politicians. With the defeat of the Kennedy Bill, after all the publicity it promoted, Nantucket was highly visible as an attractive and available place, with great development potential.

He ended his soliloquy with the question: What has all this growth, development, and promotion brought us?

In 1999, the final year of the century made time itself the subject of debate, as the world argued whether or not this was the last year of the millennium. It certainly was the end of the century, but constant publicity about the approaching millennium produced arguments about exactly when it would begin—some saying not until 2001. With the calendar change came the threat of Y2K, the acronym that symbolized the problems of the computer age: the year 2000 challenged the ability of the world's computers, which many feared could only read up to 1999.

It was a year of extremes, from the bitter cold of January through a mild winter to an unusually hot and dry summer. heavy traffic all day. This was followed by mild weather in the fall and no snow through December. Perhaps the globe was warming, but certainly Nantucket was. Amid great national prosperity, fed by a soaring stock market, the island had its busiest and most crowded summer, full of celebrities and cell phones.

This was also a year of tragedies and disasters. In January, the body of Pamela Bouchard, a 29-year-old Nantucket woman, was found floating in Nantucket Harbor, the victim of a heroin overdose. Two young men were arrested and indicted in connection with her death, but the tragedy was symbolic of many problems emerging in the Nantucket of 1999.

Peg Kelley's house in Quaise burned to the ground in January; in February, the Powers barn on Hummock Pond Road went up in smoke in a roaring windstorm; in April, a dangerous fire in Allen's Boat Shop destroyed the building, and the worst of the year's fires swept the popular Brotherhood Restaurant on Broad Street from the basement through the three-story building. David Watts, a Nantucket fireman and brother of Fire Chief Bruce Watts, succumbed to a heart attack and died after fighting the Brotherhood fire. He was given a hero's funeral.

Close to Nantucket, three disasters gained national and international attention. In July, John F. Kennedy Jr., his wife, and his sister-in-law died when their private plane crashed near Martha's Vineyard. The resulting search for the bodies and burial at sea produced worldwide grief, reminding many of the recent death of Princess Diana of England. On October 31, Halloween, EgyptAir Flight 990, an international flight from New York, mysteriously crashed fifty miles southeast of Nantucket, taking 217 lives. This crash was close to the location of the *Andrea Doria* disaster. In December, a tragic fire in an abandoned warehouse in Worcester, Massachusetts, took the lives of six heroic firemen in a single night. The services provided the occasion for an international outpouring of support from 30,000 firemen, including several from Nantucket, in the largest public memorial service ever held.

During the winter, a deer hunter stumbled upon a site in the woods off Lovers Lane, where he discovered an underground home and provoked a flurry of news from midwinter Nantucket. The creator of the novel homestead near the Boy Scout camp was a forty-year-old man named Tom Johnson, who had lived in or under Nantucket for about ten years. When investigated by the police, the underground home was found to be warm and comfortable, with heating and plumbing and water and shower facilities. Although the structure was invisible to the ordinary visitor, it was technically trespassing on private property, and in the view of the town, a threat to public health. The clever construction was reported in the newspapers and the story of "Uncle Tom's Cabin" made national TV news. Many Nantucketers expressed admiration for Johnson's skill and ingenuity, and suggested he might have found the solution to the town's housing problems. More perturbed by the publicity than anything else, the solitary builder didn't object to the destruction of his home, indicating he might soon find other quarters where he would not be disturbed. The story of "Underground Tom" evoked curiosity about the full story of this modern Thoreau, who only sought peace and solitude in the woods.

The town imposed another building cap in an attempt to limit the construction boom. With the population close to 9,000, no housing was to be found for young couples or working people, and land was increasingly expensive. The building cap was modified to give relief to first-time homeowners, who were allowed to build if they could find the money. The same town meeting voted an annual budget of $18.5 million to run the town, but rejected any expansion of the Town and County Building.

One expansion that went forward was the White Elephant Hotel, which won approval for new construction along 375 feet of Easton Street, making the 1965 hotel Nantucket's newest and most expensive hostelry. Nantucket also expanded its connections to the banking world of New England when it was announced that Fleet Bank would merge with BankBoston, thus providing Nantucket's Pacific National Bank with its third owner within three years.

In September the Boston *Globe* featured a magazine article on "Nantucket's dirty little secret," which accurately named several heroin users on the island and talked about the need for a methadone clinic in the town where there might be 400 heroin users. Rather than street drug dealers, Nantucket was pictured as having an elite, close-knit group of addicts, holdiing jobs and raising families. Among thousands of transient workers and visitors, it appeared nearly impossible for police to control the flood of illegal drugs, and many would prefer to ignore the problem or treat it with methadone.

The biggest public issue of the year, however, was again the Steamship Authority and the continuing effort of the city of New Bedford to reattach itself to the islands' lifeline. In April, the legislature held hearings on the New Bedford proposal to mandate freight service to and from the city, which the islands opposed as unwarranted and detrimental to the boatline. Then the issue was inflamed by some Cape Cod communities that sought the New Bedford service to divert island-bound traffic from their streets. By the end of the year, the New Bedford proposal had won narrow approval in the House and was pending in the Senate. The authority, which had foreseen the public demand for speedy service by purchasing a new $7.5-million fast ferry, was now threatened with sending slow freight boats to New Bedford.

The economic signs pointed to continuing boom. Now running its own fast ferry, the Steamship Authority authorized the HyLine to increase the capacity of the *Gray Lady II* from seventy to 149 passengers. The cost of rising municipal salaries indicated the town would face a deficit within a few years, while the school population went up from 1,236 to 1,270 in one year. In the biggest single parcel sale to date, Stop & Shop purchased the supermarket on Sparks Avenue from Steven Karp for $12 million—the same property that was acquired by Sherburne Associates in 1977 for $750,000.

Three churches made news this year. In August, the newly renovated African Meeting House had a well-attended dedication, featuring the reenactors of the Civil War's famous 54th Massachusetts Regiment—the Glory Regiment. In the fall, the Baptist Church on Summer Street received a new steeple, made partially of fiberglass to accommodate a Bell Atlantic cell-phone antenna. By Christmas, the restoration of St. Mary's Church was virtually complete, with new stained-glass windows and a fresh interior for the new century.

Mainland newspapers and national magazines continued to feed on Nantucket news, seeming to compete for something timely or sensational about the New Nantucket. Much of the commentary focused on the changes wrought by the big money flooding the island as the new breed found Nantucket the place to be for the summer. Gone were the days when Nantucket was a remote and low-key summer resort where old families returned each year for the love of the island, living quietly in somewhat rustic summer cottages. Now, reporters found the newcomers always demanding more—more living space, more privacy, more horsepower in their yachts and sports vehicles, and more visibility at catered cocktail parties. The symbols of the New Nantucket had become the trophy house and the No Trespassing sign.

The Boston *Globe* declared that seriously big money was turning the historic island into a playpen for the super rich. Ned Rorem complained about the people turning "a paradise into a fairground." Rob Benchley, island photographer, felt the island was becoming "one big gated community."

The New York *Times,* calling it the "Hamptonization of Nantucket," reported that private yachts were clogging the harbor, sport-utility vehicles were jamming the cobblestoned streets, and historic homes were being gutted to accommodate air conditioning and modern kitchens. Everyone was stunned by the soaring cost of homes on the island, and the pace of the building boom that brought 400 workers onto the island, workers who continued to find it cheaper to fly round-trip every day than to find housing on Nantucket.

A new subject of some concern was the reckless renovation of historic houses by wealthy visitors who purchased charming old homes and ripped them apart to provide modern amenities in dubious taste. The Historic District Commission, which controlled exterior appearances of buildings, could not control interior renovations, and found some such projects totally destructive of the old houses. Although the historic homes stood in the same location, they had lost their architectural integrity.

It was becoming apparent that Nantucket, with its strict preservation guidelines, its comprehensive bylaws, and its extensive preservation tradition, could not withstand the force of so much money and so little regard for the historic integrity of the old town—a paradox the island would surely have to confront in the future.

The most perceptive piece on Nantucket in the nineties was published in the July 1999 issue of *Town and Country* by the Pulitzer Prize-winning author and Nantucket summer resident David Halberstam. From the vantage point of thirty years' observation of the island scene, he remembered the days when people from all walks of life knew each other and treated each other with respect. Now the once remote, simple island had become instantly accessible by private jets and luxury yachts, making it an easy target for wealthy commuters and "stunningly wealthy winners of Wall Street." Beside his sharp but not strident comments, the magazine printed color photographs of the beautiful people arrayed in their island finery. Halberstam was uneasy about the effect of so much wealth on the small and fragile island, where he longed for the simple pleasures that first attracted him: the beaches, the fishing, and the outdoor life. Above all, he noticed a decline in "the courtesy and manners that are so critical to the texture of life in a small town," and best summed up his observations with this comment: "Many of the true pleasures of Nantucket are not easily gained and cannot be purchased on demand . . . they have to be like everything else in life, earned."

Perhaps it was the long dry summer, the driest since 1991, and the daily heat waves that irritated so many people in the summer of 1999. Appliance stores ran out of fans early in the season, as lawns turned brown and water consumption reached record levels. Restaurants had to be air-conditioned to attract evening business. Crowded streets and traffic jams contributed to many reports of road rage and frustration.

Amid it all, on August 20, President Bill Clinton and First Lady Hillary Rodham Clinton paid a one-day visit to Nantucket, flying over from their summer vacation on Martha's Vineyard. This was the first visit by a sitting president to Nantucket since Woodrow Wilson's visit in 1917. (Both Franklin D. Roosevelt and John F. Kennedy arrived aboard yachts in Nantucket Harbor, but had not come ashore.) Clinton spent most of his day playing golf with friends at the Nantucket Golf Club, while the First Lady toured the town, making visits to the Nantucket Atheneum, the Methodist Church, and the Nantucket Historical Association's Whaling Museum. In the evening, the Clintons attended a reception for the American Ireland Fund in the Matthews' house on Cliff Road, where Tim Russert was the featured speaker, and then attended a fund-raising party at the Eel Point home of Ambassador Elizabeth Frawley Bagley and her husband, Smith Bagley. It proved to be quite a gala day for Nantucket: the roads were blocked in many directions, Secret Service

291

agents were everywhere, and the crowds turned out in force to view the national couple. Coming at the height of the summer season, the presidential visit put a strain on the island's hospitality, but the public reaction was receptive and friendly.

There were several departures from the island scene in the last year of the century: Dr. David B. Voorhees, longtime "country doctor" who delivered many Nantucket babies, died at sixty-four in April; Theodore L. "Ted" Tillotson, respected real estate lawyer, died in May; and the well-known artist and illustrator Robert Perrin died at eighty three in April.

As the old century ended, scientists declared that Nantucket would be the first place in the United States to witness the millennium on January 1, when the sun rose from the Atlantic Ocean to strike the cliffs at Sankaty Head. At midnight on December 31, Rev. Ted Anderson rang out the old century by tolling the bell in the Unitarian Church while a crowd gathered below on Orange Street to cheer in the new one. A parade of automobiles drove out Milestone Road to Sconset to celebrate the dawn. With perfect, mild, clear weather, the sun rose in the east, right on schedule, at 7:03 A.M. on January 1, 2000.

Nantucket had survived the century.

Afterword

"IT WAS THE BEST OF TIMES; IT WAS THE WORST OF TIMES. . . ."

Within the span of one hundred years, a wave of people and progress swept the island of Nantucket into the modern world. The quaint old "Little Gray Lady" became something of a fancy place: a trophy island for the rich and famous. As the people and pace of life increased annually, many wondered about the future of the fragile island.

Not all change is bad. Nantucketers in the year 2000 enjoyed a higher standard of living than their ancestors. They had far better medical care, education, and transportation. The new residents and retirees added to the life and culture of the island. Nantucket can take pride in her past, but no community, even an island, can live forever in the past.

The Nantucket of the future will be different, but it will retain many of the qualities of life that created its special character and appeal. The climate, the seashore, and the harbor are the best to be found — anywhere. The conservation movement has preserved much of the natural landscape—forever. The charm and ambience of Sconset remains—unchanged. The beaches surrounding the island are abundant, accessible, and open. Above all, the old town has retained its wonderful appearance and historic architecture.

Many things have changed, but the important things abide.

OTHER WORKS BY ROBERT F. MOONEY

The Nantucket Way, with André R. Sigourney, Doubleday & Co., 1980.

The Wreck of the British Queen, Mill Hill Press, 1988.

Tales of Nantucket, Wesco Publishing, 1990.

The Advent of Douglass, Wesco Publishing, 1991.

The Civil War: The Nantucket Experience, with Richard F. Miller, Wesco Publishing, 1994.